NOTHING PERSONAL

Prostitution is considered to be the oldest profession in the world; yet to be caught either selling or paying for sex is considered to be demeaning. These suppositions of guilt are strongly challenged by Donald McRae in NOTHING PERSONAL. With unprecedented access to the stories of prostitutes of both sexes, their pimps, and their clients, McRae reveals the intimacies that take place at this most private of exchanges. He turns the spotlight onto previously hidden areas — who is motivated into using the services of a gigolo, or a whip-wielding dominatrix? — and explores, with sympathy, the plight of women — and men — routinely exposed to danger, with little or no protection from the law. This is a personal guide to the business of sex.

About the author

Donald McRae was born in Germiston, South Africa, in 1961. Between 1981 and 1984 he edited and wrote for two independent Johannesburg magazines while also teaching English literature in Soweto. Since the middle of 1984 he has lived in London — where he has written about South Africa, music, films, books and boxing for numerous national newspapers and magazines in Europe, America and Africa. *Nothing Personal* is his first book.

Nothing Personal
The Business of Sex

Donald McRae

CORONET BOOKS
Hodder and Stoughton

First published in Great Britain in 1992 by Mainstream Publishing Company (Edinburgh) Ltd

Coronet edition 1993

British Library C.I.P.

A CIP catalogue record for this title is available from the British Library

ISBN 0 340 60116 7

Printed and bound in Great Britain for Hodder and Stoughton Paperbacks, a division of Hodder and Stoughton Ltd, Mill Road, Dunton Green, Sevenoaks, Kent TN13 2YA (Editorial Office: 47 Bedford Square, London WC1B 3DP) by Cox and Wyman Ltd, Reading.

For Kath

Contents

Acknowledgments

Nothing Personal, more than most books, is indebted to other people. Without the generosity and patience of all those featured in these pages I would not only be without a book but I would also not have learnt or laughed as much as I did during the last few years.

Within the wide band of people who spent so much time with me, special acknowledgment has to be given to Mandy Kavanagh, Alice Teague, Lee Docherty, Leila T., David Missen and Sara Dale and Howard Lambert for their insight into prostitution and their unstinting humour.

To Shelley Power, who followed my turbulent progress from the very outset, I would like to emphasise how much I have relied on her since 1989.

Tim Binding, Humphrey Price and, especially, Bill Campbell, made invaluable editorial suggestions and, for this edition, Kath Meadows provided some unerringly accurate amendments.

Without access to my own specialized computer 'boffin', Lisa Lyhne, I would probably still be looking for deleted chapters on lost files. So thank you to her and all my other friends who, many times, said the right thing just when it was most needed – Luke Alfred, Jay and Dee Savage, Hilton Tanchum, Kate Stott, Josh Sepheto, Anne McClintock, Rob Nixon and Tessa Spargo who also gave up her 'Parisian boudoir' when it seemed like I had nowhere else to write.

Kath Meadows has done more than anyone to encourage my writing. She also provided the most crucial editorial assistance during the earliest drafts of this book and was the first person to stress the need for me to write about prostitution from a personal perspective. It is to her, also, that I owe the *Nothing Personal* title and much else since I first began writing.

I can never adequately repay my parents, or Heather and Ross Simpson, for all they have done — especially the way in which they have always accepted me with both grace and understanding. Thanks go, most of all, to them.

Preface

In March 1990, I was asked to write the biography of a London prostitute. She had been written about in the 'quality' newspapers as a woman of both strangeness and substance and was reputed to have been working for some time on the idea of a book. My first reaction on hearing this proposal was to laugh, as I felt certain that some mistake must have been made. I was then writing mostly about South Africa, my home country, and the idea of switching to a subject like prostitution, of which I could then claim to know not much more than the next person, seemed absurd.

However, I was persuaded that I was capable of writing such a book because of my previous experiences in South Africa, where I had occasionally interviewed 'banned' or 'wanted' people in Soweto. The ensuing logic, presumably, was that I would have little difficulty in engaging in meaningful dialogue with a similarly controversial 'refugee' from polite sexual norms in suburban London. Yet I still felt acutely conscious of my relatively limited knowledge of prostitution and uncomfortable with the idea of writing a biography of a living person. I imagined myself being pulled apart by my own ignorance and the compromise which is embedded in the writing of another's personal history as they peer over your shoulder. So I declined that offer with as much grace as I could muster beneath the bewilderment I still felt at having even been approached.

The subject would then have been closed if it had not been for my own aroused curiosity. As becomes clear some way into the first chapter of *Nothing Personal*, a variety of

11

circumstances opened the way for the emergence of an altogether different kind of book. Most of all, I was extremely fortunate to meet Alice Teague and Mandy Kavanagh in those first weeks when I began to seriously consider writing about the wider arena of prostitution. Their initial impact on this book was considerable − not only in the way in which they shattered my preconceptions about the subject but also because they introduced me to the darker areas of prostitution with unusual wit. They pointed out similarly that, at the crossroads of marriage and the marketplace, prostitution blurs the boundaries between the personal and the public so that money is brought into the bedroom and sex is sold on the streets. Prostitution's complex conflicts also accentuate the more subtle power struggles inherent to all relationships and Mandy and Alice, from the outset, were emphatic in the belief that empowering prostitutes empowers all women.

But they helped most of all by constantly reaffirming the need for me to move beyond the confines of their more intellectually rigorous domain. It was imperative for a coherent understanding of prostitution, they stressed, that I ventured into the more representative, if also more distressing, backrooms and streets.

They both expressed bitter regret when my increasingly wayward journey into the furthest corners of prostitution culminated with my ending up in hospital one night. That had been the seventh time I had been physically attacked during the eighteen months of my writing about prostitution and it felt then, momentarily at least, that I would be lucky to be allowed another two lives. To Alice and, in particular, Mandy, whose one client was responsible for that openly declared 'season of violence', it felt as if they were personally liable for the trouble in which I had landed. But I knew then that I was not being especially persecuted. In the context of prostitution, such violence is not strange. Neither is the fear nor the pain which that brutality inevitably brings.

12

Alice and Mandy eventually had to concede the point that they had always made to me; far from being the ones responsible for the often ominous backdrop against which they work, the prostitutes in this country are pinned to the wall not only by physical assailants but by the hypocritical iniquities of the law. It would be laughable if it were not so damaging that prostitution has still not been decriminalized in Britain. Instead, we have to deal with the ludicrous situation where actual prostitution is not illegal; rather, the *advertizing* of the act constitutes a crime, which is a curious anomaly to be applied to a billion-pound industry by a capitalistic legal system. This also results in the widespread confusion surrounding the discrepancy between legalization and decriminalization. Prostitutes are not calling for the legalization of their trade, for such a change is less innocuous than it sounds. Under legalization, the State assumes the role of an all-controlling pimp with often disastrous consequences for the prostitutes themselves. In Austria, where prostitution has been legalized, sex workers operate under an insidious kind of house-arrest system in which they have to report to the police whenever they take 'extended leave' of the area to which they are consigned. In Switzerland, women who decide to abandon their careers as prostitutes are not allowed to legally find alternative forms of work until they are in receipt of a 'good girl' letter from the police. To obtain such an official statement, the ex-prostitute has to prove herself to be a 'good girl' for three years. In Germany, prostitutes pay an exorbitant 56% tax rate and yet are not eligible for the social benefits available to the 'ordinary' citizen.

Even more disturbing in Britain is the judicial whim which sometimes appears to consider that a prostitute living in the same house as her lover is a more serious offence than rape. This is yet another consequence of the fact that Britain's business of sex is regulated within the confines of criminal rather than commercial law. This constraint means that the

State effectively considers prostitutes to be 'guilty' of a crime.

From a similar perspective, Peter Sutcliffe's 'Yorkshire Ripper' murder of thirteen women in the late 1970s was apparently driven by a divine mission to rid the Earth of the 'guilty scum' who walked the streets. Sutcliffe claimed that he could tell that prostitutes were not 'innocent' just by observing the way in which they walked. Just as Sir Michael Havers, the Attorney General, declared that the saddest part of the Ripper case was that some of Sutcliffe's victims were not prostitutes, so the Yorkshire police ran a 'the next victim may be *innocent*' poster campaign after five prostitutes had already been murdered.

As long as prostitution is a criminal offence then this presumed guilt will continue to be a given and prostitutes' lives will still be considered to be 'worth' less than others. I soon learnt that when a prostitute is a victim of violence it continues to be presumed in some quarters that 'she was asking for it . . .' This attitude is degrading not only to the prostitute but to all women.

So when those bad and violent moments came to me, any maudlin pleasure I searched for in self-pity was truncated by the store of memories I had already built up in talking to more than three hundred people involved in prostitution. If I had to find some sustenance in order to complete this book I did not have to look far, for I had witnessed much resilience and creativity from others during our interviews. Moreover, I also probably laughed more in those eighteen months than I had ever done. When all that was remembered, it was not especially difficult to continue.

And in truth, beyond my personal concern, nothing of lasting consequence occurred in those various assaults against me. They were but a pinprick when set against the severe ramifications of the political and legal establishments' reluctance to confront the fact that arresting streetwalkers night after night and breaking-up 'brothels' is not going to wash away prostitution and its endemic problems of violence and exploitation.

From the penthouses to the tower blocks, from telephone booths to suburban backstreets, prostitution is now so consuming that it shadows every facet of this society. It could be argued that such an expansive sex-for-cash spectrum has always prevailed; but against the backdrop of an enduring economic crisis, the concentration of prostitution has never before run so deep or with such drastic urgency.

Yet I was drawn deep into this subject less by failings in the law than by the very people involved in prostitution. Their extraordinary stories, often related here in their own eloquent and incisive words, present an informed platform for the change that is needed, the change that would finally drag the sex business out of the furtive and damaging world it all too often inhabits.

The lucidity of those featured in this book allowed me to use a significant percentage of the words I recorded during the many hours we spent together. However, my initial desire to keep myself out of these pages was refuted by the prostitutes themselves. They claimed that this book was different from others written about prostitution in the sense that, through a combination of chance and specific personal interests, I was able to meet and get to know such a diverse mix of people — covering virtually every conceivable form of prostitution — both rich and poor, exclusive and pedestrian, male and female, gay and straight. Ironically my South African-ness, or my comparative classlessness in British terms of accent and school education, helped enormously for I found myself able to drift in and out of the disparate strata of prostitution with relative ease. Apart from a few isolated individuals I was invariably welcomed and was the recipient of much kindness and patience when, really, those attributes should have been travelling in the opposite direction.

The structure of the book, like the style of its writing,

also underwent numerous changes. At first, in my strictly objective phase, I was planning to write a series of virtual 'case studies'. Without the necessary sociological acumen I soon abandoned this technique for a more open exploration of four distinct spheres of prostitution — namely, 'high-class' prostitutes and gigolos who mostly work alone; Soho, that traditional but now significantly altered area of prostitution; escort agencies; and street sex. While they make for convenient divisions, these barriers are easily blurred with both prostitutes and their clients sometimes moving from one sex-zone to another. So, finally, I settled on this hopefully more fluid, if sometimes amorphous, version where my experiences of prostitution are recounted as a journey, in the chronological order in which they unfolded.

Owing to my earlier intention, the book can still be read in terms of the different worlds comprising British prostitution — in broad terms, the first five chapters are set at the very top of the prostitution tree, with people who have enjoyed both impressive educational opportunities and backgrounds of relative economic stability, and sometimes extreme wealth; chapters six to eight are set in Soho; the following two are devoted to contrasting escort agencies; chapters eleven to fifteen are mostly out on the street. I was particularly interested in the fact that these worlds are not enclosed — not only do they echo the same themes but, also, they often include the same people. Inevitably, some of the protagonists move from one chapter to the next, from one section to another.

Lastly, on the crucial question of personal identity, one of my prime objectives in writing this book was to interview the clients and entrepreneurs involved in prostitution. Because of society's prevailing attitude to the commercial consumption of sex, such people, particularly the clients, are loath to have their private prostitution practices made public. Consequently, I have changed the names of those people who requested this before agreeing to be interviewed.

16

Mindful of this prevailing anonymity and accompanying sense of the unknown, I also resolved not to write about prostitutes such as Lindi St Clair and Helen Buckingham as their stories and views on prostitution have already been well documented. They are the exceptions to the rule which, perhaps up until now, has always preferred to cloak prostitution in secrecy. To all those in this book who chose to break that more typical silence I offer a heartfelt 'thank-you'.

Chapter One

The Terminator Angel

As usual, his finger pressed against her doorbell at exactly three o'clock. Mandy Kavanagh felt certain she would only find a more accurate measure of time on a Tuesday afternoon by dialling the Speaking Clock. Moreover, Alistair's metronomic arrival at her home in South Kensington every week had the same despairing effect on her as that digitalised voice.

For the first eighteen months of their 'dark tryst of pain', as he described their relationship, she had been fascinated by this precision. She used to watch him from the wide bay-window in her blue room as he turned the corner of her tree-lined street at exactly two minutes to the hour. That was all the time he needed to walk past the thirty houses before reaching her front steps.

The meticulous strangeness of his obsession with time was not unlike that which shadowed her own life. Since the age of nineteen, twelve years ago, she had also framed her darker desires within specific compartments of time. But where Mandy thought in blocks of years, Alistair's life was ordered by the hour. He kept track of the minute hand on his gold Rolex by means of a small alarm which drove her mad when it beep-beeped every quarter-hour to help maintain his intricate schedule of appointments.

As his austere 'Terminator Angel', one of the rare pleasures of her time with him was to remove that chirruping watch as soon as they got down to business. This shifted the balance of power in her direction. But, even as she humiliated him, Mandy could never forget that Alistair dictated the course of his own degradation. She also could not fool herself into thinking that this transfer of authority was anything more than a temporary manoeuvre, a kink in his otherwise impregnable psyche.

Time never flew when Mandy was with Alistair. Instead, the minutes between three and four dragged. It was not only the actual time she spent with him that was so consuming. The hours preceding and following his every visit left a trail of slime down her day. She had learnt the long way that this slippery feel of dirt did not become easier to bear with repetition.

Every week was the same, even though he was different from her other fantasists. Where they locked themselves into their adjusted personae as soon as she led them into the bedroom, Alistair always took his time. There was something eerily measured about the way he abandoned one self for another. It seemed as if he was trying to control his own fleeting renunciation of power.

More importantly, as she leaned back against her wardrobe watching him, Alistair wanted to impress Mandy. To him, she was an incredibly bright, beautiful woman. Although nearly twenty years younger than him she exuded a self-assurance he rarely encountered. For when they were together Mandy seldom allowed any emotion to cross her face, even when he dropped into his jagged whisper that she should 'call me cunt, call me cunt'. And so, as if she was reading out a familiar share price on the Dow Jones Index, she repeated the word in her cool newscaster's voice. This unyielding professionalism only made him more determined to chip some way into her heart.

He would spend the first ten minutes in her cream bedroom, slowly undressing while he spoke of his success in the City that past week. Each item of clothing duplicated a decisive anecdote of achievement. It had always been this way – him talking, her listening – with Alistair never able to fathom the extent of the impression he made on Mandy Kavanagh.

He had been a client of hers from the start of the golden years of his career, an apex of accomplishment which Alistair claimed to scale a little higher every week. When she first met him he had just fought his way on to the board of a nationwide bank after years of transforming ailing financial institutions into money-spinning corporations. Other prestigious board positions had since followed, for Alistair's talent, or 'genius' as he put it, lay in money; in manipulating it around the marketplace. The clarity of his success stemmed from the strict correlation he made between power and money. He used one to strengthen the other.

Having shared his business week with Mandy he would stand naked before her. She would continue to appraise him silently, barely concealing her disapproval. This, in one of the many ironies of her work, meant that she was already doing her job. He'd talk on, letting loose some of the secrets he had stored for himself since the previous Tuesday. Almost always, these stories involved a young girl who would be trampled beneath him.

She would start out as a real person in a position of hackneyed subservience – a secretary in his company's head office or a young air hostess on his most recent Concorde flight – and he would describe how she looked, how she moved and how she made him feel when he watched her. He would evoke for Mandy the smoothness of the girl's skin, the sheen of life radiating from her. He imagined her sweet smile twisting into a pout, then into a wet open mouth begging him to shower his moneyed power over her, to favour her over the rest.

Then his desire became entwined with anger. The girl would be reduced to his idea of a money-grabbing 'everywhore'. He breathed the word out softly while Mandy turned away and led him down the narrow stairway leading to the cellar. All the way down those eleven stairs

21

'everywhore' would follow her, a refrain as sour as his breath was sweet with minted chocolate.

At the bottom of the wooden stairway he would be on his hands and knees, crawling towards the leather and metal apparatus. He felt himself being peeled open and pinned to the black convex couch 'like a mounted butterfly', with Mandy, his 'forbidding Mandy', his very own real life whore, swinging her studded leather belt fast through the air so that he could hear the thick swish just before he felt the pain. She rarely said anything while lashing into him, preferring instead to draw breath to fan her own hurt.

She knew that to fling wounding words at him only deepened the pleasure of his debasement. Despite the £250 he paid her to play the part of 'The Terminator Angel', an avenging 'everywhore', she did not act as she did with the others. They came to her cellar for more symbolic gestures of surrender and punishment — even the sound made by the belt was often enough to fill them with regret. But, where she pitied them, she despised Alistair. For him, she wanted her black ribbon of retribution to cause suffering rather than release.

Alistair was beyond redemption and, as bleak as he made her feel every Tuesday, this thought forced Mandy on with him. Her reasons for choosing prostitution were intensely personal; but wider social issues loomed over her encounters with Alistair. He was indisputably a powerful man, a man with the capacity to devastate the lives of other people. She was 'the only one', he said, who curbed his lust for power.

Yet Mandy could never claim, like some more golden-hearted prostitutes, that she was in this business for the well-being of her clients. She took limited pride in the service she offered, despite her men's avowal of its excellence. Prostitution was merely the track she had chosen to follow for five years. Mandy often wondered what Alistair might do if he no longer had recourse to their Tuesday afternoon sessions; so she had resolved that as long as she worked as a prostitute she would maintain their 'tryst', despite his depravity.

But when she heard the first ring of the bell on that Tuesday, a heavier kind of dread drew across her heart. Mandy stayed a little longer in the blue room, rocking gently as she always did when she sat in her high-backed wicker chair. She knew that he would ring again more insistently, as he was already doing, whether or not she raced from her room, down the stairs and along the black and white hall to answer his call as soon as she heard him.

Lately, Mandy lingered before letting him into her home. In the past it had never been for more than a minute or two but on this afternoon, after nearly four years of such arrivals at her door, she continued to let him wait. At five past three, as his ringing hit a declamatory pitch, she finally rose with a sigh and closed the door behind her, still uncertain why the thought of seeing Alistair that day ground her down in a way she had never known.

She dallied down the sumptuously carpeted stairs, wondering if maybe she should end it and not open the door. What would he do then? Where would he go if not to her cellar? Perhaps he himself imagined these questions for his finger appeared glued to her buzzer.

Opening the door, she saw that Alistair's lean face was unusually flushed. Where he normally feigned an air of authority on entering her flat, he was plainly agitated as he stepped through the doorway. He plunged down the long hall, not bothering to make his typically cryptic allusions to her lateness or to comment on the way she looked as he had done on every other visit.

Mandy followed him into the bedroom and was surprised to see Alistair already undressing himself, his anger at her delay devoured by his arousal. When he began talking it was not of his weekly success story but of an incident at a local hospital. As he masturbated in front of her he asked Mandy if she had watched the news the night before. She knew immediately that he was referring to a story which had had

23

a profound effect on her. A fourteen-year-old girl had been raped in her hospital bed by an unknown male. The rape had lasted for more than an hour. The next morning an image of this faceless girl kept slipping across Mandy's mind, like a shadow over a usually clear screen. She had been grateful that before her appointment with Alistair she had seen only one client — a sixty-five-year-old retired barrister who liked to be held gently with one arm while she used her free hand to bring him to a wistful climax.

Now here was Alistair, talking of this same girl. For a wild moment she even thought that maybe it was him, that perhaps he had finally slipped into terminal darkness and raped the girl himself. But she had learnt to recognize the guilty shapes of Alistair's desire, to understand that he still only fantasized about making this final bid for what he called 'mastery' over women.

His preoccupation with domination prevented him from acting on impulse. Whatever risks he took, irrespective of their intensity, Alistair always weighed them against the threat they might pose to his long-term pursuit of even greater power.

That was where Mandy came in; for she was his 'everywhore', paid to satisfy his harshest remorse. As she watched him swell with lust she felt faint comfort in the realization that Alistair was too cunning to succumb to his most glaring weakness. He only dreamed that it was him stealing through the hospital grounds and into the children's wing where he picked out the girl for himself. Before he could reach the imagined point where he was about to force himself into her, before he could pick up his murmuring 'everywhore' mantra, Mandy turned her back on him and walked towards the cellar.

Alistair, hoarse with craving, shouted after her that he wasn't ready yet, that he still had much more to tell her. She walked on silently, forcing him to follow her down the stairs, cursing her for being 'a fucking stuck-up bitch'. He wasn't crawling either when he reached the cellar floor. She might have felt a spasm of fear as he towered over her, with the veins standing out in purple welts across his body, if her own rage hadn't felt so bottomless.

She spat some words back at him, struggling to control the tone of her voice so that he would not guess the pain he had caused her. It was as though these words were the first blows to strike him. He sank back on the black couch. This time he did not have to ask her to manacle his arms and legs for she did so before he could turn over to lie face downwards. For once it was Alistair who felt an encroaching sense of horror as the beating began.

The belt whipped across his bare legs, his now limp genitals, his stomach, his chest and finally his face for five or more minutes until his silence was broken by screaming and then by a pleading that she should stop, that he could not bear the pain. The skin on the masochistic back of his body had gathered a hardness during the years of being struck by the belts and whips of prostitutes. But his front was tenderly susceptible to pain. Even his psychological humiliation, deepened by being strapped on his back, was overshadowed by the physical pain raining down on him.

When she stopped she found no solace in his sobbing apologies. She knew that she had beaten nothing from him. Nothing had changed for either of them, even though Alistair had felt real pain rather than the imagined hurt he paid to escape from at the end of every S&M session.

Even as he began to dress himself once more in the silence of her cream room the strap marks faded from his whitened face. Soon they would be gone, leaving the surface smooth and pink again. When he finally walked down her hallway, his composure regained in time to match the singing alarm on his watch, he was back to his old self. 'I'm not sure what got into you today, Mandy Kavanagh,' he said as a way of parting, 'but you were at your very best. You should surprise me more often, it does us both the world of good. See you next Tuesday, my love . . .'

She wordlessly closed the door behind him. He was gone for another week from her home, but not from the bleak vistas of her heart. Mandy felt as if she were about to crack open under the weight of that one word, 'Why?', which followed her down the hall, up the salmon-shaded staircase and into the centre of her favourite blue room, in the place where she shut herself away from the world outside. It was still light out there but everywhere looked dark beneath her steady, lowered gaze.

'Mandy Kavanagh,' murmured Alice the following Sunday afternoon, 'is the strangest, most beautiful woman I have ever met. There's no-one else like her; she does things in a way the rest of us haven't even dreamed of. When you're with her you realize that she's living her life like it's a story, like some savage story that's told to you in the most exquisite language you've ever heard. And, yeah, I can already tell — you fucking want to hear this story, you want to meet this girl. I'm right, aren't I, sweetie?'

Alice Teague was almost always right, as she was then. Yet just a few hours earlier it had been hard to imagine anyone looking as strikingly unusual as Alice did while walking towards me with her own strange kind of sinewy grace. It was my first time, my maiden meeting with a prostitute. All I could think was 'So *this* is what "*they*" really look like?'

Alice looked so good that I tried to force home the reminder that she was actually a former prostitute, as if it was an impossibility that she could ever have looked this free when she worked the streets, the parlours and the agencies. I also would never have guessed, as she moved closer towards me with such careless fluidity, that she was listening to John Coltrane on her pink Walkman, to a beautiful song called *Blues For Bechet*. Instead my head kept swirling with its banal wondering as to whether this woman could *really* once have been a prostitute or whether I'd mistaken her for someone else, someone completely different.

26

The despondent tennis players, the kite-flying families and the roller-skating lovers along this stretch of Hampstead Heath were apparently even more at a loss. They could not guess who Alice could possibly be: a fearfully bolshie feminist or merely a brash slut? The only certainty was that they didn't have a clue, for they all stopped to stare. Their eyes hooked into the sight of Alice walking, as only she knew, in time to Coltrane. Her blonde stream of hair was pulled back loosely from her sharply featured face by deep blue ribbons while her Doc Martens were tied with red laces and topped with fluorescent green socks and immaculately faded 501s. But, amid all this colour, the large black words on both the front and back of her crisp white T-Shirt stood out, forcing Hampstead's gently unco-ordinated Sunday afternoon activity to lapse into a perplexed pause. As the gaping mouths and furtive whispers indicated, 'Vindication Of The Rights Of Whores' and 'Prostitutes In Paradise' were not part of the bantering lexicon usually used in this picnic-friendly zone.

Yes, I breathed a little more quickly, this was Alice all right; a different kind of frisbee-flinger from the rest of us watching her meander down the tarred path which was warm with sunshine for the first Sunday in months. She soon stood right in front of me, raising an inquisitive, immaculately lined eyebrow.

'Alice?' I asked tentatively.

'Who else?' she laughed.

With my stare pulled back towards her T-Shirt, her laughter curled into words: 'I wasn't sure what you looked like so I thought I'd better wear something so you couldn't miss me! Anyway, what else is a bad girl gonna wear across her chest? You know where this comes from?'

'Vindication Of The Rights Of Whores', I said clumsily, came from the title of a book featuring an international cross-section of prostitutes who gathered together at the 'Second World Whores' Congress' in Brussels in 1986. They had adapted its title from Mary Wollstonecraft's ground-

27

breaking book, *A Vindication Of The Rights Of Women*, published at the end of the eighteenth century.

As if I had passed an opening test question, Alice patted me on the cheek and said, 'Good boy.' She then proceeded, humming with her Walkman, to lead me across the Heath. I was intrigued that a prostitute, even a *retired* prostitute, would have known about Coltrane. My shameful amazement must have been obvious for she flashed a pitying smile when I asked her if this was why she chose to use 'Alice' as a pseudonym, since it was the name of Coltrane's wife. 'No, sweetie,' she said, 'it's 'cos I make men think they've discovered wonderland when they fuck me.'

Apparently galvanised by the success of this prelude Alice set off a bubbling burst of questions relating to my muddled opinions on sadomasochistic sex and Britain's current legislation on kerb-crawling. By the time we had reached the edge of South End Green I was reeling beneath the weight of her interrogation and the curious stares from the Sunday strollers.

Alice appeared oblivious to such attention for she guided me into a crowded Hampstead pâtisserie, full of cultured colour-supplement readers, pipe-smokers and beret-wearers. While pondering her choice of cream cakes, Alice sealed with certainty my suspicion that she was less shy than I was. 'Boy,' she said in a loud voice, 'you've got a lot of catching up to do on bondage and kerb-crawling.'

The sidelong glances aimed at our table froze in disbelief. But these hipsters were so cool that their eyes soon thawed under arched eyebrows and averted noses. The magazine flipping and cappuccino sipping resumed, as did the burr of more sensitive conversation.

Finding a table in the most obscure corner, Alice's own talk was muffled by the adjoining walls and by her fantastic demolition of a walloping Black Forest gâteau. In between mouthfuls, she confirmed what I had already heard about her past. After three tedious years at Sussex University, during which time she gained her English degree, she accepted an offer to join London's most exclusive escort agency. After a further three years she left the agency to work on her own. For nine months, 'during my golden days as a prostitute', she worked the lucrative streets of Mayfair before branching out into her final venture, as a massage-parlour owner in Camden.

Although it initially appeared as if she had descended through the ranks of the sex industry, the longer Alice Teague worked as a prostitute the more control she carved out for herself. From being merely a cog in a large agency to owning her own business, Alice had seen prostitution from all tangents. After seven years she decided that she wanted a break, for 'there were a lot of other things I wanted to do with my life'.

Although now ensconced in a new career and a steady relationship, Alice maintained her links with other prostitutes. 'It wasn't a conscious decision to keep in touch with prostitution but I found that I had made so many friends over the years that it's just happened that way. Girls phone me up from all over the place, usually just to say "Hi" but then other problems creep into their conversation – they've been rumbled by the police again or there's a problem with a fucked-up client. Having stepped back from the day-to-day work I'm more able to be sympathetic. In the past maybe I would have just said, "Get on with it. This shit goes with the job, honey." Now I listen more, I try to offer practical solutions. Maybe I'm going to have to take this up another notch or two and go more high-profile.

'But, you know, that's a huge personal step to take. If I come out publicly as an advocate for the rights of prostitutes then you can be sure I'll drown in a river of hypocrisy. That typical British hypocrisy will ruin my other work, it'll put a terrible strain on my current relationship. So, in the meantime, I just go my own way, doing what I can, deciding if I should come out and take on the

Establishment. Who knows what I'll eventually do? In the meantime, my sweet, tough whores keep on calling me.'

Alice sentimentally called her 'sweet, tough whores' names like 'Gloria', 'Alicia', 'Roberta', 'Lola' and 'Shana'. She laughed long and hard when I asked if every prostitute she knew had a name ending in the letter 'a'. 'I'm just as big on the 'y' girls too, baby. You know there's "Cand-y", "Mand-y", "Sand-y" and even a "Rand-y" on my list. Then there're those more exotically-named whores — like "Angel" and "Harp" and "Lightning" and "Storm" and even "Enema Lady". But a special favourite is my one friend who gives the best escorting head in London while calling herself either "Germaine" or "Greer". It depends on her mood which name she uses with a new client. Some names just stick. I stuck with "Alice" as mirrors were always my kind of erotic aid.'

Alice, intent on parading through her gleaming array of prostitutes, spent the next hour and a half telling me about the kinky sex tricks and psychological dents of almost everyone from 'Gloria' to 'Germaine', or 'Greer'. Only one name was excluded — Mandy. When I asked her why, especially as she had started her 'Prostitutes In Paradise' litany with that reference to Mandy as 'the strangest, most beautiful woman' she had ever met, she looked meditatively at me. The frivolity of her chocolate gâteauing and whorish name-checking was forgotten.

'Here you are,' she eventually said, 'sitting with me, recording the sexy stories of a retired jazz and cake-loving ex-whore and you know I don't even have to ask why. I know you're sorta waiting for me to give you the nod, to say, "Yeah, write a different sort of book, baby." But I think you've already decided. So before I tell you anything about Mandy, tell me what you think you might write about us.'

That was the type of question which could only be answered confidently after a few hours of steady drinking. As our intake had been limited to a polite pot of herbal tea,

I bumbled about not being certain why I had even asked to meet her. I was more interested in writing than prostitution. Yet, ever since I had passed on the chance of ghosting the story of an escort agency queen, I had been unable to shake the subject from my mind. I started thinking about what it might mean to be a prostitute, about the stories which lay beneath the clichés and about the women who lived beyond the stereotypes of the 'Lolas' and 'Candys'. And then I began to wonder about the men who made up that secret other half of prostitution.

Despite the British public's enduring fascination, as attested by the media's propensity to seek out 'sex-for-sale' scandals, it seemed to me that prostitution's real stories were still to be told. Perhaps this perception had much to do with the fact that I saw myself as being a kind of outsider in this country, as a disenchanted white South African with a heart lost somewhere between Johannesburg and Arsenal FC. I wasn't sure yet how I could write these prostitution stories but I wanted to hear as many as possible. To do this I knew that I would have to be something more than a 'ghost-writer'; I would have to move much closer to the core of prostitution than I might have done during an arm's-length recording of one particular Madame's memoirs.

Alice listened pensively. Then suddenly she started laughing, as she already had done so often that afternoon, and leaned over and patted me once more on the cheek. 'You'll do just fine, sweetie. So, yeah, I think you should write this book and I think you should start with Mandy because she's so different. She's the last type of person who's supposed to become a prostitute. There seems to be some dark secret to her life.

'But hell, I don't really know. I've only met the girl twice. She called me up, right out of the blue. She says she's heard about me, that she wants to talk to me. She says she's been working for three-and-a-half years and that she's only got another eighteen months to go. She won't explain completely what she means by that. She doesn't say too much about

31

herself. She asks me more about other prostitutes — girls on the street, girls in parlours. "How are things for them?" she says, with those big, grey eyes of hers opened up wide and beautiful, like she's never turned a trick in her life.

'All this time she's been working completely on her own, running things just the way she wants them. She doesn't sound or look or act like any kind of whore I've ever met but she says that's what she is — "a whore". I call her "Crystal-Whore" 'cos she's like shining, quality cut-glass. But there's something else about her, something that I can't understand yet, something that makes me unsure whether her life is a thing of beauty or tragedy. Maybe you'll find out for me, sweetie. All I really know is that you start with Mandy Kavanagh and who knows where the fuck you'll end up? But you can bet you're gonna run through some peachily fucked-up stories . . .'

I learned for a second time that Alice Teague was invariably right when I spoke to Mandy Kavanagh the following week. She sounded different from any prostitute I had dreamed up in my head. Her telephone voice was, as Alice implied, crystal-like, but with an edge to it. It set me flicking back and forth between mazy images of what type of face a voice like this might emerge from, as if she could actually be an eloquent singer or an actress rather than the 'whore' she claimed to be.

But, if nothing else, I was learning to recognize that my preconceptions were hopeless. I remembered my surprise at the way Alice had looked on that sunny Sunday afternoon and tried to concentrate instead on the words Mandy was actually saying. They were chosen carefully. Our conversation faltered awkwardly between her precision and my rambling before she finally said that it would be best if I wrote to her, telling her something about myself and my reasons for wanting to meet her.

It seemed much easier to write than speak to her over the phone and so I sent her two single-space pages of typeface that same night. I told her that I was from South Africa and that I guessed I would always think of it as home even though I wondered if I'd ever live there again. I wrote about what it had been like to spend the first twenty-odd years of my life in a country as beautiful as it was blighted, in the suburban surrealism of a town called Germiston, just outside Johannesburg, where there were a handful of girls at my school who worked as afternoon hookers in the reeds along a set of railway tracks when they were fourteen or fifteen years old. I remembered being interested in them. But as a sixteen-year-old imagined stud, I thought that I only had to observe them at a distance like I had already done with the young black 'domestic servants' who sometimes, for a couple of rand, would shed white teenage boys of their virginity.

That had been the first time I had ever thought about prostitution. It was twelve more years before its reality sank in with any lasting impact. I had returned briefly to Johannesburg in 1990, having left for London in '84 when the South African military could be evaded no longer. I went with a friend to a hotel in Hillbrow, Johannesburg's most recklessly bohemian quarter where black and white people began living alongside each other years before they did anywhere else in South Africa. It was around two in the morning and we were both drunk, but with that delicious kind of drunkenness where the only sensible thing seems to be the hunt for yet another bottle. We knew that The Quirinale was the one hotel where we were sure of finding drink all night, for it was Johannesburg's most notorious brothel. The hotel's residents were exclusively young black women who had left the townships for the more profitable, if similarly hard, life they led as prostitutes to an unbroken stream of white men, many of whom were defiantly bearded Afrikaners.

My friend and I found the murkiest corner of the lounge and, smiling our pissed 'Not tonight, thanks' smiles at the slickly questioning Quirinale girls, we settled back with a few more drinks. It was a good, hazy feeling being back

33

home again, as strains of township pop blared across a dance
floor heaving with nervous Afrikaans men and seductive
black prostitutes dancing towards the 'New South Africa'.
Then, as if in a dream, a young woman appeared from the
shadows of the bar and knelt down in front of me. 'Don,
it is you, isn't it?' she asked. My friend gave me a knowing
look as if to say he had always been hip to my liaison with
prostitution. The night's drink tumbled through me and I
looked at her blankly, until she spoke again. 'Don't you
know? It's me Grace! You know, Grace from Bop . . .'

'Bop' was Bopasenatla High, a school in Diepkloof,
Soweto, where I had taught English, prior to the township
being engulfed by a State Of Emergency. Grace had been
my star student, a girl my own age who loved Keats, Hardy
and Eliot, even though the sun would be baking down
outside our prefab classroom and the desks were lined with
dust. Then, she too wanted to be a writer. After we had
hugged each other we were suddenly shy for we were both
unsure what to say about her working there as a prostitute.
But somehow, as I wrote to Mandy Kavanagh, I felt the
same as I had always done about Grace from Bop as we
drank through the early morning. She was coping, despite
the Afrikaans clientele and the undeniable fact that her
life had gone through a terrible upheaval to reach that
point.

That was one of my own stories, I wrote, but having
returned to London and spent the previous Sunday with
Alice Teague I was now interested in meeting her, Mandy.
In the last line of that letter I made the barest allusion to
the type of book I might write about prostitution, a subject
I felt I was being pulled inexorably towards.

Two days later, a postcard of Camus wearing a raincoat
in Paris dropped through the letter-box. It was from Mandy
and she wrote, simply: 'I liked your letter and, yes, I think
it would be interesting if we meet. This Friday evening seems
right. Alice has my address. Come see me around seven.
Mandy K.' It was as if she knew there was no question that

I would be there that Friday, as if the story had already begun, as if it were a river down which all we could do was drift, mapless, towards our unknown destination.

Mandy Kavanagh's house, the place she also worked from, was reminiscent of the set an advertising director might use for a turn-of-the millennium commercial about easy access banking or provocative perfume. White fans hung from the ceiling and dark venetian blinds lined every window. Apart from the cellar, the starkly tiled kitchen and bathroom, each of the rooms contained only one primary object. There was a music centre in the first room, a TV/VCR system in another, a computer in the third, a big low slung bed next door to that and an outlandish metal bookcase in her lounge. This was her favourite room, her most private place. As if in recognition of its special slot in her heart it was slightly more cluttered than the others. Here there was also an old oak table, a battered Turkish chair, her high-backed rocker and a lush black velvet sofa which appeared to be her lone stab at opulence.

Every room was painted a different colour – bright yellow in the music suite, pale grey for the video den, light green for the study and rich cream in the room with the bed. Mandy's favourite room, with its overflowing book case, was dark blue. Along the white passages leading from one room to the next there were elegantly framed prints – by Klee, Picasso, Mapplethorpe and Cartier-Bresson – and black and white photographs of Franz Kafka, Samuel Beckett with Buster Keaton, Miles Davis and a young Iggy Pop. At the end of this stylish gallery of alienation there was a smaller but much more intensely personal photograph. Although it was also attractively framed, this photo was nothing more than an over-exposed, blown-up Polaroid print. It was the most shattering image in the whole house.

The photograph had been taken thirteen years ago, on Mandy's twentieth birthday, when she looked much older than she does now. Then her hair was cropped short and bleached with peroxide. But her face belied her age, with all gloss and tautness struck from the skin. It hung shapelessly above her thin neck, literally ghost-like in its whiteness.

She sat on a single bed in a small white room, lit by a bulb above her head. Her eyes were wide and heavily ringed as if it had been weeks since she had last slept. Lower down, on the pitted surface of her upturned arms, the cause became clear. Her skin was covered with yellow and purple blotches. They were raw with needle marks. She held her emaciated arms up to the camera like she was making some kind of sacrifice. No matter how many times you walked down that passage it was impossible to pass this image easily, as though it was an adornment rather than some harrowing statement of personal history.

'That's me turning twenty,' said Mandy Kavanagh the first time I stopped to stare at the picture. It was just after seven on that Friday evening in August 1990, and my nervousness on her doorstep had changed into something different by the time we had reached the end of her hallway. Her voice was so matter of fact, so impersonal even, that she may as well have been talking about a distant cousin's wedding snap as of this depiction of herself at the ebb of life. Yet she looked at the photograph with such self-absorption that its significance to her was obvious.

Mandy had acquired a serenity which enabled her to look back with equanimity at that blackest of times. Her face shone with a soft tug of remembrance rather than with any marked sense of hurt. In the passing years, her face had regained the sculptured lustre found in glossy make-up spreads. Her hair, back to its original colour of black, curled round the edges of her mouth in a relaxed bob. She had given up the dirty white T-shirt and torn jeans for designer clothing.

We had been sitting in the blue room for a couple of hours, her rocking in her wicker chair and me sitting on the

velvet sofa, before she spoke again of the photograph.
Through the bay window, from where she used to watch
for Alistair, the sun was flattening out against the orange
outline of the trees as we emptied our second bottle of wine.
After so long, after I had talked and talked and she had
prompted me here and there with a question or a comment,
it finally seemed right for me to ask her something. Despite
the drink and the sun, the image of her which hung in the
hall had not slipped away.

She was quiet when I asked her about the photograph,
as if she was deciding whether I deserved an answer longer
than a few words. I had already told her so much about
myself, about Johannesburg and Soweto, about arriving in
London and not knowing a soul in the city, about my cheery
evasions of the moustached men of both the South African
army and the British Aliens' Office, about lost girlfriends
and dead friends, about the feelings of attraction and
bewilderment I had felt when first seeing Alice Teague, that
it was as though I was there to be interviewed by her.
Perhaps my willingness to talk instead of question touched
a chord in her because she at last ended her silence with a
story so strange that I did not have the breath to interrupt
her.

'It was my birthday, that day,' she said in her
characteristic murmur, 'the day I turned twenty. Six months
before, to the exact day, on the twentieth of December, I
started taking heroin. It wasn't the usual sort of scene, where
you fall into it at a party or because of a boyfriend. I took
it on my own that first time; and I deliberately chose heroin.
There's little in life that's more extreme than being addicted
to smack. But when I started I was like a child. I didn't have
a clue as to what I was really letting myself in for. I thought
it would be the ultimate test of will-power, of desire if you
like, but it was only much later that I realized the horror
of what I was doing.

'Essentially it was a very simple experiment. When I was
nineteen-and-a-half I decided on this test. For six months,

not a day more and not a day less, I would take heroin. Then, on the twentieth of June, the day I turned twenty, I would stop. As pure as that.

'I guess, if you really wanted, you could uncover any number of psychological reasons for doing such a thing. I was just fascinated by the idea of heroin and of course it was hopelessly romantic. I wanted to experience this thing which gave such a rush that people laid down everything for it. And even more than this, I wanted to know if I could survive heroin. I wanted to know if I had the desire to overcome the craving.

'When I started I wasn't quite sure what to expect. I began quite slowly, shooting up every ten days, trying to measure the full thrill of it when I felt the smack going right inside me. The first five or six times were truly wonderful and I realized then that there was a chance that I wouldn't want to come off it. I made the mistake of imagining that it was just about will-power. But heroin has much more to do with the body than the mind. I was fucked by the absolutely mindless need for physical relief every day. There were days, maybe weeks even, when I never believed I'd be able to give up on the day I said I would.

'I was burying myself in this white junk and if I hadn't started from such a weird tangent maybe I would never have found the motivation to cut back a little, just a little, every day during the last six weeks. But still, when it came, the twentieth of June, I didn't know how I was going to come off. If you look closely at that photograph you see how devastated I was. There's real terror there. Not the fear of dying but the sheer terror that my body would be denied heroin, which had become my whole life.

'But I came through that day, and the next, which I thought would be the worst, only to find that the third and fourth days were even more excruciating. It was also midsummer and unbearably hot. But by the fifth day the need eased a little and I could think about what was happening to me and what I still had to do. By the end of the next week

I knew that I would never go back to it. I was off, and really lucky to be off it.

'I'm now, I guess, scrupulously healthy. I don't smoke — and although you might not believe it the way we're sinking this wine tonight, I rarely drink. I exercise every day. I feel pretty strong. But that photograph stays in the hall because it's from a time which was very real to me. I sought out that experience knowing that, if I survived it, it would be something to remember rather than to forget. And I've tried to remember it as clearly as possible so that it remains as something more than a sentimental memory.

'Everything about those six months is there in that photograph. I came through it intact but the truth of that time is not glorious. Endurance is not glorious, it's not romantic. And that's what I did, that day of my twentieth birthday; I decided to endure, to go on, as best I could . . .'

There had been moments earlier in the evening, with me talking urgently and her rocking silently, when Mandy looked like she was from a chillingly beautiful autistic world. She seemed content to sway back and forth, until my words dried up and she would replenish another stream from me with just the gentlest question which again diverted attention from her. But now it was if some latch had been lifted from her own casket of stories. The next three hours were filled by her voice outlasting the batteries on my tape-recorder as she took me through the different stages of her life.

She began by answering my bemused question as to why she had felt the need to actually prove to herself that she could overcome a junkie addiction. Surely you could be curious about heroin without having to test your inner resolve to survive its shattering effects for a specific period of time? Why hadn't she just tried it once or twice, for pleasure, if she felt so compelled, and *then* tested her resolve never to try it again? 'I don't think that's really the key question, do you?' she retorted with a withering stare. 'Surely it's more puzzling that most people just fall thoughtlessly into addiction, that they're just random victims of some "accident" they claim to have had no control over? Isn't that more fucked — that you become a junkie without knowing it?'

I remained unconvinced. While it would certainly be more interesting to know why someone chose to drive at top-speed into a brick wall on a dry afternoon instead of guessing why another person spun off a wet road and smashed into that same brick wall on a rainy night, it'd be difficult to argue that the accidental crash was the product of a less controlled mind. Mandy smiled at my 'facetious analogy', saying that it was similarly difficult for her to think that she had been uncontrolled when she began her 'six-month affair with smack'.

I thought it peculiar that she described her addiction as an 'affair' but, as she traced her first twenty years, it became increasingly apparent that love or, to be more exact, the absence of love, had shaped the seemingly smooth curves of her life. She had been born into an extremely wealthy family and had lived with her parents, two older brothers and a sister in a Hertfordshire mansion until she was seventeen. They were a family with a considerable political and military heritage and so it was preordained that Mandy would follow her sister to the country's most prestigious school for 'young ladies', an institution favoured by those who dreamed that their daughters might, in Mandy's words, 'one day become a real-life princess or, at the very least, the wife of some fucking terrific captain of industry'.

'It's trite, I guess,' she continued, 'to pin everything on those years and on my family but that doesn't stop me from wondering if I would have done less extreme things with my life if it hadn't been for them. It's not that I wish we had been poor or that I had been an abused child because when I look around I see how lucky I was to have had such a comfortable life. I never had any problems about coming from the wrong side of the tracks. I've never had a day of hunger in my life. I've never wanted anything materially that I couldn't get if I asked long enough. I hated the school I went to but it gave me some kind of start in education and I had friends. It wasn't like I felt desperately unhappy or anything — Christ, even then I knew I was lucky.'

But money and luck, as another homily suggests, do not always bring love and Mandy Kavanagh's teenage life was one of secure lovelessness. 'I can't remember any spontaneous show of love in our family. My mother and father were mutilated by their good manners, so much so that they were incapable of feeling anything as uncontrollable as love. Or looking on the bright side, maybe they did love us but were unable to express it. Whatever, it made no difference. My life with them always felt cold. But as I got older that seemed to bother me less than the complacency of their lives. I remember how they would just try to "smooth things over" all the time. If I was snotty in my teenage rebel phase they would hardly notice for it was too embarrassing for them to look beneath the surface, to see if there was a problem of some sort. That just deepened my cynicism and so I escaped into things like books and records.

'But the fact that I became a junkie and that I am now a prostitute is not just because of my upbringing. I don't need any excuses to justify the way my life has gone. The heroin decision had as much to do with my obsession with certain songs and books as it did with just a basic rejection of my past. When I decided to shoot smack for six months I had already moved away from home and I had no intention of returning to our village to shock Mrs Mitten, the tweedy next-door neighbour, or to upset all those girls called Clarissa and Rowena-Jane who I used to go to school with and who're now married to stockbrokers and polo players.

'It was always much more personal than that. It was nothing to do with revenge. Instead it was all about my own heart, about letting loose everything that was swirling around in there. You know I was just a young girl living in a Holloway bed-sit on bacon sandwiches and chocolate biscuits while out of every pocket some book would be jutting.'

'What kind of books?'

'I dunno . . . books by Rilke and Baudelaire and books like *Nausea* and *Notes From The Underground*.'

'It sounds like you were a hip kind of Holloway girl,' I said.

'Yeah, I was pretty hip. It was 1977, after all, and I was also into punk and, even more so, into Iggy Pop and The Velvet Underground. I used to just love that wasted glory that shone off Iggy, the most beautiful junkie there's ever been. And my favourite song was the Velvet's *Heroin* which, 'cos Lou Reed used a needle or two round that time, came pretty close to sounding like the rush that smack gives you. So I found all these nihilistic ideas to be echoing my life up until then. To you it must seem kinda crazy but then you had a completely different life to me – what with those years in Soweto and all those cute teenage prostitutes along the railway tracks? You can laugh but, really, you had other choices to make. And, with me, six months of heroin seemed the right thing to do at the time.'

Having had a romantically existential adolescence myself, I could identify with some of the reasons behind Mandy's heroin experiment. Yet I was more interested in trying to link those six months with her decision to become a prostitute. She, meanwhile, moved ahead at her own dreamy pace. With the aid of a battered old sewing basket which acted as her crate of memorabilia she took me through her subsequent four-year career at London University, during which time she acquired a Master of Philosophy degree, and two more years as a professional model. She dipped in and out of her sewing box to produce pictures and certificates as if to quell any scepticism that a prostitute could ever have, in orthodox terms, achieved so much. The photographs clearly meant more to her than the 'meaningless' academic qualifications. But the attraction of well-paid, jet-setting modelling waned within the first year. After another twelve months, in which she gritted her teeth through the unremitting boredom of seeing out her contract, she could hardly bear the thought of having to hang around for a photographer to give her the command to 'pout girlishly' or 'go sultry' for the benefit of his camera.

'So there I was at twenty-nine-and-three-quarters, after philosophy and modelling, unsure of what to do next. For a mad moment I even thought about marriage. I had been seeing this man, someone who was mildly famous in "entertainment circles", while I had been modelling. I guess my brain was so fried by all the smiling and strutting that I allowed myself to get mixed up with this geek. He was exactly the sort of man a model is expected to "go with" and, in his way, he was the best of a bad bunch. When I gave up on the modelling he broke down and said he loved me and asked me to marry him. I quite liked him at that moment and the thought of having a baby then was quite a spur.

'But I knew that I didn't want to live with him for the rest of my life. I'm sure we could have had a comfortable marriage by conventional standards but it was never going to be enough for me. And I wasn't sold on the idea that he had that he was going to be the economic "powerhouse" in our partnership. He kept saying things like, "but you'll never have to think about working again if you're with me." I'd had enough of that kind of dependence with heroin! So I politely said "No" and decided on another course in life.

'That particular year had been crucial to me — what with the modelling and the marriage proposal. I'm not trying to say I had some sort of unique dilemma because I know there are thousands of other women in this city who feel like I did. Many of them do their own thing in an admirable way. But the whole economic structure of this society is still tilted towards stripping women of the independence that men have. There just seem to be too few women out there equipped to live on their own, free from doubt and fear because they haven't got a husband. It's still not the done thing to live alone for more than a few years. To me that's a fucked-up morality. Women should have the power to choose the way they want to live. But it isn't easy.

'If you live in a society like we do then you need money – otherwise you're just powerless. And marriage to a wealthy man or finding a high-powered job just 'cos the money's good always struck me as being refined examples of prostitution. That set me thinking: why go in for the hypocrisy when you can go it alone and do the real thing on your own terms?

'So early in March 1987 I decided to become a prostitute. I thought back then to my heroin time and resolved that I wouldn't let myself be destroyed by prostitution. The heroin experiment was, as I said, wildly romantic. This move into prostitution was more considered. It was planned. It was mercenary. There was nothing personal about this decision, just the fact that I knew prostitution could earn me the money I needed to live the way I wanted. I worked out that I could probably earn around £70,000 a year as a prostitute. Five years of that would free me from worry about money for a long time. So, I decided that I would be a prostitute for exactly five years – not a day more, not a day less – and tonight, you know, there are only five hundred-odd days to go. Let's have another drink to that, boy . . .'

As we opened another bottle of wine, all my previous speculation on prostitution appeared redundant. Before meeting Alice Teague and then Mandy Kavanagh, I had been under the spell of the liberal assumption that 'prostitute' was merely another word for 'victim' and that any woman who worked in the sex industry was inevitably subject to nothing but crass exploitation and abuse. Yet there was little doubt that both Alice and Mandy, with their degrees and past pedigrees, their sharp minds and strong characters, had had other choices at their disposal besides prostitution. Mandy, in particular, as Alice remarked, was one of those few women who could legitimately make that tenuous claim of 'having it all', as her success as both a model and post-graduate student suggested. That night, if Mandy Kavanagh was to be considered a 'victim' it would only have been of her own mythology.

Despite exploding traditional concepts of 'the prostitute', there was something unsettling about the extremity of her life. She seemed curiously fated to flip between 'good girl' and 'bad girl' roles — from 'poor little rich girl' to 'junkie', from 'model' to 'whore' — which were more society's constructs than her own. While absorbed in the execution of choice, she lived under an especially harsh personal vision. As I left her South Kensington home of coloured rooms and haunting photographs, knowing that I would soon return, I could only question the personal cost entailed in her dramatic bid for economic 'freedom'.

There is much turmoil in prostitution. This becomes apparent from that first moment when the idea of working as a prostitute is no longer confined to the abstract. That initial step, so different from the hypothetical imaginings women may have about the possibility of their becoming prostitutes, occurs with a tangible move towards the business of selling sex. For Mandy Kavanagh that entailed the concrete decision to advertise herself to prospective clients as a prostitute.

'I remember that I made my decision on a Friday morning. That same afternoon I phoned up this man, Alistair, who I knew had had the hots for me for years. He was just becoming well-known as a big city financier and his wife was interested in fashion. So he used to come to some of the fashion shows and that's where I met him. He was charming, in that unctuous businessman-of-the-year way, and he made it clear to me from our very first meeting that he wanted to take me out. He herded me into a corner and breathed his chocolatey breath all over me. He said I was the most irresistible woman he'd ever laid eyes on. And I was going, "Oh yeah, I wonder what your wife would think about that?'' He got really creepy then and said that their marriage was effectively over and that they just kept together for the sake of appearances. Then he came right out with it and made it clear that he fancied me so much he'd do anything I wanted, he'd give me anything I needed.

'He backed off when I told him I wanted nothing from him. He left me alone after that 'cos I was firm with him, but I always knew that he wanted me. So the very same Friday that I decided to become a prostitute I called him at his office. He hadn't seen me for about a year and at first he was very debonair on the phone. I said to him that I had a business venture to discuss with him and I wondered if he'd come over to my house the next Tuesday afternoon. He tried to stay cool but he was literally choking with excitement. I guess that's why I started with him. I knew he would take the bait.

'Over the whole weekend and on the Monday I'd stayed fairly calm. Of course I was thinking about it all the time but I was also certain about my decision. I never felt that I might be making an awful mistake for I'd considered the situation very carefully. It wasn't just impulsive, in the way the heroin thing had been. It was only on the Tuesday that I began to feel panicky. I woke up before it was even light and those nine hours before his visit were hell. I just wanted to get it over with but at the same time I was determined that I was going to control our first session. I knew that everything would hinge on the way I dealt with him that first time. If I was vulnerable, if I was nervous, he'd rip me apart. I wanted to be sure that I would dictate the mood of that afternoon.

'I didn't wear anything special – just a black dress and black stockings – and I didn't plaster myself with make-up. I wanted him to remember who he would be dealing with. I was coming out as a whore, but that whore would still be me. He had been a little frightened of me in the past and I didn't want to give up that advantage. But, shit, I was still shaky and feeling sick while I looked out this big window and waited for him to come. And sure enough, at two minutes to three, he turned the far corner. That set the pattern of our next five years of Tuesday afternoons.

'As soon as he walked down the hall I felt a little stronger. He was making all these jibes at my photographs — "Who are these *clowns*?" he sneered — and I said, "That's *Kafka* and that's *Beckett* and you'd better take your fucking hat off when you look at them!" He liked that, he always likes it when I swear, and so I started to feel my usual disdain for him. He took a seat and I got straight down to business. He spluttered into his coffee cup when I told him I was going to be a prostitute. I think he thought I wanted to be his mistress! I remember him saying, "There's no need to call yourself *that*," and I said, "But, Alistair, *that* is what I now am. I am a prostitute."

'I said this would be a purely business arrangement between us. I told him I'd charge him £150 to have sex and he agreed straight off even though that was quite a steep price to pay in '87. I gulped then because I knew the crunch point had come. So I took him into the bedroom and told him to get undressed. It was more nerves than anything that made me seem so decisive. He did as he was told and soon he was standing naked before me. He wasn't the prettiest sight I'd ever seen and, although I was a little repulsed by him, I felt in control. It was all over in about a minute and I thought "Phew, is that it?"

'Of course it wasn't because I felt pretty bad about having him inside me and when we got dressed again he seemed full of himself. Me being a whore was a great idea, he said, and before he left he wanted to discuss next week's session with me. I was a bit taken aback because I thought he'd just want to scuttle out of the door. Not Alistair though. So back we went to my blue room and he told me about his sexual desires. He was tactful about it in the beginning but it still came as a shock to me. He asked me if I had ever whipped anyone before, if I'd ever dominated anyone. I remember saying, trying to stay as cool as possible, "I could whip you all right, Alistair." I was in way over my head — I didn't know the first thing about bondage but, again, it seemed essential not to yield any ground to him. I told him that I would charge more for punishment and he said, "Of course, my dear, money's no problem with me, as you know."

'He talked on and on about his need to be dominated and disciplined. My mouth was just about falling open — after all, the most extreme thing *I'd* ever done sexually up until then was "69" a couple of times with my last boyfriend and even that had made me blush a little. Anyway I just brazened my way through with Alistair and he never had a clue how much he had disturbed me. It was only after he left that I cried a little. But it was more to do with relief that he had gone than with shame for myself.

'I had made my mind up about prostitution so there was no going back. But it was really hard that first time — especially all his bondage talk. I remember I had a bath and then I went to bed for the rest of the day. But I felt OK the next morning and I went down to the Ann Summers shop in Charing Cross Road and I bought my first whips and belts and, *voila!*, there I was — "The Terminator Angel", a leather-bound Dominatrix!'

And so it was 'The Terminator Angel' herself who first uncovered for me the struggle for control which beats at the heart of prostitution. Money and lust may keep the wheels of the sex business turning but the sparks which those wheels inevitably shed come from deep within the prostitutes' unequal strife with their clients, pimps and the police. Yet I had begun at the very top, with Mandy Kavanagh, where the struggle tilted in her favour.

Even though she was the first prostitute I came to know well it was never possible to imagine that Mandy could be anything but an exception to the usual rule. Her iron grip on her own business as a prostitute was soldered during that initial encounter with Alistair. By choosing to work alone, in her own home, rather than taking the more typical routes of escort agency or massage parlour or pimped street sex work, Mandy resolved to prostitute herself, as far as possible, on her 'own terms'. She risked danger in seeking out such independent control, for her very apartness from other prostitutes left her isolated and potentially open to unnoticed abuse. But Mandy intuitively knew that prostitution was more about loneliness and that quest for control than the jokey, girls-together camaraderie from which more ordinary hookers draw sustenance.

She also knew that the brutalities of this business mean that there is no such thing as a perfect operation, no such thing as absolute security, no such thing as an effortless life in prostitution. All it takes is one man to destroy everything. If that was the risk then she wanted to be the one who would choose her own clients, who would decide which chances were worth taking.

Through Alistair, she met another man whom she interviewed before deciding to take him on as an additional client. She then also called up a further long-time admirer, someone she had kept at bay in the past, and offered the same business terms as she had to Alistair and his squash-playing colleague. As she emphasized, 'I've always stuck to the same procedure. If a man wants to become a client then he has to apply to me, through one of my existing clients, for an interview. That means I get to pick and choose who I'll see, which I know is a very rare privilege for a prostitute. But I don't think I'm as strong as the women who work in more typical circumstances. I would buckle under the strain they endure. For me to work as a prostitute I need to retain as much control as possible.

'So I've turned down as many men as I've accepted as clients. I've stuck with ten for the last two years and so these boys think they belong to the most exclusive club in town. But I'm in charge. They know that I only take men who accept my terms. I see two men a day, five days a week and they all have their regular appointments. Two of them are retired while the rest of them are still working so I show a little flexibility. It's only Alistair who has turned his three o'clock Tuesday appointment into a kind of fetish. It takes a really important meeting, once or twice a year, for him to have to change that time. With the rest of them they stick to their day of the week. So if it's a Monday afternoon man then he knows I'll slot him in for an hour anytime between one and eight. Those are the hours I work, Monday to Friday, and I make few exceptions. Anyway none of them ever seem to miss an appointment. They know that if they do I can always show them the door, for there's a whole line of prospective clients waiting to take their place. So I have this routine, this Monday to Friday routine and it goes like clockwork, like £1,500 a week clockwork.'

For all its psychological ramifications, prostitution is essentially a business and, like most money-spinning endeavours, it depends on routine for its stable profitability. While Mandy enlivened my second visit to her home with a witty breakdown of her weekly working hours, I also remembered Alice Teague's grimmer delineation of the routine that less fortunate prostitutes endure. On the streets, it's usually a 10 p.m. to 2 a.m. shift, whatever the weather, while the bed-sit prostitutes of Soho and those advertised in the surrounding telephone booths face a longer 11 a.m. to 11 p.m. span of unremitting visits from anonymous clients. The escort agencies and the massage parlours have their own distinctive working patterns. So even as I listened to Mandy's exotic rendition of her own working week, I could sense the bleakness shadowing my future acquaintance with different routines of prostitution.

'You know,' said Mandy, 'in this job time takes on all sorts of weird shapes. The days blur into each other and time seems to move at different speeds. With some clients the hour passes like any other. With others, especially Alistair, when I have to smell his sweet breath on me as I whisper "you cunt", "you cunt" over and over again while

I whip him, the hour drags like nothing else on earth. Five years can seem like an endless period.

'But routine keeps me going. Instead of looking at this long stretch of time that lies ahead I've always tried to focus on my routine. I knew when I started that there would be days when I would feel dead inside. I knew that it was possible that every day would feel exactly the same. Because prostitution is like that — it's Nietzsche's theme of "eternal recurrence". The same thing happens again and again to prostitutes. A man comes in one door, fucks the prostitute and goes out another door, only to be replaced by another man who does the same thing before his place is taken by another man. Or else if you're a street-walker you get picked up by a man in a car, he fucks you, drops you off and then the same process is repeated again and again, year after year.

'That's why prostitution is also about deadening yourself. The routine can be so remorseless, with the prostitute on a conveyor-belt, that she has to blank herself — otherwise the repetition, the invasion of her private self, might drive her fucking crazy. But if you are going to make money as a prostitute you also depend on your routine. If you do it only when you feel like it you'll hardly ever work. In a strange way it's like the discipline you need to be a writer. You write every day, no matter how you feel, for you have a routine — it's essential. So it's the same with me, except I have a different routine as a prostitute. I'm luckier than other hookers because I'm able to control my routine — I know who and what to expect when. That may be boring but it is also a source of stability in this business, and it can be such a savage business.'

Mandy remembered that when she first began working as a prostitute she felt 'like the guy in this film I loved when I was a little girl — *If It's Tuesday, This Must Be Belgium*. I'm sure it's a terrible film but it tickled me when I was seven years old. There are days when I wake up and think, "Where am I? What am I doing today?" And then I'd remember. "I'm whoring again today so what day is it?" After a while it would sink in that it was a Tuesday. If it was Tuesday, it might not be Belgium but it certainly must be me jerking off the retired barrister and then whipping Alistair at three in the bondage cellar. If it's a Monday I'm a sexy vampish fuck to the advertising yuppie and a dildo-waving nun to my ex-politician. On Wednesdays I'm a governess and a strap-wielding Dominatrix to a weepie old judge and a corporate chairman who likes to wear a suspender belt and one of my old dresses. If it's Thursday I talk dirty and give head to a Comparative Literature lecturer and beat a leathery City man while he watches the same old gay porn video. Friday means the week's almost over and to a naughty architect I'm a bisexual honey with kissable feet while a rich painter likes to watch me eat fruit in the nude. Then he jerks off into a half-empty bottle of wine which he slugs from after he's "mixed the juices"! Actually, Friday's the best day as it happens; even now I find it a bit of a giggle . . .'

Then, as a novice in prostitution, I had to giggle myself at the vicissitudes of Mandy Kavanagh's clientele. Another basic assumption of mine, that prostitution automatically meant the exchange of money and fucking, was riddled with misconception. Out of her ten clients, Mandy only had regular intercourse with one man, her advertising executive, and even that would be preceded by a fifty-five minute massage and fashion-show routine which left only the last few minutes for sex. Her two hard-core bondage clients, Alistair and the leather-clad video-watcher, were content to receive their punishment from Mandy without any form of obvious sexual contact with her. The wine-mixing painter also refrained from actually touching her. The remainder of her consumers were mostly recipients of hand and blow jobs and only occasionally would the 'corporate chairman' request intercourse – a change which would cost him a further £100.

'I'm far more likely to take on a man as a client,' Mandy remarked, 'when he's looking for an "imaginative" kind of service rather than straight sex. I *am* a whore so I will

52

fuck for money but I prefer it if penetration's not involved. Richard, the yuppie who does want to fuck me every week, is my youngest client — he's in his late thirties and claims to have this idyllic family life except for the fact that, apparently, his wife will only have sex in the missionary position. I keep telling him he must be doing something wrong if she's so uptight. Anyway he comes to me so he can do it "doggie" and "side-on" and whatever — "Ho hum" is what I say to myself but he's all right I suppose. It doesn't take him long to get his rocks off, I'll say that for him.

'But the rest of them are in their forties and fifties and they're looking for something different. Of course they're all married and they're sheepish whenever I ask them about their wives because I'm scathing about their hypocrisy. In the beginning they were also frightened of me because they said I didn't look like too many other prostitutes they'd been to. I don't know about that but I settled them down and I've kept on playing these characters they fantasize about — you know, "the nun" or "the governess" or "the foot lady" or the "Dominatrix" or the "foul-mouthed bitch" or the "fruit-eating virgin nudist". It's like being in a Repertory Drama Company in a way — one day you're doing "Lady Macbeth", the next you're "the witch", then you're "Lolita", then you're "Miss Jean Brodie" or, God forbid, you're having to do *The Mousetrap* again in the cellar.'

For all their sardonic mockery, Mandy's theatrical analogies uncovered an essential truth about prostitution — that acting, and fantasy, are never far from the surface. Yet the various roles she plays are as reductive in their masculine-coded ways as those of 'junkie' and 'model' which she chose before embarking on her five-year career.

But in prostitution, where the most personal act of intimacy between two people is reduced to a repetitively impersonal business exchange, the survival of the woman living within the timeworn shell of the 'whore' often depends on the skill with which she manipulates her various personae. 'Mandy Kavanagh', after all, is not her only pseudonym. To her clients she is also 'The Terminator Angel', 'Ms K', 'Madame M', 'Miss Pussy Boots', 'Amanda-Jane' and, even, 'Mandsy-Girl'. For their fat weekly fee, some of which is paid by standing order into a Jersey bank account, the men get to choose Mandy's alias while she gives their fantasies, and an hour of her time, back to them.

As Mandy said a few Tuesdays later, 'At first I found it demoralising that the names I had to use were either these harsh Dominatrix words or these infantile "Mandsy-Girl" virgin titles. Then, as you do in this business, I became inured to it. The names are now meaningless to me, as are the personae. I'm more concerned about keeping myself together when I'm around someone like Alistair.

'And *you're* also going to find this the further you go into prostitution — that there's always this jarring conflict between the whore and the john, between the woman and the man, between the person and the persona, between the personal and the impersonal.

'I felt that terribly today when Alistair was here. He went back again to that horrific hospital girl rape fantasy of his. I was hoping he had forgotten after all these months — but he never will. And I was so frightened of what he made me feel. He has such anger towards women, towards our sexual power, and so he wants to demean women ceaselessly. But because he's sharp enough to know that his true power over women lies with his money and status he comes here to channel his worst desires.

'When we're in the cellar together I sometimes feel almost deformed by my own rage at him. There're times when I feel I could happily beat him to death. But there's this restricting struggle of morality between me and "The Terminator". He knows I'll only go so far. You know, he thinks he's really winning our struggle. I asked him today what he'll do when I'm no longer his "Terminator Angel".

'He just laughed in my face, with his foul minty breath,

and said, "Who do you think you're kidding, Angel? You're a whore for keeps. *My whore*. All this five-year talk is complete crap. Once a whore, always a whore. Once a woman, always a whore. You're *mine*, Terminator," he kept crooning as I started hitting him with the belt again, "You're mine, you're mine . . ." '

Chapter Two

The Cellar of Pain

A month had passed since Mandy Kavanagh first led me through the multi-coloured rooms of her home. In that short time it seemed as if everything both around and inside me had changed. It was not just the fact that the cold rains of the previous month had been replaced by the enervating heat of a belated summer. Neither was it merely the point that my own routine had been reshaped by the numerous visits I made to her house during August; by the end of which time I knew I would write about 'The Terminator Angel'.

There were deeper shifts, more elusive to name and more difficult to interpret, within these seasonal and writing permutations. Primed by Alice Teague, I had arrived at Mandy Kavanagh's home that first Friday evening expecting to meet someone different, someone who existed beyond the stereotype of the victimized prostitute. But nothing could have prepared me for the physical deconstruction of prostitution which Mandy embodied. She tore up every preconception I had nurtured about the way a hooker should look and sound, about the background she was meant to creep from, about the relentless humiliation she was supposed to suffer day in, day out. These *were* factors, if sometimes only for the exceptional difference she brought to their existence, but their true weight could only be felt once they were regarded from her personal perspective.

In those first visits, instigated more often by her than me, she revealed that perspective with a terrible intimacy. Apart

57

from helping me, she also used the inexhaustibly whirring tape-recorder for her own purposes. After four mute years, she finally felt able to give voice to herself as the 'Terminator Angel', 'Madame M', 'Ms K' or whoever else she had chosen to be on a given day. There was a kind of unspoken agreement between us that just as I was blatantly unsuited to any sort of priestly or psychiatric role she was not in need of confession; for she had no admission of guilt to make. Rather, we narrated different personal histories. In this way we told each other about ourselves. If these conversations were interviews it was the presence of the tape-recorder which made them so, rather than any rigid definition of roles where I was the interviewer and she the interviewee.

She made another implicit decision to avoid the professional routine which comprised the rest of her week — so, outside of her strict working hours, I visited Mandy at different times and on different days. Through all of this she made me look at prostitution and its attendant practitioners and consumers from a blank start, with that impersonal blankness which every prostitute has to call upon at some time every working day.

But she also made me see more ordinary lives in a clearer light. The generic struggles for dominance in all relationships no longer appeared removed from her own work, streaked as it was with role-inversions and game-playing. Inverted echoes of her S&M stories were everywhere. Even on a crowded tube to South Kensington I could see the subtle manoeuvres for space unfolding as a woman found herself hemmed in between a man and a shut door. He would invariably be the one to thrust forward knowingly, she the one to back up against the door, anxious about this uneven temporality of space in the steaming underground. I would look at the man and wonder if he ever needed the taste of a prostitute's whip to redress that imbalance; and doubt if the woman was as in control of her life as Mandy Kavanagh claimed. Perhaps these were ridiculous comparisons but against the backdrop of the stories Mandy had already told me, I felt acutely aware of the coded reactions that take place between men and women in public places.

I tried to check these observations by deliberately noticing summery flirtations. In this search for more innocent pleasures there was a seeping fear that my eyes had been jaundiced by even a lone month's exposure to prostitution. But I was seeing what I had always seen.

Whenever I made the short walk that September from the South Kensington underground to Mandy's house, the pubs and cafés spilled out onto the sunlit streets with women in cool dresses and men in shirt sleeves drinking and laughing together as if an endless holiday had just begun. While it appeared as if every sunny face around me was slick with thoughts of love, their flirtations were so full of coquettish promise and grinning anticipation that they seemed to parody prostitution's own caricature of sexuality.

Yet this random game-playing was disturbed by murky images of Alistair. I had the barest physical description of him from Mandy — tall, lean, 'distinguished-looking' with only his mouth and eyes revealing a trace of the cruelty she knew her whipping just about curbed. I found myself imagining him everywhere, while knowing all the time that he was already elsewhere.

I felt him most of all in Mandy's home when she described it as her 'house of pain'. She said these words with a laugh that was impossible to pin down, falling from her mouth with bruising irony. For all the extraordinary control she exerted, her life was ringed with sadness. She told me on the last Sunday of September it was exactly four years to that very day since she had last had 'cashless' sex. Her words came with neither arrogance nor despair but with a softly resonant sense of pain. She knew that feelings of love do not flourish easily in her world, distended as it is with stories of caustic masochism. But she also knew that in the world outside, in that everyday world of apparently 'ordinary'

people, love was ringed with hurt too; and so in her telling
of these stories, not everything had to be personal.

Mandy remembered her breath being taken away by the
shimmering brightness of the first outfit Robert wore for
her. It was a skin-tight cat-suit made out of glistening red
leather and covered in golden zips and buckles. Under the
spotlights of her video room the suit crackled as if full of
a life of its own. It stretched upwards from the ankles to
the neck, biting down into his flesh. The only exception to
this constriction was the ring of space cut away to allow
Robert's buttock-cheeks to pout from the squeezing embrace
of leather.

Stunned by the sheer visceral force of the uniform, it took
Mandy a moment to register that Robert was also wearing
a matching red hood and condom. The mask was pulled
down so tightly that he had trouble breathing. A slit of space
had been left for his mouth, no larger than the hole opened
up over each eye. His breath came in shuddering bursts just
as the surrounding leather creaked with the effort of his
movements. The effect would have been almost sickeningly
sinister if it hadn't been for the saving touch of the red
condom. Robert's cock, struggling through the constricting
leather, peered valiantly out of his golden trouser zip even
though its low-slung eye was covered by the red mist of his
Mates' protective hood.

Robert could not move easily or make any comprehensible
sound but it was obvious that he was literally suffocating
with lust and, more problematically, lack of oxygen. The
video was already rolling and Mandy watched for a minute
as a slim-hipped Californian surfer learnt a new 'Hang Five'
variation as he was fist-fucked by a Dennis Hopper lookalike
wearing a black stetson and smoking a thin Indian reefer.
At the same time the boy was also giving head to a beefy
lifeguard who moaned a suitably surferesque 'Tube that
fucker, tube it!' mantra over and over again.

Robert had fast-forwarded *Surf Butt Bandits* to one of

60

his favourite moments. Even through the slashes, Mandy could see his eyes gleaming as he watched the screen. Eventually he turned to her and with the slightest jerk of his head indicated that it was time that she swapped her wide-eyed astonishment for the chiselled anger of 'Ms K'.

With his last decisive act for the hour Robert spread himself over her black leather 'Lazy Boy' rocker which she had tilted into an inverted, downward-sloping psychiatrist's couch. As he had requested during their original interview, Mandy manacled his bare feet to the special hooks inserted at the back of the chair and hand-cuffed him to the front legs. She thought that it looked as if he was tied to a comfortable ironing board, sloping towards the floor. His chin sank down onto the foot rest which she yanked up a notch so that he could watch the next scene in which a muscular Hispanic toilet cleaner deflowered another prime example of the blond American surfing dream.

As the video unfolded its stock of porn clichés, Mandy's task was to punish the helplessly pinioned Robert with a strap until his flesh was as red as the endlessly sighing leather of his uniform. He had said the week before that she should 'bleed the red' from him but his words were furtive, without the messianic zeal Alistair used when demanding his hourly share of discipline. So when it came to the point where she had to swing her belt in studded arcs over Robert, Mandy bent her wrist back and forth so that a whipping sound sang through the air. She saw how he twitched beneath the flapping tumult. Even the sound of the belt moving through air was enough to fuse his desire with guilt.

Mandy had not expected homophobia to be the shaping restraint of Robert's life. When they had first met he had appeared wryly sophisticated − even when he said that he would pay her £200 to beat him while he was strapped down and 'forced to watch filthy videos' it had been with a tone of knowing irony. But bound up in his leather suit and hood it was clear that this mummified version of Robert found the idea of gay pornography 'filthy' − it

61

was the kind of erotic dirt that both aroused and repulsed him.

When she punished Alistair he was always naked, leaving no doubt in her mind that it was him her belt was slashing into. But Robert disappeared into the taut folds of his red outfit. She felt uncertain that it was even him she was standing over with the belt whirling around her head. It would have been easier to lay into a depersonalized homophobic, to send her studs swinging heartlessly into the open flesh of a uniformed figure she had never known; for she had liked Robert's wit from the moment they met and it pained her to think that she should have to hurt him.

She focused on the ominous hood he had stretched over his hidden face to find some well of detachment into which she could sink her raised arm. But then he raised his buttocks with a muffled groan and she caught a flash of his red condom. She couldn't help her shortened laugh as she imagined Robert in his pin-striped suit carefully packing his matching uniform, hood and condom into the Sainsbury's packet he then placed in one of the myriad compartments of his briefcase.

From then on he was Robert to her again and she concentrated more on zipping the belt back expertly so that it merely stung his absurdly expectant posterior. As requested she also abused Robert verbally, switching back and forth between his own desired 'faggot' and 'queer' choices and her improvised 'closet-case' and 'pin-striped prick'. She found it hard at first to sustain this momentum of defamation but the video helped with its ludicrous mix of crusin' and surfin' porn slang and she built up a repartee with the screen. She was unsure how any of this went down with Robert until his stifled moans were finally accompanied by the jerking of his hips against the leather chair. As he at last came with the belt circling above him, Mandy doubted if she'd ever laze on that particular chair in quite the same way again, even though Robert had had the good taste to wear a condom.

After his curious climax, Mandy lent over to loosen him from his manacles. Robert shuffled from the video room with the spotlights still gleaming on the red leather and the slowly drooping, now filled, condom. The video was nearing its end with a mass beach-hut orgy accompanied by an ersatz funk soundtrack which grew louder with each culminating thrust until the star surfer pulled out of his pal's mouth to crank out his 'cum shot', captured in slow-motion replay by the artistic *Surf Butt Bandit* director. Over a freeze-frame of gushing semen, presumably meant to reflect a foaming wave, the video credits rolled. Amidst all the 'Jeffs' and 'Joeys' and 'Johnnys', Mandy was staggered to see that one of the actors was called 'Gregor Samsa', the name of Kafka's own beetle butt bandit in *Metamorphosis*. For her, as the Kafka-loving 'Ms K', this seemed to be post-modernism taken to its most ironic degree. But it left her in dazedly good humour as she waited for Robert to return from the blurred fantasies of his leather world.

Fifteen minutes later she knew she had a satisfied customer. Robert glided into the suitably grey room in his formal financial analyst uniform with a shy smile on his face. He said, 'Thank you, Ms K, thank you,' graciously and shook Mandy warmly by the hand. She tried to talk to Robert about his gay-leather desires and the 'Gregor Samsa' video star but he skilfully evaded her questions. He said that she had been 'just perfect' and that he would see her at the same time the following week. And so another routine was set in place – the only difference being that Robert would appear in a new uniform every other month, with a different colour matched by his perennial hood and condom.

For Mandy, 'compared with Alistair, clients like Robert are bliss. He's obviously got some strange hang-ups but I've always liked Robert. He can be a very witty guy although he doesn't like it much if I kid him about his homophobia. He gets very defensive whenever I try to talk to him about it. When I interviewed him he was excruciatingly embarrassed about describing the service he wanted from me. He never even hinted that we'd be watching *Surf Butt Bandits* or that he'd be wearing this bottom-squeezing red leather number. He just said that he needed to be beaten whenever he watched these "disgusting" videos. It's the word he uses more than any other when he talks about pornography — "disgusting". But he gets a kind of stilted pleasure from just saying the word.

'Robert was only my fourth client and I was surprised by the uniform and by his homophobia. But I soon loosened up and gave Robert what he wanted — which was more verbal than physical abuse. At first I found it hard to churn out these obscenities. I wanted to counsel him instead and to say sweetly, "It's OK, Robbie, for you to like men. Why don't you just try it instead of getting me to beat you up while you dream about it." But that's not what Robert wants to hear. It's impossible for him to admit that he's gay. When I tried to get back onto the counselling tack by suggesting he go to a gay bar one week instead of visiting me, he said, "Are you out of your mind? Don't you remember that I'm married, that I am a father of three teenage children, that I work with million-pound deals every day. Do you want me to give everything up for a filthy fantasy that afflicts me every now and then?"

'It was almost a poignant moment, even though he chose to use a horrible word like "afflicts". He'd come out of his submissive role and he was the Robert he is outside this house — rigid and uptight about respectability. For him, being gay means certain ruin, the end of everything. He just refuses to even contemplate coming out. By paying me, a woman, a supposedly wrathful woman who's going to sort him out, he thinks he's "dealing" with his desire. Of course he's not — we just continue our merry way week in, week out.

'For Robert, there's such deep shame that he tells me he can't even jack off in front of his own video screen. He has to be punished for his pleasure. But there're still moments of real wit and creativity. I like the matching colour technique whenever he unveils a new uniform — bottle-green suit and hood, bottle-green condom; baby-blue suit and hood, baby-blue condom; polka-dot suit and hood, polka-dot condom. I think he searched long and hard to find a packet of polka-dot condoms — imported from Scandinavia. He also goes out of his way to find different kinds of leather and PVC contraptions so I'm never really sure what he'll turn up in.

'The same goes with the videos. Sometimes he'll arrive and say I've got a new "Gregor Samsa" video for you. It's for him really but he does go out of his way to hunt down videos with "Gregor Samsa" 'cos he knows how amazed I was that a Californian porn actor would call himself after a Kafka character. With Robert it's the thought that counts. I find it touching in a way. Whereas with Alistair our S&M sessions are built on nothing but brutality . . .'

The way Mandy spoke about Robert provided further shifts in my perceptions of prostitution. Whenever she saw Robert it was obvious that he was more the 'victim' than her. Although there was hurt in Mandy's separation from love, in her apartness from people existing outside her 'house of pain', it was Robert who needed help.

Mandy's revelations of her differing S&M sessions with Alistair and Robert also pointed to the fact that prostitution in Britain is patterned with themes of bondage and fantasy, repression and role-reversal. Sex, especially amongst the professional clientele, is often merely an introductory gesture or a vague after-thought to the more urgent currents of guilt and retribution.

Although I could make a cerebral linkage between Alistair's misogyny and his culpable need for punishment, as well as between Robert's homophobia and disappearance into leather-cased anonymity, I felt emotional incomprehension whenever I tried to imagine myself wanting to either whip or be whipped. Having had a life so far devoid of sado-masochistic fantasies I alternated between feeling smugly self-congratulatory at my supposed normality and then mildly disappointed in my comparatively mind-numbingly dull sex-life — with not even a single manacle, studded belt, leather cat-suit or polka-dot condom to remember.

'Of course it's gonna seem strange to you at first,' Mandy remarked, 'because it *is* strange. S&M goes to the root of people's darkest fears and desires. It's about domination and submission, about control and abandonment, about pleasure and pain. These boundaries are closer than you think and they blur in the mind rather than in the body. That's where this extreme strangeness comes in, with the mind. But that's what also makes some of it so fascinating.

'Most of the clients I see need mental rather than physical relief. There's a morass of contradictions inside them and they come here, in a way, to recover some sort of clarity, some kind of balance. Even Alistair. It's a mistake to try and just conjure up an overview from the start. These S&M desires are deeply personal — they come out of people's bruised psyches. One wants to have me walk over his face in six-inch heels, another wants to be flogged, another wrapped up tight in a uniform, someone else only wants verbal rather than physical abuse. The reasons for each desire are different and they can shift as well.

'What my S&M service seems to do is provide a framing device for confronting these men's unnameable longings. They choose the frame, they set the limits and I play their game in the persona they most fantasize about. I don't really feel I'm curing anyone of their repression because, for the most part, the S&M fantasies stay unchanged year after year. But I attract a particular kind of client, I guess . . .'

Then, I felt it was time for me to branch out of Mandy's blue room and to hear from some of these masochistic clients themselves. As tarnished as he already was in my own mind, I knew that I would have to test this grotesque image of Alistair against a personal encounter.

When I suggested this to Mandy she almost seemed to growl a low 'No!' rebuke.

'Why not?' I asked.

'You're not ready for Alistair yet — you're still a baby when it comes to dealing with someone like *him*.'

Of course she was right and although I tried to feign an air of hard-boiled mockery at her maternal 'baby' tag, I was mightily relieved when she suggested I start with Robert instead. There was plenty of time for Alistair — he was out there, somewhere, not even dreaming, as I was, of a clash between us one day.

It has always been difficult to break through the anonymity shielding the consumers of prostitution. This became apparent during Mandy Kavanagh's ensuing weeks of negotiation with Robert. He listened to her talking about me while slipping back into his 'married financial analyst with three children and 7-series BMW' mould. Although he trusted her implicitly, having been a client without any trouble for nearly four years, Robert was riddled with anxiety at the prospect of meeting me. Visions of tabloid-infested scandal haunted him.

Mandy tried a variety of charming and domineering techniques to persuade him to phone me. Even though he contorted his sexuality further by telling Mandy that he was 'half in love' with her, Robert refused to make any contact with me. Considering the history of scandal smearing prostitution in Britain, neither Mandy nor I felt able to question his logic. Tradition has determined that it is always the client, and never the prostitute, who receives the luxury of anonymity. It is inevitably the woman who is exposed in the dock, while the man's name is protected. This, it is said, is in the interests of his family and career, a sensitivity from which the prostitute never benefits. Despite the lucidity of Mandy's stories I could not forget that, in the world outside, prostitution is the dirty old 'p' word. The stench of its stigma is meant to stick to the whores only. So we accepted Robert's refusal with some resignation. I even felt a little foolish in half-expecting that he might have spoken to me.

But a few days later, Mandy called to say that Robert had had a sudden change of heart — he would meet me the following afternoon, the day of his next appointment. He had given no reason to her for the shift and so I arrived at her home once more not knowing what to expect. She also looked nervous when she opened the door and whispered that he was waiting upstairs, in the video room, where we would do the interview prior to his changing for their latest 'Gregor Samsa' session.

Mandy held my hand tightly as we walked up the stairs together. She was worried that Robert might be getting the wrong idea about her mild liking for him. His garbled declaration of love for her the previous week had unsettled her. As with all prostitutes, it was imperative that her clients' emotions were kept sufficiently in check to avoid any 'unnecessary confusion'.

Robert was evidently seeing me as an affectionate favour to Mandy. All kinds of compromising situations sprang to mind as she knocked gently on the pale grey door. There was no answer from inside the room. After a slight hesitation she opened the door and walked inside, only to stop in mid-step so that I almost careered into her. She swallowed a gasp of surprise and said, as neutrally as she could, 'Why, Robert, you've changed already . . .'

Through his eye slits, Robert must have seen a comical sight. Mandy, all arched eyebrows and pursed lips, hovered uncertainly around the gaping statue that once was me. Robert wore a black leather cat-suit which had a broad gold zip running up the middle from crotch level right into his shiny black hood. The thought crawled across my mind that if this was *only* Robert then how much worse could Alistair possibly be? It looked as if his head was split into two sides by the zip and could be peeled apart to reveal a hideous face of flesh. Having once been a delinquent fan of the manic 'Leatherface' in *The Texas Chainsaw Massacre*, it seemed a cruel come-uppance that I should be turned to stone by a financial analyst in a South Kensington video den. As the black hood shone a few feet from me, it was as if 'Leatherface' had been brought back from the grave into awesome life.

Yet instead of the whirring whine of a chainsaw blade, Mandy's composed voice cut through the silence. She drew Robert by his black leather glove towards me and said, 'I think you two had better meet after all this time. Robert, this is my friend I told you about . . .' 'Leatherface' and I exchanged stiff handshakes and he made a muffled grunting noise in reply to my inappropriate 'Hello, how're you?' greeting.

As even I could see, Robert was not doing too well within his creaking leather encasement. His breath hissed painfully from the small round hole covering his mouth as he tried to drag air down these suffocating confines. He gestured painfully to the 'Lazy-Boy' couch which was still in its upright position. Mandy interpreted this as an indication that I should sit there while Robert leaned awkwardly against the wall opposite. She retreated tactfully, saying she'd wait in her room until we had finished our interview.

I stared into this hooded nightmare of gurgles, relieved that he hadn't shown me the extent of his colour co-ordination by whipping out a black condom-clad penis. Perhaps that was yet to come. Noticing my discomfort Robert made a guttural series of noises which I could only manage to answer with an apologetic 'Pardon?' He repeated himself with a sound that emerged as a disconcerting mix of a gargling Teutonic hum and a crackling death-rattle.

Trying to remind myself that this was meant to be my first exclusive interview with a significant consumer of high-class prostitution, I suggested to the supposedly submissive Robert that he move a little closer to my chair and speak more slowly through the thick leather hood. He inched forward towards me until I could feel the heat rising from the shining black surface. He spoke again and the noise broke from him with intimate fury, more incomprehensible than ever.

In desperation I nodded sagely. 'Robert,' I said pleasantly, 'do you mind just nodding either yes or no to my first few questions?' Robert shrugged his shoulders, a stifled movement which set off ripples of light across the smooth black surface.

And so off we went with a series of nods either up and down or from side to side. Robert's hood revealed that while Mandy was not the first prostitute he had visited she was the most satisfactory Dominatrix he had yet encountered. He now had no need to visit any other prostitute and his wife, with a vigorous shake, most certainly did not know where he spent his late Thursday afternoons. While he gave a shaky no-yes-no answer as to whether he enjoyed pornography, he was emphatically clear that he was not gay but that he did deserve punishment from Mandy's belt.

Thinking that we were proceeding swimmingly I decided to delve further into this more complex area of sado-masochistic uniform sex. Did he feel simultaneously more secure and more excited behind his anonymous black mask? An affirmative nod was quickly followed by a long burst of black zipper talk which I had to ask him to repeat. Robert released an equally indecipherable series of tortuous exclamations.

Not having the heart to go through the entire process again I asked Robert, seeing that his anonymity was assured by the uniform and that there was a 'slight distortion' of his voice behind the hood, if he would mind if I taped our conversation. After a few wavering moments, the hood shook from side to side and so I placed the recorder between us in the hope that I would be able to make some sense of Robert's speech when replaying the tape later on Mandy's monstrously high-definition speakers.

A bizarre half-hour followed. I reeled off a list of prepared questions to each of which Robert delivered a thick gush of crackles and hisses. I reverted to my sensitive nodding technique at the end of Bob's every burst of hooded noise without understanding more than one word here and there — 'Ms K', 'belt', 'leather', 'hood' and 'video' — to reassure myself that we were still on the right track. Eventually, worn down by my own nods and futile efforts to keep up with Robert's strangulated voice I shook him by the glove, thanked him for his time and assured him that his secrets were safe with me.

As I shut the door behind me and sank against the wall in fatigue I heard the video begin with the unmistakable thud of a pornographic soundtrack. Trying to block out the thought of 'Leatherface' reaching for his black condom I walked down the passage to Mandy's serene blue room. She was rocking in her usual chair, reading, and as I walked in she looked up hopefully.

'How did it go?' she asked.

'Don't ask.'

'Why?'

I slipped the tape into her cassette desk and wound it back a few minutes. The room resounded with the sound of Robert's leathery chainsaw voice. It reverberated from her speakers with a bizarre ferment of sighs, moans and grunting growls.

'But that's like the noise he makes when he's jerking off to Gregor Samsa,' murmured Mandy thoughtfully. 'Whatever did you ask him?'

Before I could answer her, my own recorded voice burbled through the speakers. 'Yes I see,' I lied. I imagined myself nodding furiously. 'But why do you want to feel pain so badly, Bob?' My voice sounded terrible in such definition and I squirmed while Mandy laughed — 'You called him "Bob"? I'm sure he went for that in a big way . . .'

We listened to Bob going for it in his own ubiquitous way as a twisted stream of white noise whined from his mouth before lowering itself into the sound of a rubbish truck grinder.

Mandy was still laughing, her own words struggling to be heard as she said, 'Welcome to the secret world of sado-

71

masochism, boy. This is what £200 an hour sounds like. But, baby, how're you ever gonna understand the language of bondage?'

Even though my comprehension of that language was still in its infancy, I could no longer fail to acknowledge the power impacted into its rituals. Standing alone in the silent 'Terminator Angel' basement a few days later I imagined I could hear the excruciating intensity shaping the language of S&M. As if lost in a chamber of horror, I listened for an echo of the cries I knew had reverberated from one white wall to another. The more I strained to penetrate the sound-proofed cellar the deeper its concentrated silence began to hum. In my head that hum slowly mutated into the faint din of pain that must have been felt by the men on the black leather and gleaming metal apparatus set diagonally opposite each other.

The convex mounting-couch where Alistair spent much of his hour between three and four every Tuesday afternoon stood in the far corner so that it was the first object to be seen when the door swung open. Across the full expanse of the cellar's twenty-square-foot cement floor, an even more imposing contraption demanded attention. Like an eight-foot-high metal doorway, embellished with a complicated system of pulleys and chains, this innovative stretching rack had been constructed by one of Mandy's former clients, an engineering genius. He liked to dangle from his steely invention for twenty minutes at a time, occasionally requesting that 'Madame M' should either spin him round or lash him with one of her whips. When he left London for a high-paying academic post in America he had to abandon his rack. Not having much use for it any more, 'Madame M' rarely oiled its complicated cranking system and so its effectiveness had rusted slightly in the two years which had passed since the creator's departure.

In less hi-tech mode, a long wooden rack filled most of the adjoining wall. Mandy sometimes used it not only to manacle an expectantly submissive client but also to house her assortment of shiny boots, belts, chains, handcuffs, hoods, rods and whips. Surrounded by this full range of bondage paraphernalia, reflected in the large revolving mirrors standing in the two remaining corners of the cellar, it was perhaps inevitable that I felt intimidated.

I had not been on my own there for more than ten minutes when I heard Mandy and Alice Teague walking down the stairs to the basement. It felt as though they were dispensing the surreal relief visitors must bring to a prison. While the two of them had been upstairs looking at Mandy's chic Nicole Farhi and Pam Hogg wardrobe, I had ambled down ahead of them. But where I had seen only grim retribution they both found touches of levity in this, to them, familiar place of bondage. Mandy was dressed in an incongruous sun dress and sandals while Alice wore a more apt outfit of thigh-length boots, a leather mini-skirt and jacket whose blackness was offset by the bright pink of her halter-neck top and the inevitable ribbons in her hair. If Mandy, with her sun-glasses perched on top of her head, looked like she was heading for a picnic, Alice appeared set for an infinitely more rousing encounter.

'Oh yeah, kids,' she sighed as she strode across the cellar, 'this is like coming home! Mmmmhmmmm! Not bad! Pretty nifty in fact — do you have them face up or down on this?' she asked Mandy as she stroked Alistair's convex couch.

'Down — unless they've been acting worse than usual,' Mandy replied softly.

'That figures,' said Alice distractedly as her attention fixed on the line of whips wedged into the wooden rack. 'Yes, oh yes, "Crystal", you've got some great stuff here. I've used most of these in my time. You only seem to be missing some of those huge sets of forceps . . .'

'Somehow, I've never needed to use them,' Mandy said, smiling reassuringly at me in the huddled shadow of the stretching rack corner.

'Aahaaa! Here we are! This is what I've been looking for!'

Alice exclaimed as she picked out a thin whip which made a whippity-whappity sound as she flexed it back and forth through the air. 'I used to be brilliant with one of these — even if I say so myself!' Providing the proof of this, she went through a drum-majorette twirl which rolled into a series of clipped kung-fu jabs and chops before, with an apocalyptic cry, she brought the whip crashing down into the leather couch. 'Yes! Kinky Karate Kat! I like this one!' she almost whispered in confirmation as she slipped off her leather jacket and lovingly curved the whip back in both hands. Finding the mirror-prop she had used in her own bondage work Alice entertained us for a few more minutes. She sent the whip whistling round her while watching herself closely in the mirror for any false moves. 'This your favourite whip too?' she asked Mandy when she'd worked up a light sheen of sweat.

'Oh yeah! I've always been a bendy-girl!'

'Me too — definitely! You can't beat a bendy for fun! It's those short truncheon type monsters I never liked using. With a bendy you always feel you can control things a little better. Are most of your "johns" bendies too?'

'About a third, I'd say. But I've got as many into the belt as the whip,' answered Mandy.

'The belt's OK, I guess. I just go for this bendy-type noise more!' To reward herself, Alice produced a particularly ferocious set of swishing slashes through the air which left her breathing quickly. 'Whew, you tend to forget that this gives you a better work-out than any kind of aerobics class!' As she reluctantly replaced the whip in its proper place on the wall Alice, as if in an afterthought, asked, 'You got lots of "sniffy-tasties"?'

'Two, I'd say. I seem to attract more of the "dressie-feelies" . . .'

' "Sniffy-tasties"? "Dressie-feelies"?' I asked helplessly.

'Fetishists, sweetheart,' Alice murmured kindly. As she had travelled across town to ensure that I was 'making progress' with 'The Terminator Angel', Alice was glad to be able to help out further with a child's guide to the diversity of fetishism. 'Basically, at least in my experience, there're two kinds of kinkies. The "sniffy-tasties" are, as you can probably guess, into bodily functions. The simplest "tasties" can be kinda cute. I had this one guy who could only get off by giving me head when he'd smeared strawberry yogurt inside me. He never actually wanted to fuck me. Yogurt was his thing until he wanted to graduate to ice-cream. *That's* when I said we'd have to part company. Otherwise, the "tasties" are more into being given "golden showers". I enjoyed a few big earners having to pee into some "tastie's" mouth. Not really my style, actually. I always thought it was a bit degrading having to squat and pee over someone. Sometimes I'd get all blocked and couldn't pee so I was glad I didn't get asked too often. And I didn't like the "sniffies" much either. I don't particularly want *anyone* sniffing my used knickers even if they offer a lot of money! Luckily, I was also much more appealing to the "dressie-feelies", anyway! It made life easier 'cos those leather and rubber and plastic boys are always most interested in their uniforms and the way it rubs against their skin. I didn't have to work too hard with them. I actually thought most of it was a bit of a giggle rather than just work — which is the way it should be, I think. What do you think, "Angel"?'

'Well, my painter client with the fruit-fetish makes me laugh. And so does my foot-sniffer!'

'Yeah, I always liked feet-guys,' Alice smiled fondly. 'They're often very shy and sensitive . . .'

'And always respectful!'

'You bet they are! Jeez, I dunno, this is making me nostalgic!'

'Do you miss it?' Mandy asked Alice curiously.

'Yeah, I do. The only thing I don't miss is the sneering of some goody two-shoes who thinks she's better than me 'cos I'm a whore. You know a few months before I gave up I went to this swanky dinner-party. Real *Late Show* types

– my kind of people as it turns out – and we were chattering about this and that – Salman Rushdie, Algeria, boycotting The Body Shop, Charter 88, Miles Davis, whatever. Now don't you two laugh – it's true! Then this one woman, this fucking advertising floozie, leans over the table and she says, "and what *exactly* do *you* do?" Now my friend knows what I do and, normally, I would've just lied and said I was a "designer" or a "model". But this snooty little madam got to me. I just looked her in the eye and said quietly, "I'm a prostitute!" '

'That's great!' laughed Mandy.

'Well that's what I thought at the time. It sure shut her up! But it made everyone else terribly uneasy and my friend felt so embarrassed. She kept trying to steer the conversation on to safer ground. She kept saying, "Anyone for some more Pavlova?"'

While Alice acted out the remembered serving of copious helpings of Pavlova, Mandy couldn't resist asking, 'What happened then?'

'It back-fired on me basically. I started to feel terrible and I left early, long before anyone else. The ad exec gave me a stiff handshake and a sneer before she called out "Good luck!" in this fucking sing-song voice. I know I shouldn't have let someone like her get to me but she did. She made me feel ashamed and I got angry – more with myself than her because I was usually proud to be a prostitute . . .'

'Well it's a more interesting and useful job than an ad exec's . . .'

'You bet it is!' said Alice with renewed zest.

'But that's not why you gave up being a prostitute, is it, Alice? Because of people like her?' Mandy asked.

'*Never!* I just wanted to do something different for a while.'

'Uuuuh, I don't mean to lower the tone of this conversation . . .' I began slowly, '. . . but going back to these fetishists . . .'

'Yes, kinky,' Alice said slyly. 'I thought you might be a

bit of an enigma. Are you a "sniffy-tastie" in disguise, maybe? Naaah — maybe not. What do you want to know, kinky?'

'Well I was wondering about the feet-fetishists. Do they worship the foot because they see it as the ultimate submission?'

'Yeah, that's certainly part of it — but the bottom-line's a bit more basic than that. It's the smell that most of them go for — don't you think so Mandy?'

'I wouldn't know — my feet *never* smell!' Mandy said lightly.

'Oh yes they do! At least more than your hands do! The odour's everything for these guys! Can you imagine a "sniffy" hand-fetishist?'

'I quite like looking at women's hands,' I ventured in a vain attempt to live up to my new 'kinky' tag.

'You said "eyes" last week!' Mandy laughed.

'And I've seen you looking at legs too!' Alice exclaimed triumphantly.

'Well aren't "kinkies" supposed to be versatile?' I asked as I backed into my stretching-rack corner.

'No! It's just the opposite!' said Alice. 'The whole point for the fetishist is that, for him, only certain parts of the body or inanimate objects are exciting. If you're a pure rubber fetishist then you've got to get into your uniform to really get a thrill. If you're into feet you're not bothered much about the vagina. Now I'm not usually big on all that Freudian stuff, but with my fetishists the obsession began when they were really young. All my guys felt a lack of love when they were babies or young kids. So they transferred their affections to something that gave them more comfort — a rubber duck, a high-heeled teacher, a nurse, whatever. It's a bit like Pavlov's dogs — you know, whenever they heard a bell being rung they went crazy 'cos they associated it with being fed. It's the same with sexual responses sometimes. A guy gets locked into this one fantasy he had as a nine-year-old — he got the hots for his teacher then

77

and she wore red shoes. So this stays with him and whenever he sees someone wearing red shoes, the bell still rings and he goes "boing!"'

'But what about severe domination — when people need to get flogged?' asked Mandy. Both Alice and I knew she was thinking of Alistair.

'Shit, I'm not the psychological expert I'm pretending to be! Maybe as a kid you get cuddled and given a cookie after you've been smacked and you make that association. Maybe it's the feeling of having someone interested in a bare part of your body. That explains the bottom-spankers. But, fuck, when it comes to darker stuff you start talking a different language. You start saying words like "guilt" and "loathing" and "degradation" . . . it's not so much of a giggle then . . .'

'I know,' said Mandy as the room went quieter and we all felt a tug of the pain bound up in that more tangled language. 'It's frightening sometimes to even think about it and that's why I wonder about Simone; I wonder if she really knows how deep and dark that place can get . . .?'

Chapter Three

Languages of Loving, Screaming and Boot-licking

French, Czech, Italian, English and Swedish words rolled off Simone Maillard's tongue with soft-accented fluidity. When she was alone the words looped around each other as if they belonged to a sixth language which only made sense inside her own head. She sometimes caught herself thinking in that curiously musical composite. It took a while then to remember which language she had been using before the boundaries blurred and other words slipped in from different places out of her past.

Switching from one language to another Simone still remembered, at arbitrary moments, the time when her tongue felt thick and useless inside a sulky mouth. She had been just a little girl then, in her first year of school. The laughter of the others whenever she tried to say their strange words made a cruel sound, a sound she had never forgotten.

Although born in Paris, just across the river from Nôtre Dame, she moved with her family to Prague when her father was transferred there as a diplomat. She was six years old then, in 1965. Her parents decided that she should enrol in one of the better Czech schools. While they would ensure the development of her French at home, the school would offer Simone the opportunity of learning a new language.

For nine months she tried to speak as little Czech as possible. She preferred to nod or shake her head, or merely to shrug. That way she could avoid at least some of the sniggering which accompanied her rudimentary attempts at

79

Czech speech in the playground. While her classmates skipped in the street after school, she sat at the wooden kitchen table with her mother as they translated her Czech homework into French and then back again.

That hour with her mother was the happiest of every day; and with each passing week it became obvious that Simone was gradually taking over the role of language teacher. When she found herself able to laugh, gently, at her mother's struggling Czech pronunciation Simone knew that she was nearly there.

Then came that glorious half-hour during the end of year Czech test when she sat quietly over her paper and filled in the correct word next to every picture. When the ruddy-faced teacher made a speech the next day in praise of Simone, 'now a true Czech girl', for finishing at the top of the class she found herself propelled to unimagined heights of popularity. The girls in her class offered her boiled sweets while the boys pushed each other around whenever they saw her looking at them. Suddenly, language, for Simone, meant pleasure rather than pain.

They left Prague for Rome in 1968, just after the Soviet tanks had crushed Dubček's Spring Uprising. Despite the tears she felt exhilarated at the thought of starting all over again with a new language. After the rigours of Czech, Italian came easily to her. Within a year she was revelling in its richness and even outswearing the thirteen-year-old boys who would call her all kinds of names while she fed her favourite stray cat at the top end of their new road.

After two sun-filled years in Rome, the Maillards returned to Paris. Her Czech and Italian experiences had left her with the barest trace of an unusual French accent. Rather than trying to eradicate this exoticism she strived to maintain her links with other languages by writing to her friends in Rome and, less often, in beleaguered Prague. At the same time she had uncovered two new passions – English and, more urgently, teenage boys. She did well with both and the years flashed by until she was reading English literature at the

Sorbonne and living with her lover, a student from London, in the Marais district.

Simone followed him to London after they both qualified in 1980. She has been there ever since, even though she left her boyfriend not long after they arrived. Simone decided to take a French philosophy degree at London University. It was there that she met Mandy Kavanagh who had made a similar decision the year before.

'I was a little frightened of her at first,' Simone remembered in her inevitably immaculate English. 'She stood out from everyone else. Even then her reputation was, you know, *formidable*. I always watched out for her. But it was only later, after we had both finished with philosophy, that I got to know her well. Not long after that she became a prostitute and, well, I guess you know the rest — she is *L'Ange Terminator* and I am *La Chienne de Souffrance* . . .'

With a delicately raised eyebrow Simone called herself more directly then, in English, ' "The Bitch Of Pain", of "Suffering" if you like.' She was a small, pretty woman and when she wore her large owl-like glasses for reading it was hard to imagine anyone looking less like a Dominatrix. Instead, she appeared more like a personification of Parisian academia. Before becoming *La Chienne de Souffrance*, Simone had worked as a freelance translator of academic journals from French into English, Italian and Czech. She was good at her job but the supply of translation work was both inconsistent and poorly paid. Eventually, Simone chose to follow Mandy into prostitution — as one highly qualified university graduate after another.

But there was a further, more telling, irony. Simone Maillard, the elegant technician of language, was made voiceless by the change in her work. After all, what words could she reach for when she pressed a burning poker down onto the flesh of a man's inner thigh? What could she say, even silently to herself, when she threaded a needle through the nipple of another? In the terrible wake of their bellowing and shrieking, with sounds coming from their flapping mouths which would not have been out of place in an abattoir, Simone was struck dumb. She felt her tongue wagging hopelessly, like a bloodied stump, near the back of her mouth. Then she thought back to those earliest days in Prague when she was also despairingly lost between languages.

Her mind, like her heart, froze when she heard the men's screaming. She was stunned by the fact that it was their choice to suffer. Simone struggled to find the resilience to go through the process each new time; particularly as the screeching from the time before made it seem like the top of her head had been ripped open. But numbness also emerged as her prime source of endurance whenever she confronted her most arduous clients.

'To be able to do this kind of work,' Simone almost whispered with weariness, 'you don't have to be cruel, you don't have to be a bitch. I don't ever really think of myself as "The Bitch of Pain". If I did I would go crazy. So to stay sane you have to remember your own reasons for doing this work. You have to block everything else out. I block out language first of all, because if you have language then you are going to want to look for meaning; and I'm not sure how much clear meaning you could ever find in this kind of S&M.

'With a lot of the men I see, everything begins and ends with the scream. That sound says it all. No word is ever as articulate as a scream. For them pain is everything, language is nothing. So my mind empties and I do what they ask me to do. And if there are no words for me, a linguist, then there can be no names for any feelings I might have. So I am remote when I have a needle or a poker in my hand; I am empty when I do this work . . .'

Simone said these words with such ragged fervour that I felt certain that nothing could have been more difficult for her to do than to drain herself of feeling. Even though I had only met her earlier that day, she had spoken tenderly about her parents and Mandy, about Prague and Rome and about her enduring love for language. It must have been a pitiless struggle to nullify these emotions within prostitution's most extreme domain.

Mandy Kavanagh had told me nothing about Simone before I met her apart from the fact that they were friends and sometimes worked together as prostitutes. It was only after I had heard Simone's personal history from her own mouth that I realized the significance of Mandy's restraint. She had realized that Simone was ready to talk; and so Mandy allowed her friend to tell her story in her own way.

She began, naturally, with her childhood; and so there was the grace of accuracy in Simone's account of the way in which sado-masochism can transgress existing boundaries of behaviour and language. Against the backdrop of her persistent search for new words ever since Prague, Simone's inarticulacy in the face of her clients' screams assumed a rare poignancy. In becoming a mute technician of punishment, Simone had given up what had once mattered most to her. She had learnt to dominate language so that it became a reservoir of, as she said, 'pleasure rather than pain'. Her life had been defined by language and then, instead, it became reshaped by wordless mutilation.

Before we sat down to speak in the bare room where Simone worked, she had shown me around the old maisonette she and her boyfriend, Kyle Johannsen, rented in the least gentrified quarter of Clapham. The flat was filled with books and ceiling-high piles of paper — 'The place of words,' Simone said — and only the very top and bottom rooms were empty of books. Kyle painted in the attic, which he had converted into a studio, while Simone worked in the cellar.

Her place of punishment lacked the professional conventions of Mandy's basement. There was only a wooden table in the middle of the room, a fire grate and chimney and a small reprint of Edvard Munch's painting, *The Scream*. It was a simultaneously ironic and disturbing picture to pin against the wall of her *Chienne de Souffrance* room. In the painting a whitened, disembodied face screams with suffering which appears almost unknowable; except perhaps to Simone and her men as they went about their unspoken business.

'It's one of Kyle's favourite paintings,' she said. 'He thought it would be a nice touch to hang it here. I think it's a very powerful painting but I find it scary to look at some days. But still, better that than a torture rack! The men like it too, for it says everything about them and this place – in a way words could never do. Look at it and you'll imagine the sounds I sometimes hear . . .'

It was hard to drag my eyes away from the painting. Yet, having done the screaming routine in Mandy's dungeon, I was more interested in trying to find out why Simone had chosen this type of Dominatrix work, where branding and piercing were the specialized components. As if sensing my question, and much to my relief, she suggested we move instead to the living room. There, she suggested, she would feel more expressive.

This room gave off a warm, lived-in feeling. Old leather-backed armchairs and a beautiful Louis XIV chaise-longue provided a comfortable resting point for Simone's collection of five heavily overweight cats. They appeared to do little apart from sleep and devour tinned Salmon Gourmet, with only an occasional night-time chase of clawing activity up the room's ochre-coloured curtains for exercise. Everywhere you looked there were paintings, full of wild splashes of colour, and books overflowing from wooden cases.

'This is our room – mine and Kyle's,' Simone said with softness opening up her face. 'I'm sure it must look untidy to everyone else but I love it. There's nothing I like more than coming in here, alone with Kyle and the cats, after the money has been earned and the day is over.'

This mention of money gave me the unsubtle opportunity to ask Simone about the exact motivation behind her conversion from academic translation. Was it just for money that she worked as a Dominatrix?

'The aim is to make money, sure! I wouldn't be doing this if the money wasn't so good — I can promise you *that*! I can make up to £1,000 an hour for the hardest bondage work. To earn that as a translator I would have to work day and night for two months probably!'

While £500 a month is not much to live on in London, I wondered if she ever thought back nostalgically to her poorer days. Did she not sometimes envy her own past freedom — freedom, that is, from the emotional price she has to pay while inflicting chronic pain on others?

'But it's not *me* who is really doing that to them. I numb myself so that when I am out of there, the cellar, I forget it. It's like any job you don't like much — when the day is done you shut your mind to it. You get on with your other life.'

This distinction between 'real' and 'fake' selves is tenuous at the best of times. Comparing the violence of her prostitution with her own private history, where identity was inextricably bound up in empathy with language, it seemed a particularly difficult trick for Simone to pull off irrespective of how rigorously detached she claimed to be as *La Chienne de Souffrance*. How certain could she ever be that her 'true', compassionate personality would remain iced over in the cellar and that her 'counterfeit' 'Bitch Of Pain' persona would stay locked away when she was with Kyle?

'You're right. I can never be certain. It's too complicated to always be sure that you're in control. With Kyle I don't feel I have too many problems in switching the Dominatrix side off — I am too in love with him to ever let that happen. It's in the cellar that the problems start. I'm not very good at hurting people. The men all say that I should be tougher with them. But I can't. I hear their pain and, even though they say this gives them pleasure, I draw back. I only go so far. It's not that I'm squeamish about pain — how could

I be doing this work? It's just that I draw the line at a certain point. And of course it is me, Simone, and not *La Chienne de Souffrance*, who steps back. In that sense, yes, the real me, *la compatissante*, is in the cellar then and I can stand it no longer.'

Yet all this talk of compassion only accentuated my own uncertainties. I trotted out what must have been a familiar line to Simone — that I didn't feel I would ever be able to bear a girlfriend of mine working as a prostitute, let alone in the area of severe domination where she found the work so disturbing.

'Look, that's OK,' she said sweetly. 'I never imagined once that I would be doing this work and Kyle never thought that he would be with someone who was a Dominatrix in her spare time. But things change and you adapt according to circumstances.'

'What has changed for you?' I asked

'I found love — it's as simple as that.'

'How exactly does *love* lead you to this kind of pain?'

'You know, for a lot of prostitutes love has nothing to do with their work. If anything, it is the lack of love in their past lives which makes them sell sex. Even Mandy — that was surprising to you, no? Mandy is my favourite woman in the whole world — a role model for me in many ways. Except when it comes to love. As beautiful as she is she can't give herself to love a man in the way that I love Kyle. And that is sad. I think she is maybe too strong for her own good. With me it's different; I'm doing this out of love, it's one way forward for me and Kyle, for us to change our lives . . .'

'What does Mandy think of your relationship with Kyle?' I wondered hesitantly.

'That,' she sighed, 'you must ask her. I don't think she understands our love in a way.'

'Is that because she doesn't like Kyle?'

'Did she say that to you?' she said sharply.

'No, she told me nothing except that you were a very good friend to her.'

'And so she is to me — *certainement*!'

'What does Kyle do — apart from painting?'

'Well, you know, painting is Kyle. That's what he is — a painter. And I think he is going to be a very great painter. We're hoping he'll be able to put on an exhibition soon.'

'So that's why you took up domination — to enable Kyle to paint full-time — out of love for him?'

'Yes.'

'But can't Kyle find a part-time job and paint during the rest of the time?'

'Our life before this was not too good,' Simone reasoned. 'I was making nothing as a translator. Kyle was working in a pizza restaurant every day. He would come home exhausted. How could he paint then, at night, when he would have to be up again the next day to make those awful deep-pan pizzas?'

I suggested that it had been done before — many times, perhaps even with deep-pan pizzas.

'But we didn't want to struggle for the rest of our lives. One burst of the work I now do can change our lives. It's important to me, too, that Kyle succeeds as a painter. When his work goes badly then we go badly. He doesn't like the fact I do this work but he accepts it. We decided together that I would do it while he concentrated fully on his painting.'

'And what about your career, Simone?'

'Being a translator is not much of a career — it's not exactly work to give your whole life up to. It's hard to do and it's badly paid.'

'At least it was *your* work.'

'Maybe — but Kyle is more important to me than translation. I wouldn't do this for any man. I'm doing this for us — me and Kyle. That's also why I do this type of prostitution. It has little sex in it. I have never ever fucked a man for money. I don't even do blow jobs. How could I — when I love another man, a man who is my lover?'

'But still,' I plodded on, 'isn't it damaging both to you,

87

personally, and to your relationship with Kyle when you come upstairs after branding a man on his inner thigh?'

'There're two answers to that. First, if you don't allow penetration as a prostitute then you already know that you're calling for a hardcore kink audience. It is hard to deal with — but the money is great. I earn more than Mandy for a single session and she is much more beautiful and skilled than me. But Mandy refuses to do piercing or branding. I refuse to do sex. That's why we have different types of men and why I have only six regulars. My service is for the most unusual, if you like — and there are just enough of them to keep us living well.

'Secondly, you must keep the work in context. Only two out of six regulars want real pain. The branding man only comes every few months and he does not always want to be branded. That has only happened twice in eighteen months. He pays me £1,000 for an hour-long dance and whipping session which ends with me branding him for a few moments. Another client likes to have his nipples and his cock pierced. That is clinical work — I am like a nurse then. He says it hardly hurts the way I do it! The rest of them are much more like Mandy's men — it's fantasy and pretend-punishment . . .'

It still sounded grim to me and, sensing this, Simone strove to change the tenor of our conversation.

'But, *mon cher*, it's not all terrible. I have this one wonderful man — "Maxwell Montague" is what he calls himself. He comes to see me every second Friday and every time he comes to the door I know that he has made a new uniform for himself. He is like Vivienne Westwood or Gaultier to me! He is so imaginative. He makes dresses and capes for himself out of anything and everything. Leather, rubber, tin foil, rubbish bags, light bulbs, flowers, fruit, metal, tyres, whatever! I'm telling you this man is a genius sometimes. Dali would have loved him! All he wants is to model for me while I go, "Ooolala, Maxie, who's a clever boy then?" Then, after a while, I must wrap clingfilm tightly around him so that he can hardly move.'

'Clingfilm?'

'*Voila*, clingfilm! It is the womb-like feeling. Then he licks my boots and tells me he worships me. Before I know it he has come and he scurries away like a little church mouse so that he can get working on his next outfit.'

'He sounds like an unusual sort of guy,' I said politely. 'Why do you think he goes for this particular kind of layered fantasy?'

'Who knows? But he is very talented in his own way. I like him.'

Although memories of Robert were still fresh in my mind, I wondered if Simone thought she could arrange a meeting between me and 'Maxie' to at least see some of his outfits.

'Oh no, Maxie is very secretive, I'm sorry. There's no chance he would ever see you. But I think you should meet Kyle — maybe he can answer better than me some of these questions you've been asking. What do you think?'

What could I do but murmur agreement? There was more than ample evidence that Simone loved Kyle deeply. To decline a meeting with him would be to offend her in the most personal way. But that still did not undermine the feelings I had at the thought of talking to him. I had already dismissed Kyle as the post-modernist equivalent of a 'bounder'. It also struck me as a peculiar aberration that the first man I should meet face to face — Robert's leather hood having precluded him from that honour — in the course of writing this book should fall outside the ritualised 'p' zone of punter, pimp or prostitute.

Despite these reservations, I succumbed to a sneaking susceptibility that this might not be such a bad idea after all. In the few days which passed between my first meeting with Simone and a second visit to Clapham, I was haunted by a comment she had made with illusory casualness. At this early stage in our friendship, as she warmly described what I would have then probably called a 'liaison', she asked me to be careful in talking about her and Kyle to other people. I made a flippant comment that it was probably a conversation-stopper at a Clapham party to admit that you worked as 'The Bitch Of Pain'. 'Oh no,' she said demurely, 'it's not that. We don't have any problem in talking about what I do. I'm not ashamed — it's just that Kyle and I could go to jail for living together. That's this ridiculous British sex law for you!'

Kyle might be some kind of rogue but it did not seem right that his living with Simone, who loved him, should be an offence technically more serious than rape. In the eyes of British law, Simone and Kyle were running a brothel and he was living off her immoral earnings. The fact that he might be exploiting her did not appear to enter the judicial equation; instead it was the supposed 'immorality' of Simone working as a prostitute in the house where she lived with another person which tipped the scales in favour of their being certified as 'criminals'. I knew Simone was even less like a criminal than she was a cruel 'Bitch Of Pain'. In judging Kyle even before I had met him it felt, at least in conjunction with this 'brothel' law, like a similarly smug conceit — a vanity that I was, by definition, morally superior to him.

Naturally, this righteous advantage returned bang on cue when our evening meeting finally arrived. Kyle stepped over a couple of cats to shake me by the hand. Simone and I had spent the preceding few hours talking and we were enjoying that otherwise inconceivable intimacy which an interview can sometimes elicit. Kyle looked awkward and apologized for breaking up our tête-à-tête. 'Don't worry,' I said too cutely for my own comfort, 'we were just talking about you . . .'

'Good things I hope', he said with a lop-sided grin.

While I shook his hand silently, Simone crooned, 'What else, *cherie*, what else?'

Kyle, I think, could guess the contents of my 'what else' but he gave me a reassuring pat on the back and soon, like

long-lost chums, we were drinking Guinness and talking
about being foreigners in London. Before long, Kyle was
whipping out sharp jokes along 'Have you heard the one
about the Swede, the Frenchwoman and the South African
who were lost in London?' lines. Despite everything I found
him laconically funny and after our third bottle of Guinness
I started to agree with Simone that his paintings exuded a
special spark — particularly when she tilted the living room
spotlights so that they shone down on his colourful canvases.
They then looked like the kind of paintings Jackson Pollock
would surely have splashed down if he had been a Swede
living with *La Chienne de Souffrance* in Clapham, *après* a
spell in a deep-pan pizza restaurant.

Kyle concurred, graciously, and flipped off the top from
another black bottle.

But our swinging mood hit a rut when the doorbell rang
and, with a sad smile, Simone went to administer the whip
to one of her masochistic clients.

Suddenly unshackled from cheeriness I turned the tape
recorder on and asked Kyle if it bothered him to be just
sitting here with me while Simone had to spend an hour in
her 'Bitch Of Pain' guise.

'Well, I can see it bothers you,' he said with a tart smile.
'I can understand what it must look like on the outside. But
if you weren't here, you know, I wouldn't be sitting around
drinking. I would be upstairs working. I know my work is
not difficult in the way that Simone's is, but look, it's not
exactly what they call a fucking picnic either. I work hard.
I'm desperate for my work to sell so we can start a different
life — a life where Simone doesn't have to work at all if
that's what she wants.'

But in the meantime, while he was painting their way
towards this often elusive dream of fame, did he not agonize
over the work she did as a prostitute?

'Simone is the most special person in the world to me —
I only think of her in that way. She is never a prostitute to
me — only the woman I love.'

Doubting the reliability of Kyle's slick answers, I pointed
out that Simone called herself a prostitute.

'Ah, but Simone is a semanticist — she always looks for
a different kind of word to me!'

'But the men who pay her also think of her as a
prostitute,' I countered.

'I don't think so. Prostitution means selling sex. Simone
is not selling sex. There is never any desire on their part for
penetration. They're too fucked up — they need a different
kind of therapy. It's quite interesting when you think about
it. They must be so numbed in their ordinary lives that the
only way they can feel is through extreme pain. They need
that violence. These men do not even touch Simone — so
she's more a therapist in a way than a prostitute.'

I expected to hear this 'therapy' pitch first from a
prostitute with a more legitimate right to make such a claim
than from someone like Kyle. While the men did not touch
Simone she was certainly touching them, with pokers and
chains and needles. Surely the inflictor of pain can become
afflicted with hurt herself?

'Again it's an interesting point. But, my friend, you must
understand that we have thought these things through
together — as a couple. None of this is new to me — or
to Simone. And it has always been Simone who has led us
down this route. It was she who started with Mandy, it was
she who asked me if she could work on her own, it was she
who decided the type of work she would do in her cellar.
And here she is — back so soon. You can ask her for
yourself.'

Simone's session was over, far earlier than expected. She
looked happy again and so I changed the subject; for
whenever we spoke about her prostitution it seemed to open
a window onto her distress. But she drew a curtain across
this when she was with Kyle. Then, she was just simply
delighted to offer me another Guinness and to look down
at Kyle, lovingly, as the fattest cat of all stretched across
her lap with a yawn.

Outside, I saw the shadowy figure of her client walking quickly away into the night where, Simone said, his own wife would be waiting for him to return home. She would be unaware of the fact that he had just paid £300 to be punished by a silent 'Bitch Of Pain', by *La Chienne de Souffrance*, by Simone Maillard who was then chattily elated that this forty-eight-year-old man, this woman's husband, had left *her* home; the home she sometimes called 'the place of words'.

Back in Mandy Kavanagh's more ironically named 'house of pain' a few days later she finally gave vent to her feelings about the effect of Simone's relationship with Kyle. 'It disturbs me,' she sighed, ''cos their relationship's built on a basic S&M premise. Simone may work as "The Bitch Of Pain" but outside her cellar she's dominated by Kyle. She's given up mastery over language to be mastered, instead, by him. And that's not just on any old superficial level — it goes far further than that, it goes into her submitting herself to the cause of his painting. I think he's a creepy, crappy piss-artist anyway! And here Simone is, she's the one suffering for *his* art! It's ludicrous. She's given up translation completely and yet she's a fucking brilliant linguist.'

People, I said to Mandy, would no doubt say similar things about her — that she had sacrificed some of her own talents for these five years of work as 'The Terminator Angel'.

'But at least the choice was made for me alone,' she retorted. 'I became a prostitute for *my* benefit. I think Simone has given up language, to become a Dominatrix, for Kyle's benefit. That seems wrong to me. And I suppose I feel a little guilty about this because if it hadn't been for me, Simone would probably never have started in prostitution. When I told her there was easy money to be made, that this top-range of prostitution often had nothing at all to do with penetration, I got her thinking.

She saw a way of "buying time", as she put it, for Kyle to paint.

'I don't think Simone would ever fuck a man other than Kyle, no matter how much money was involved. I admire that fidelity but then I also have to see the type of things she does instead. Her boundaries are very different from mine. I would never brand or pierce anyone — not just because of what it does to them but because of what it would do to me. It would fuck me up and I'm afraid it's beginning to fuck Simone up — but I tell her this and she just gets all hurt. She takes it too personally. She thinks I'm gunning for Kyle rather than thinking about her.'

I was curious about this idea of guilt, that Mandy should somehow feel responsible for leading Simone into prostitution, almost as if she had led her astray — away from her previous focused path of linguistics. While Simone might be under a spell of love for Kyle were we not doing her a gross injustice in thinking that she could not make a decision for her own benefit — especially when we were continually lauding her intelligence?

'I feel partly responsible because I encouraged Simone to do some work with me. Having worked for three years in domination, I should have pointed out some basic truths to her. I should have said, "Stick to fantasy — avoid the extremes of S&M, avoid the crazies." After all those years of Alistair I should have told her that. Instead I painted a softer picture where she'd do some work with me and make a quick £150 without a man even laying a hand on her.

'Simone and I have a very special relationship but it's complicated too. I think she always looked up to me in a way, or so she says, and this was mixed up with some small infatuation too. As for me, I learnt how extraordinary she was when I set out as a prostitute. She wasn't amongst my closest circle of friends then and she wasn't with the four women I first told about my prostitution. They were my best friends and after my first few times, when I was certain that I could cut it as a hooker, I invited them all round for dinner.

'We had a great evening for a while. I'd made this huge pot of pasta and we drank one bottle of wine after another. Finally, over coffee, I made this pathetic little speech. I told them that they were the people I was closest to in the whole world and so I wanted to tell them about this change in my life. They were giggling, "Go on, tell us, Mand, go on!" They thought I was going to tell them that I'd finally met the man of my dreams. When I told them, and they knew right off that I wasn't joking, there was dead silence. The evening disintegrated. Two of my friends left in tears, another wouldn't speak to me and the fourth kept saying, "But you've got everything, Mand, you could get *any* man you want." The one crying friend just kept saying, "I'm so disappointed — you, Mandy, of all people, a *prostitute*!" It was like I had just told them that I was a thief or a murderer.

'Well, now I can be blasé. I can think, "Shit, a lot of ordinary women have a hang-up about prostitution. That's their problem — that they see us as enemies, rather than as their wisest allies. Maybe that's because they fear or even envy the prostitute? Because which woman knows more about men, about their fears and weaknesses, than the prostitute?" But *then* they hurt me terribly. They literally abandoned me. Of course they're the type of girls who still send me Christmas cards every year but I only speak to the one now and she's full of "So what's it *really* like then?" gush.

'And that's where Simone came in — she became my best friend soon after that night. I was worried about telling her because I didn't want to lose her friendship as well. But she was lovely. She was just compassionate and interested. After all the hypocrisy of my other friends — who used to go on about finding men with lots of money before *they* turned round and called me mercenary — Simone was like a breath of fresh air. And with Simone I'm allowed to have another life. I'm her friend above everything else, her friend who also loves books and Paris and Prague and Rome, like her.'

As they grew closer over the years, Mandy began to talk more to Simone about her prostitution. Although naturally inquisitive to hear about the sexual services Mandy offered in her various hooker roles, Simone could not help but compare their very different lives. She felt that she could never live the isolated, if independent, life led by Mandy. Instead, she was thankful that she lived with Kyle. But when she saw how little money she and Kyle had in contrast to Mandy she began to wonder if she too should not go down this path of prostitution. Besides, Mandy always seemed to have whole mornings and afternoons free while she and Kyle were slaving over, respectively, academic translations and pepperoni pizzas.

I remembered recording Simone's own description of the day she decided to start work as a prostitute. 'We were sitting around drinking in Mandy's blue room one Sunday night — just the two of us. We were a little drunk and we were talking about sex when we were young. And I told her that when I was at university in Paris I had made love to two different women. With the second it had been a long-running affair. I said that I knew that I was attracted to women and that I'd always kind of fancied her. Then I said quickly that I knew she was straight. I must have gone bright red and said something about being drunk because she was very sweet to me. She said she was flattered but she knew how much I loved Kyle. But she also said that she still had a proposition to make to me.

'When she said she needed to open another bottle of wine first, I got very interested. So then it came out. She had this client, Christopher, a nice man, she said, who kept offering her a lot of money to put on a "show" with another girl. She told me she would never allow him to bring a stranger in off the street so the whole idea had faded. But then he started asking her again — so she was asking me now, would I work with her this one time. She said it would mean £150 each and that no "real" sex would be involved.

'I wanted to say "Yes!" at once but I thought I should

think it through. I talked it over with Kyle and, to tell you the truth, I think he wanted to come to the show too! I know he likes Mandy; but he always says, "No way, *non, niet, nein*, never!" He mocks me like that. He's mad sometimes. Anyway, Kyle said I should do it. I was very nervous beforehand. Not of the man — but of being with Mandy in this situation where we would be dancing and stripping together and fooling around. But she was wonderful.

'She showed me the way from the very start. We had to stay in control. She would say, "This is work — let's be professional about it, it's not us doing something intimate or private. We can't ever forget that a man will be paying to watch us all the time." But she also made it fun. She's really funny. I had to fight to stop laughing out loud because she acted out these crazy porn movies. "Ooooo, mademoiselle, my big melons are aching for your touch" and "Ze pussy — she is on fire, baby!" He really got turned on by that stuff. He thought we were being serious. Mandy says we're getting paid all this money just to be "girly". Sometimes, you know, it's fun to pretend you're a young girl again. But Christopher only has us do a few shows a year now — he says we're too expensive for him. And he likes Mandy more than me anyway. He loves her boots. They drive him wild.'

From that farcical pastiche of porno lesbian lust it was only a short step for Simone to branch out on her own. But without Mandy to parody male desire Simone found herself being drawn into the better paid but more sombre quarters of sado-masochism where, as she now knows, there are few words to be said, let alone 'ze pussy on fire' laughs to be had, amidst her cellar's bleak soundtrack to *The Scream*.

Everywhere I looked in this enclosed world of friends and prostitutes I seemed to see swirling contradictions. Mandy Kavanagh, so strong and controlled and yet, ironically, too vulnerable to think of succumbing: to even the idea of love; Simone Maillard, 'The Bitch Of Pain', being left wide open to hurt by her love for a man she was supporting; that man, Kyle Johannsen, debating the semantic point of whether non-penetration meant non-prostitution while his linguistic lover mutely flogged another man for money; Mandy's ceaseless, apparently futile struggle with Alistair; all those wives wondering, or not, where their husbands might have been while they were actually paying for pain; Gregor Samsa in *Surf Butt Bandits*; Simone, again, suffering for *Kyle's* art; Kyle, again, musing over the 'agonies' of artistic creation; that, by living together, Simone and Kyle were criminal brothel-keepers; that Mandy had been abandoned by her women friends for the 'unforgivable' act of becoming a prostitute. On and on they rolled ambiguously, entangled together, these almost mythological reinventions and justifications of self.

But there was a singular problem for me then, after nearly two months, as late summer flattened out into sticky heat. The different truths I had discerned about 'high-class' prostitution had yet to be checked against the coherent words of any of Mandy's or Simone's clients. Without access to their consumers, Mandy's and Simone's prostitution would stay suspended in quotes and in my own imagination.

The extremity of masculine sexual and psychological desire with which they worked appeared as far away as ever – until the day Mandy Kavanagh phoned me to say that one of her clients had agreed to meet me. 'And he's not a uniform-wearer, either,' said Mandy helpfully, 'so you won't have the hood problem that Robert gave you . . .'

'So if he's not a uniform-wearer,' I asked, 'what exactly is he?'

'Well, it's Christopher, the lesbian-fantasist . . .'

'Oh *him*! Could be interesting . . .'

'It will be, I can promise you that,' Mandy breathed down the phone. 'Especially as he's basically a fetishist.'

'What's his fetish?'

'Feet.'

While I waited for Christopher to call me I wondered what

a foot-fetishist would look and sound like. I had not got very far when, about five minutes later, the phone rang again.

A deeply respectable, radio-announcer voice said my name. It was Christopher. After a few minutes of amiable, eloquent formalities on his part he confirmed that he would talk to me. 'How about early this evening?' he suggested.

They were obviously fast movers when they got going, these foot-fetishists. I asked him where we should meet. 'Why don't I drive over to you? It'll save you the walk in all this heat.'

He was already thinking about my feet, I thought wildly; in reality he was merely being considerate and, of course, careful that he should meet me where he could be sure that no-one he knew would see him.

At exactly seven o'clock that summery evening I heard his feet clipping down the stairs to my front door. I looked down at my own feet — they were unerotically covered in my one pair of sensible shoes.

Christopher, I noticed, was wearing expensive Italian shoes. They matched his elegant summer suit and fedora which shielded his face from both the sun and any prying newspaper photographers I might have hidden in the neighbouring bushes. We were both very nervous. I cracked open a few cans of beer while Christopher ran his hands anxiously through his full, ginger beard.

It was only after we had drunk down our beer, opened another and spoken blandly about these 'blistering' days that we both began to relax. We talked about writing and about architecture, Christopher's 'line', as he described it. Despite the recession, of which most architects were the first victims, his business was steady.

He hoped, he said suddenly, that he could trust me not to reveal his identity.

He must have been convinced, probably more by Mandy than me, for he allowed me to switch on the recorder and we began speaking about prostitution. He explained that he

99

had been visiting prostitutes for more than twenty years — he was about to turn fifty the following month. He also said that he had been married for five years longer than he had been seeing prostitutes.

'I love my wife,' he murmured with a slight quaver in his otherwise resonant voice, 'but ever since I can remember I've been drawn to prostitutes. I was always too frightened to visit them when I was younger. I think I expected to be beaten up by a pimp or to catch some disease. But the lure was very strong.'

'Why are prostitutes so alluring?' I asked.

He thought for a long time before answering. 'I find women very attractive. I think you could say I am a little in awe of women. I know it's ridiculous in a way but I have always put women on pedestals. My mother was a very strong and special woman. I was also taught by a beautiful and authoritative governess. There's no doubt that my first sexual feelings were towards her.

'And when I grew up I found that I was not so free and easy with girls my own age. I lusted after them but there always seemed to be obstacles in the way — my shyness or their haughtiness towards me. Of course it was just in my own mind, these problems. But even after I met my wife I was still fascinated by the idea of visiting a prostitute. And their allure, to go back to your question, is their availability. I was always turned on by the fact that they were there. Whenever I wanted they'd be willing to see me, even if I was shy and awkward — as long as I paid them. It seemed a fair enough exchange without any undue complications.'

It took him a long time, with many pauses, to fashion this answer. I liked the fact that he thought so carefully and spoke so directly. The honesty of his complex fear of 'real', and therefore not always 'available', women seemed to trouble him — even at the moment he said these very words. He was thinking so hard, as if it were the first time he had considered this question, that he had yet to give my feet a second glance.

'You're a man,' he continued, almost as a way of explaining this neglect of his fetish in my company, 'and so you know that it can be very difficult to have an ordinary relationship with a woman. Of course it can be very beautiful too but often the day-to-day problems seem uppermost. These problems, to me at least, have a lot to do with responsibility. It's my responsibility to keep my wife happy and secure. It's my responsibility to ensure our lives run smoothly.'

'Surely your wife feels a similar responsibility towards you?' I said.

'I think less so. Maybe it's because we're from a different, older generation to you and Mandy and Simone. With my marriage I feel the burden rests on me.'

'Do you think that's because you like to put a woman on a pedestal, as you said.'

'I'm sure that has something to do with it. But I've always felt with ordinary relationships that the onus is on the man to keep things together. Things are different with the prostitute. She is more in control — I can let go.'

I asked Christopher, who was speaking more quickly as he warmed to his theme, if this was why he liked Mandy — because she was so clearly in control.

'Absolutely. She takes care of everything from the moment I walk in. She can be very commanding.'

'Like your governess, perhaps?'

'In a way, yes, but with Mandy it's more *her* that turns me on. The other prostitutes I saw before her were fine on the whole. But I liked them to wear uniforms — with Mandy I like it most when she's just herself. Then I think this absolutely beautiful woman is a *prostitute* and that means I'm with her for this hour. I don't have to perform for her — I can just drink in her beauty.'

'It sounds quite poetic, if a little confused,' I said slowly.

'Of course, it's totally romantic! I know that — she knows that. Again that's the allure of prostitution. The honesty of the arrangement — plus the fact that I can worship at her feet without having any real-life commitment to her.'

'So prostitution allows you to escape your everyday reality?'

'Yes — fantasy being brought into temporary reality. That's it, in a single phrase. For example, I always had a fantasy that two beautiful women would seduce me at the same time. It's a stock male fantasy. I know it's never going to happen in "real life" — but with prostitution it's possible. And so it's happened — with Mandy and Simone. I know they're only doing it for the money but it still turns me on just to look at them. They're both very attractive, as you know. And I find that as I get older I'm aroused by the prostitute who doesn't actually look like a prostitute.'

This enabled Christopher to muddy further the distinction between fantasy and reality. While they looked like 'good girls', Mandy and Simone were really 'bad girls'.

'But it's also the fact that I'm now less interested in straight sex with a prostitute — no matter how "good" or beautiful she might look.'

'What,' I enquired with a gulp, 'has taken the place of straight sex?'

After his now familiarly extended pause, Christopher said the word with an accompanying flush rising up his face. 'Feet.'

With shamefully mock surprise, I echoed his favourite word. 'Feet?'

'Yes, feet — and boots, too.'

'Why?'

'Women's feet are beautiful. It gives me such pleasure to kiss the feet of a lovely woman. I feel I'm worshipping her in the correct way.'

'This sounds like a religious experience, Chris.'

'It's an experience like no other — when I lick Mandy's boots it both soothes and arouses me.'

Baffled, but still interested in the strangeness of his reaction, I asked him when he'd first discovered this particular fetish.

102

'With my governess — she wore the sexiest boots imaginable.'

I was tempted to tell him a filthy joke Kyle had recited to Simone and me about a Swedish governess the week before. But that would have been a cruel toe-stepping jibe. Instead I offered this bearded, earnest fetishist another beer and opened up a new can for myself.

As we drank quietly for a short while, I looked across the room at him. To my as yet unfoot-fetished mind it sounded most like his declared 'awe' of women meant that he preferred to evade their most basic sexuality — defined by the vagina, the cunt, or 'that gaping hole' as he said anxiously. There was something safe about worshipping a foot; for that foot, certainly, was less 'demanding' than the feared wet, 'gaping hole'. There was obviously little real responsibility to womanly pleasure when kissing a prostitute's foot.

Yet I knew that he was growing weary of this intimate investigation of his most private fears. So, instead, I settled back for a little trivial boot-room talk to round off our evening. 'Tell me, Chris,' I said airily, 'what's so special about Mandy's feet then?'

'Ah, Mandy — she has such beautiful, such elegantly tapered feet. They look like intelligent feet and they look like feet that could dance wonderfully all night long.'

Before he went on to tell me that if they weren't such 'intelligent' feet they could probably have danced in *The Red Shoes*, I asked Chris about Simone. What sort of feet did she have?

He looked wistful for another long moment before he replied — 'To me, it looks like she has feet full of pain. I think she should dance more, for that's how feet talk . . .'

Chapter Four

Cool on the Cross

I thought again of those strange, feet-dancing words a few months later. In the middle of a small room in King's Cross, surrounded by black and white photographs hanging from every wall, I stared at the print of a young girl dancing. Barefoot and wearing a flower-patterned dress, she was caught in a ballerina pose. Her weight rested on the ball of one scrunched-up foot while the other leg piked up towards her head which was already encircled by her bangle-dangling arms. She had such long hair that a strand had twirled its way round the flexed toes of her free foot. Her face, turned towards the camera, glistened with sweat and laughter. She couldn't have been more than sixteen.

Although it lacked the painterly quality of some of the photographs around it, this frame stood out from the rest for a different reason. The others, without exception, were of prostitutes who walked the streets of King's Cross. Like the photograph of the dancing girl, who I soon learnt was Docherty's sister, the prostitution prints were shot with an almost unbearable intimacy. Even when they weren't horsing around together for the benefit of his camera at two in the morning, even when they were seen alone and in a mood as black as any January night, the prostitutes looked back at Docherty, and out of the frame, with a curious kind of interest that he should find them worth remembering. Depending on the time of day and the shade of light falling across them, these images of the Cross looked either austere or luminous. But, always, the effect of walking into that room was like entering a shrine.

He liked me to call him 'Docherty', the name he had chosen on the day he changed his life. While he had always been attracted to ideas of transformation it had once been enough for him to merely listen to such talk at drunken late night parties. There, his friends had spoken often about avoiding the banality of ordinary life. It seemed as if each of them was going to be great at something, as someone different to the person they already were. They were going to be painters or politicians, millionaires or serial killers of the rich. But the more they talked the less likely it became that they would ever change. Docherty stood slightly apart from them. For one thing, he never voiced their exalted kind of ambition. Instead he would shrug a little and say that he had no specific thoughts on the future they already celebrated. Yet within this apparent emptiness he found the belief that he could invert the very essence of himself.

And one day he did become someone else, different from anything imagined by his friends during their precocious time together. On a Sunday morning in September, years ago, he sat down at the plastic-topped half-moon table in his King's Cross kitchenette. He positioned his chair so that he was warmed by a thin band of sunshine shining through the flat's only window. The sunlight reached the new yellow pad where he had written twenty potential pseudonyms for himself.

He thought then, drawing more pleasure than usual from his first coffee and cigarette of the day, that there could be no finer moment to reinvent himself. It was still early, before nine even, and he was conscious of the quietness both in and outside the concrete block of flats. He was aware of a similar stillness within himself. As much as he relaxed into the sensation he wondered if this was the serenity which comes only to the utterly bereft.

He had not slept much the previous night. It had been

typical of most nights he had endured through that terrible year, a year in which his life slipped away to the point where there were days when he no longer cared whether he lived or died. Earlier that fateful week he had visited his doctor. He was told that his sleeplessness was a symptom of acute depression. The doctor, an amiable but overworked man, did not press him on the source of his sadness. As he would not have known what to reply, Docherty was relieved by this absence of compassionate questioning.

So he sat silently in the doctor's green clinic, listening to the advice that a holiday might cure him of his insomnia. Having neither the money nor the inclination to leave his flat he requested a course of sleeping pills as an alternative arrangement. This was refused. He was, after all, 'fighting fit'.

Docherty sank even deeper into despair. Some of his friends suggested that he should 'lighten up'; that he should get drunk or drugged-up every once in a while so that he could 'forget' himself again. When he was younger he had tried this diligently. On ragged jags of Jack Daniels and acid he thought that it sometimes worked, this method of illumination, this fragile art of forgetting. But it was never himself that was truly forgotten; it was never a way of sustaining that initial feeling of lightness, the lasting release he imagined only his own death would bring.

He knew that retracing these steps would remind him of that other death which still pierced him: the death of a girl he had only realized how deeply he loved when she kicked a chair from beneath her feet and, in that fine floral printed dress, swung slowly out of his life. He had done enough drinking and drug-taking to see that, far from releasing him into oblivious refuge, they could unleash the most wretched visions he had buried deep within himself.

These thoughts had welled up inside him the night before. At the seemingly appointed darkest hour, around four in the morning, he finally had had enough. Sitting upright in bed and drinking from a plastic bottle which leaked tepid water onto his old *Taxi Driver* T-shirt, he recognized the absurdity of his anguish. If it was to be suicide then he might as well get it over and done with at that supposedly dramatic moment of realization. And if he really did not yearn for death then he would go on, but in a different kind of way. He would change what he hated most about his life − he was sick of never having enough money and he was sick of dead-end work.

By the time the emptied bottle had soaked the bed he had decided to postpone further thoughts of death. A few hours later he had his list of names. He'd picked them out from the shelves of books and films lining the wall opposite his rickety table: 'Bickle, Carver, Caulfield, Dedalus, Docherty, Kane, Malloy, Malone, O'Neill, Travis . . .'

There were other names besides these but they have long since vanished from memory. Some belonged to writers but most were taken from within the books and films themselves, from characters he had seen and understood. But the significance of their source was neither particularly literate nor literary. It was more an intimate gesture to his previous self to set out a list of possible new names by looking at his own shelves than by flipping through the telephone directory.

'Docherty' was one of these characters, a big man from Scotland. This was the name he finally ticked. The way 'Docherty' resonated from his mouth, with a guttural first syllable softening into a sigh, was what he liked most about his new name. It had a sound all of its own, a boom and a breath, which could be used either to echo a portentous past or to whisper a mysterious future.

To front 'Docherty' he added the first name 'Lee', after his favourite Kung-Fu movie icon − Bruce Lee. He had the pseudonym he needed for his new start; and ever since he's been known as Lee Docherty or, most often, just Docherty.

By the time I met him I had interviewed twenty prostitutes and a quarter of that number of clients. Despite the

comparatively cheap and unspecialized services offered by
prostitutes other than Mandy and Simone I was struck by
the way extraordinary themes resounded from one life into
another, the most telling of which was the need for shifting
identities and exaggerated personae wherever sex was
considered a business. I had begun to understand that
prostitutes call upon hidden resources to withstand both the
personal rigours of their work and the hypocrisy of public
perception towards its existence. The latter is generally so
scathing that the prostitute is virtually compelled to seek out
a double identity.

This distinction between the private and the professional
reminded me of the eulogistic way in which Norman Mailer
claimed that some boxers 'begin to have inner lives like
Hemingway or Dostoevsky, Tolstoy or Faulkner, Joyce or
Melville or Conrad or Lawrence or Proust . . .' Instead of
articulating the disciplines and dreams of boxers, Mailer
ultimately only provided an admiring emphasis of their
'otherness', an 'apartness' which has as much to do with
a fighter's past as his present.

Whatever their romantic limitations, I'd always been a
sucker for such concepts of secret history, of fantastic
'interior landscapes'. It was this which drew me in irresistibly
towards prostitution — for it was impossible to escape that
similarly necessary 'otherness' most prostitutes reach for
when they set themselves up for work. While the lives led
by hookers besides Mandy and Simone were less cerebral,
they were equally adept in calling up divisions of self to
separate their 'real' from their 'whore' identities.

Docherty's photographs spoke most of this extravagant
inner life — both his own and that of the women who looked
back into his camera. Mapped coarsely on their faces,
personal histories curved through them like dark rivers in
unknown countries. These shadowy expressions depicted a
furtive sex-world lending itself naturally to such mysteriously
personal mythology.

Transmuting itself into this outlandish journey, my

exposure to the wide arena of prostitution became increasingly compelling. Yet as an outsider, my initial comprehension of the sex business was obscured by my own interest in the distinctiveness of its practitioners. Until I could penetrate their separation from other people it appeared futile to even attempt to give voice to the lives, whether lived internally or not, of the prostitutes I knew.

So I repeatedly found myself skirting around this subject whenever I was asked that 'What are you doing these days?' party-going question. Much of my earliest reticence to speak about prostitution had a lot to do with the arch 'Mmmmm . . . interesting' observations I had already encountered. I also preferred to imagine that I was living out my own secret identity – a polite bumbler in the real world, but a relentless traveller in prostitution's kinky life of the mind.

Yet I buckled in the face of one particularly assertive American girl, called Lesley, at a party so dull that it could not even boast any visible signs of outer life. With that open-faced curiosity even hardened New Yorkers can assume abroad, her questions persisted until I at last mumbled that I was 'sorta writing something about prostitution, maybe . . .'

'What do you mean – "sorta" and "maybe"?' she asked.

'Well, I guess I mean "probably" . . .'

'When you *finally* decide "definitely",' she said, 'give me a call.'

'Why?' I asked, wondering if this dead party had forced her to admit an enigmatic career as a prostitute.

One of my old lovers became a prostitute a few years ago,' Lesley said less forcibly.

'Oh . . . well, um, how's she finding it?'

'It's a "he" . . .'

'I see,' I must have said knowingly.

'No, you don't – he's not gay. He's what they call a "gigolo" – you met any of them yet?'

'No – but I'd like to meet your friend.'

'I thought you were only "maybe" writing about prostitution!'

'It's not really a "maybe". It's been definite for a while.'

'Good for you!' she laughed. This was a refreshingly different reaction. Up until then, apart from my closest friends, the few English women I had told about this book had tended to smile nervously and take a step back from me as if they might be similarly contaminated by perversion. Most people imagined that such sustained exposure to prostitution would be 'bad', rather than good, for me. Lesley, meanwhile, not only appeared interested in the subject but was also a veritable fountain of knowledge on the price a woman might pay to have sex with a man in New York, Amsterdam or London. She also said some incisive things about the way in which this kind of prostitution represented an unspoken taboo, only varying in depths of silence from city to city.

Yet her acumen carried an undercurrent of anguish. While her friend's immersion in prostitution a year or so after their break-up had opened up her previously closed interest in the idea of a man selling sex to a woman, she could not easily hide the pain she felt in having lost him, Lee Docherty, 'so completely'. Although he had left her for no apparently specific reason, she also knew that he had loved her while they were together. But he preferred it now, said Lesley, if they didn't even meet as friends. Everything he did after their split centred around his becoming a prostitute.

'It's not him being a "gigolo" which makes me sad. It's just that I'm not sure if he thinks of me as his friend anymore. He's cut me right out of his life now . . .'

'I'm sorry,' I murmured, not knowing what else to say.

'Me too − I really loved him. He's an interesting guy. But I'll call him for you. At least it'll give me an excuse to phone him. Maybe he'll meet you and, for me, you can find out how he really is . . .'

Having survived her early brashness, Lesley exuded a gentle kind of American charm. I can't say that I was completely surprised that it worked once more on Lee Docherty — so much so that before the next week was through he met me for the first time because, as he said, 'Lesley asked me . . .'

Docherty lived in King's Cross, close to the station and the surrounding streets along which prostitutes have walked for more than a hundred years. He had lived there since 1987, long enough for him to think of the place as home. In King's Cross, where there were people and places which interested him, Docherty found a rhythm to life. He called it his 'routine'.

That was not the word which sprang to mind when I walked into his council flat early one November evening. There was something almost ghostly about the pattern of life Docherty focused on in King's Cross. Only the grace of the dancing girl spoke of another life beyond the Cross. Otherwise, the reason for my visit shone down from every framed prostitute.

Docherty's flat, on the fifth floor of a concrete high-rise, was small but functional. The kitchen had been turned into a darkroom and a ceaselessly sighing fridge doubled up as an alternative chair in the lounge. Despite its constricting size, the flat had been organized in such a way that there appeared to be plenty of space in which to walk. This lack of furnishing was made more noticeable by the many photographs hanging from every wall and by the absurdly large surrealist print covering the outside of Docherty's darkroom door. It was a copy of Salvador Dali's ghostly image of three clocks melting and folding over a bare branch, a table and a blurred face against a backdrop of fading sunlight. Its effect there was made all the more surreal by the surrounding photographs of night-time prostitution beneath the Cross. I later learned that Docherty intended no glib irony in choosing to hang *The Persistence Of Memory* in his flat, which was more a photographic museum than a conventional home for living in.

112

Although they could hardly have been more dissimilar in terms of layout and value, Docherty's flat made me think of Mandy Kavanagh's house across town. The contrasting homes were both dominated by dramatic photographs from their respective pasts. Just as Mandy's heroin Polaroid loomed over her tastefully colour-streaked 'House Of Pain' so Docherty's animated shot of his sister literally pirouetted over everything else in the room.

They were also linked by their reinventions of themselves along that secluded path of prostitution. Extending the comparison even further, Docherty not only lived alone but he was also, like Mandy, good-looking. Six-foot-two tall, lean and with short black hair, he appeared all the more striking to his female clients because he had that rare ability, at least for vagabonds like me, to make the most of whatever clothing he happened to be wearing. He looked cynically crisp whether dressed in his baggy 1950s-style cream suit or his faded 'Cool As Fuck' T-shirt and black 501s. Docherty said that he didn't care much about clothes, a claim borne out by his overt reliance on these two outfits as his personal response to 'smart' or 'casual' invitations from his clients; but he always wore them with a nonchalance which passed as his own definitive bash at style.

Apart from being fashionably dressed, a gigolo, at least according to cliché, is expected to be fawning and sycophantic. Whether from the shards of his own persona or out of instinctive professionalism, Docherty acted differently. He was almost curtly forthright, an enemy of small talk and banal compliments. This fascinated his women patrons because, beneath the surface good looks, it appeared to them that he was offering his real self. Docherty was reputed to be the best gigolo in London because women said he made them feel that, like him, they were 'serious' and 'contradictory'.

But I also thought of Mandy when I saw how nervous Docherty was during our introductory meetings. Whereas she was assured in both her home and in talking about her work, he was much more apprehensive. Docherty was unconvinced about both the suitability of his flat for our interviews and his capacity to talk about himself. Moreover, when I tried to deflect attention away from him by describing the type of prostitution practised by Mandy and Simone, he became increasingly distraught. 'Man,' he groaned at one point, 'this S&M stuff is pretty distressing. These are the type of men some of my women are probably married to — it's little wonder they seem so unloved . . .'

A vulnerability seeped from Docherty — a feeling held in check by Mandy and even to an extent by Simone, despite the ferocity of their more difficult S&M sessions. Whereas Mandy had developed 'The Terminator Angel' with an icy clarity and Simone claimed to slip into her 'Bitch Of Pain' guise out of love for Kyle, he had become Lee Docherty on a dejected whim.

It was only during our fourth meeting that Docherty finally felt able to give some coherent reason for his becoming a prostitute. Until then we had only flitted across the subject, our conversation punctuated by his stilted silences and my wayward monologues. 'When I became "Docherty",' he finally said, 'when I became a "gigolo", I wanted to find some kind of freedom. At first I thought I just wanted the kind of freedom that a lot of money gives you. But then I saw that I needed something more than just being free from having to hassle about the gas bill. I've got enough money now to live well, if that's what I want. But I've had that before, I've had jobs where I earned a lot of money.

'I was looking more for the freedom that comes from starting a new life. I could have left everything behind and gone to live in Cuba or somewhere. But I wanted to change the inside of me much more. I wanted to tear out the past. New name, new identity, new job, new life, new person. "Lee Docherty, prostitute" — that was as fresh a start as I could dream for myself.

'I always knew I was different. We all have that feeling

114

when we're kids. It's just that that fades for most people as they get older. They feel pressure to be like their friends, their neighbours. They worry if they're not married by a certain age, if they don't have a steady job. I get depressed by the thought of living with one person my whole life, working in one job for hours on end every week, every year. Even the idea makes me a little crazy. I wanted freedom from all this so I became someone else — "Docherty".

'And in becoming a specialist type of prostitute I did find some freedom. I only have a few clients and I charge them a lot. Except for the short time I'm with them I do exactly what I want with the rest of my life. No one tells me what to do, when to get up, who to see. Everything's down to me. That's the way I like it.'

This speech surprised me, not only for the way Docherty echoed Mandy in selecting a strict rota of clients but also for its length and passion. Considering that he had previously said little more than two or three sentences at a time, this block of words virtually qualified as a confessional address. Just as he had opted for prostitution on impulse, so he decided to trust me on apparent chance. The reason for this conversion, he said, was that he had seen me the weekend before at a double-bill of *The Texas Chainsaw Massacre* (parts I and III, subtitled *The Return Of Leatherface*) at The Scala, just down the road from his flat. Now my usual problem in being identified as a horror-splatter *aficionado* is that I invariably feel compelled to let it slip to the liberal accuser that I had sandwiched 'Leatherface' between, say, Renoir and Kurosawa triple-bills in the weeks before and after such a Texas excursion. Docherty, to his credit, was oblivious to such niceties. He was more interested in hearing that *Basket Case II* did not match the dark humour of its original and in telling me to seek out low-budget 'masterpieces like *Deranged, Motel Hell* and *Nekromantik II'*.

Although I couldn't help wondering what Docherty's refined women-friends made of his cinematic tastes, I was relieved that he had at last begun to talk to me as if I was someone other than a fearsome interviewer. After hearing how I tried to discuss pornography with Robert, sporting South Kensington's sartorial answer to the *Texas Chainsaw* look, Docherty lightened up sufficiently not to worry about the impression he made as a shy interviewee. Over the next couple of months, in between the odd Scala sojourn to reaffirm our new-found splattering solidarity, I was told the full Lee Docherty story.

Even before he made his 'Docherty' choice he had thought often about prostitution. When he had been too young to know what the word really meant they had called his sister 'a whore'. His father, with a face like silent thunder, and his mother, hushing him anxiously, had refused to answer when he asked them why they were calling her by this word, a word whose gravity terrified him even though its exact intent eluded him.

He had even asked her, his sister, to her face, to explain the meaning of 'whore' and had felt himself reeling back when her hand struck him and when he saw that the tears splashed down not from his own eyes but from hers. He felt then that this one word must be the most terrible thing a person could say, worse even than saying that God spelt backwards was 'dog' or that the school head was an old fucker, a creaky wanker, or any of the other profanities they loved to whisper to each other at the back of his classroom. 'Whore' to him then, just twelve years old, and his own sister barely four years older, became an unspeakable word — especially when he learnt its precise meaning from a dictionary and knew that it could never be applied to her with any degree of accuracy.

But that time passed, even though he had sometimes wondered if he and his family would ever survive the trauma induced by that first whisper of 'whore'. He moved on, beyond that frozen frame in his memory of them falling apart together in Hitchen, in Hertfordshire. For a while he forgot. Those were the five years when, after they had moved to Buckhurst Hill to make a fresh start, he came closest to skipping the past, when he lost himself in a ravishing world of speed, teenage girls and garage parties.

Even then he was separate from the others. As much as he tried he could never quite complete their circle of shared insecurities and preoccupations. Instead he was just there, ironically near the very centre of their group, almost as if he was the necessary hole in the middle of their otherwise minted milieu; minted, because they were stuck on sex and sweet on fame and felt like they could have much of both if they dreamed hard enough. Docherty already had something of each, although his fame was based on a boyish notoriety as a killer with the suburban girls. They seemed ready to do anything for him, these girls, if it meant that they might strip away his cool aura which was never quite understandable as either adolescent reserve or a stranger kind of adult resolve to be alone. But he liked kidding around with the girls and wondering what it would be like to score the winner at Wembley or to vomit before a sickened nation on *Top Of The Pops*. In those respects, at least, he was a lot like his sneeringly spotty friends.

'When I was a teenager it wasn't really a conscious thing that I kept a little apart from everyone else,' Docherty says. 'I was always there — at the games and at the parties — but I never felt like I could just lose myself with anyone. I always seemed to be watching others, never really letting go with them. I wouldn't say that I was unhappy — just a little detached. But I did like sex and I always liked being with girls. I never seemed able to fall for anyone though. And I also never "applied" myself to any single ambition. It wasn't like any big social statement but I just didn't believe much in anything.

'So when we left school I didn't see much point in doing anything else but following two of my friends who went to the LSE. Before I knew it I was doing this degree in

Economics and being bored to tears. Fuck it, it was terrible. That's when I was drinking and taking two caps of acid a week. I was wasted. Somehow I passed my first year and then, in the middle of the second, something weird happened. I was asked by this group of girls if I knew any male strippers. They were having this "post-feminist hen night". This friend of theirs was getting married to one of the Commercial Law lecturers. I was pretty cynical about that so I asked them why they were asking me. There were three of them and one said, "'Cos you look like you'd know a few dark characters." I said something like "I'm a dark kinda guy myself" and they all laughed and said, "We know, boy!" This went back and forth for a while and suddenly I found myself agreeing that I might as well do the strip. I liked them and I thought "why not?" But I wanted to be paid. They were a bit surprised when I said I wanted £100. There were going to be twenty of them there so it wasn't too much to ask. They tried to get me down to fifty but I stuck to my price. Without even knowing it I was setting down a ground-rule for myself in later years. But to get my hundred I had to agree that I'd throw in a kiss-a-gram and a full half-hour strip! They were pretty hard bargainers, those girls, but we had a deal.

'I was terrified on the night of the party — I'd never done anything like that before. But by the time I arrived they were all pretty drunk — just screaming and giggling and being outrageously "girly". I didn't have to do too much to make them laugh. They laughed at me and with me and I even laughed a little myself — 'cos I was surprised that I could pull off a stunt like that. I kissed the main girl a lot, I danced around to James Brown, I took off all my clothes to Barry White and the bride-to-be rubbed cream all over me during *Sexual Healing*. They went mad then and I had to duck away quickly. I was relieved to get out. I never did anything like that again but, I guess, it gave me the confidence to know that I could eventually turn to prostitution.

'I left university soon after 'cos I was sick of being a

student. I found this flat in King's Cross and I wangled this job as a runner at the Stock Exchange. It was in the peak yuppie-boom, big-bang time. I hustled, I made some money. I was there a year — hanging round guys who're like miniature versions of your pal Alistair. It was fucking gross. I was better at making money than most of them but I couldn't find the thrill in it. I wanted to buy my own chainsaw, I wanted to be "Leatherface" in the city, I wanted to carve up some of those smug fuckers. But I opted for a redundancy settlement instead. I could have saved my job. There were lots of other guys they wanted to get rid of. But I wanted out. I got six months' pay which was really lucky, a bit of a scam to tell the truth, and I just chilled out here, at the Cross.'

Docherty wallowed in his solitary space. He did little but spend time there, doing things which now he can hardly remember beyond the fact that they were dominated by sleeping and reading and video-watching. When he did go out it was invariably down the Pentonville Road, to triple-bills at the Scala Cinema. It was curious that the films which interested him most were of a certain kind. He loved and watched, again and again, *Taxi Driver*, *Hardcore*, *Ms 45 – Angel Of Vengeance*, *Driller Killer*, and the inevitable *Texas Chainsaw Massacre* trilogy. These were bleak, grainy films in which images of sex and violence and morality and death were pushed to the forefront of the screen. Yet he also found them, overflowing with images of retribution and redemption, to be moving rather than lurid. Even though he was from Hitchen and Buckhurst Hill, rather than Brooklyn or the backwoods of Texas, these movies said something intimate to his otherwise dispassionate heart.

Taxi Driver was his key picture in life. He had first seen it, in 1975, as a twelve-year-old boy. Fifteen years later it still carried a seemingly personal message for him. Docherty could even understand how John Hinkley had used the film, and his obsession with one of its central characters — the

twelve-year-old prostitute, Iris, played by Jodie Foster —
as the justification behind his attempted assassination of the
then President, Ronald Reagan. Robert de Niro acted out
the part of Travis Bickle, the taxi-driving vigilante
attempting to purge the streets of prostitution and
pornography, with a measured balance of vulnerability and
violence. Docherty felt that de Niro uncovered a stained
truth about his own life in England, about the equation he
had struck between fragility and fury to emerge as some kind
of quintessential outsider. And Jodie Foster, hauntingly,
reminded him of his sister, even though they looked and
dressed completely differently.

But the film struck Docherty so forcibly because Travis
Bickle, attempting to save Iris from prostitution, and
Hinkley, trying to win the eternal remembrance of the real-
life Jodie Foster, appeared to be defying the mediocrity
of the everyday. Docherty himself did not dream of
emulating their terminal violence; rather, he was fascinated
by the attempted eclipse of their original selves. In this
way he also imagined he could transform himself into
something other than the mundane person he had seemingly
become.

The renewed impact of *Taxi Driver* on him during the year
that his redundancy pay lasted was such that he even took
to imitating de Niro's austere Mohican and, most bizarre
of all, eventually working as a mini-cab driver. For all its
absurdities, Docherty's extreme immersion in *Taxi Driver*
struck a chord with me. I remembered being similarly
affected, if not quite to this degree, when I saw the film as
a mid-1970s' South African schoolboy. My friend and I were
so impressed by de Niro that we decided that at least one
of us should take it on himself to arrive at school the
following week with a mean Bickle-like Mohican. We spun
a coin to decide who would be honoured with the shears.
Although I would not have described myself then by this
word, I was lucky. I called, naturally enough, 'heads' and
the five cent piece turned up 'tails'. The outraged reaction

my friend's Mohican caused staggered both of us and it was only the thrashing he received from our uncinematic headmaster which deterred me from letting my head follow my heart into the *Taxi Driving* wastelands. I was, after all, riding a yellow bicycle in a town called Germiston rather than a yellow cab round Times Square; I was fourteen years old then. It was mildly disturbing that Docherty should identify so passionately with Travis Bickle's psychotic rage when he was in his late-twenties.

'It wasn't *that* bad!' Docherty grinned.

'Becoming an actual taxi driver is sort of extreme!' I said.

'Well my Mohican had grown out by then and I was looking ordinary again. I packed it up after a couple of weeks anyway.'

'Too much scum on the streets?'

'No!' laughed Docherty. 'It was just that I could hardly find the fucking streets. I thought I knew London but I got lost hopelessly night after night. I'd have these passengers screaming at me while I tried to read the A-Z in the dark. It was a total disaster and when this second-hand car I'd bought a few weeks before started to cut out at every corner I gave up being Robert de Niro . . .'

A few weeks after this that he went to see his wearily cheery doctor. How could he even begin then to talk simply of his life without spilling everything that he had held in for so long? He felt that once he started to talk he would never be able to stop. Unwilling to allow that to happen he decided on his radical gigolo change.

'But don't you find it disturbing,' I asked Docherty, 'that you became a prostitute not long after all this *Taxi Driver* stuff?'

'Why?'

'Because Travis Bickle's mission is to wipe away the "scum" of prostitution, to save Jodie Foster from being sold on the streets.'

'Well . . .' Docherty paused for a moment's thought. 'Don't you find it strange that after also loving the film you're now hanging out with prostitutes, that you're writing about them? Where's your Mohican now?' As I tried to think of a snappy reply, Docherty ploughed on. 'Come on, we didn't identify with Travis Bickle's morality. Christ, the guy's insane. But, shining through the madness was the way he tried to transform himself, the way he sought salvation through change. That's what got to me. That's what the film's about — madness, violence, revenge, redemption. It's not about prostitution or pornography.'

'But you do still walk around King's Cross at night,' I said. 'You *have* become friends with some of the younger prostitutes on these streets outside. I know you're not going to blow their pimps away but isn't this also spookily like *Taxi Driver* — being repelled and drawn to the street at the same time?'

'Christ, I really do think you've got me down as a psycho! But the main thing to remember is that *I'm* a prostitute just like they are prostitutes. We're very different kinds of prostitute but that's what we all are — hookers! You shouldn't lose perspective on this whole *Taxi Driver* thing. If anything it was a romantic identification with the film. When it comes to prostitution there's no place for romance; only professionalism.'

Knowing that Paul Schrader had written *Taxi Driver* and directed *Hardcore* before making *American Gigolo*, I asked Docherty if that film had had any effect on his sexual decision.

'Uh uh. Schrader's great but I don't like *American Gigolo* much. Richard Gere's not my boy. Anyway, it was more business sense than the movies which got me working. Sure, I'm a prostitute, a gigolo, a stud, a hired gun, a toy boy, whatever the fuck anyone wants to call me. But more than anything else I'm a professional. To succeed in this business you've got to be professional in who you see and what you do with them. I'm not doing this for fun. This is not just my job, it's the way I live and so I make sure it retains a sense of order. I follow a routine.

I have the mornings to myself and the women know that if they want to date me they must do so between noon and midnight. Sometimes I'll stay the night if they pay the £250 rate — but I prefer just to spend two or three hours a time with them.'

£250 sounded an impressive fee to me until Docherty pointed out the discrepancy between his nightly charge and that of a female equivalent.

'This is *not* an equal opportunities business,' he said ruefully. 'I know that if I was a woman I could add another thousand on to my all-night fee. I bet Mandy Kavanagh would add on even more than that . . .'

'Is that because women paying for sex, or companionship, is still such an oddity?'

'Yeah, of course. But the real reason is that women have little economic clout. My clients are at the top end of the scale but where their husbands might be able to spend £1,500 without anyone noticing, it's much harder for the wife to even get away with £250. It's not their money. They have to depend on their husbands for income. They might pretend that it doesn't matter but it gets to them. The woman who's most at ease with me is "Molly" and that's because she's single and a company director. The money she spends in seeing me is her own. She has more sense of worth than the others. But even "Molly" earns nothing like she should. She's on about £40,000 when, if she was a man, she'd probably have been earning that ten years ago. So in this business I get a close-up look at the economics of the system. My problem is that I don't earn the same as my female contemporaries . . .'

'But then you don't have to deal with the type of male clients they do,' I pointed out.

'That's true! Thank fuck!'

'It also seems that where most women are driven into prostitution with the specific purpose of making money your choice to become a gigolo was more random . . .'

'Yeah, in the sense that I know I could find a job where

I would make more money than I do as a gigolo. I like the freedom and the time this job gives me. But when I do work I'm very professional. I know I can't do this indefinitely. It's like being an athlete. I've only got so many years in this business. I'm turning thirty soon − OK, so I'm in shape and I look all right and I've got a roving tongue and a vivid imagination − but there's gonna come a time when someone younger takes my place. I'm under no illusions about my life-span as a prostitute.'

One of the mysteries surrounding the gigolo's clandestine world concerns the physical demands of the job. While a woman prostitute can feign arousal, the gigolo's job inevitably requires a certain amount of genuine involvement. 'How do you keep it up − all this sex work?' I asked Docherty unambiguously. 'You don't have to take any strange pills called "Stallion" or "Stud Man" do you?'

' "Stud Man"?' laughed Docherty. 'No way! I pace myself. I've done this for three years. I stay cool as fuck. Otherwise I'd just burn out. If I can get away without fucking a client on a date I'm happy. It's like if you're a real hired gun you don't waste a bullet if you can help it. You don't just shoot for the sake of it − and I'm speaking metaphorically here, as in semen-shooting . . .

'Sometimes a woman just wants to be held and told that she's special. I push sex to the side then. Man, I can do that understanding trip in my sleep but, and this is when it gets tough, there're those days when you don't feel like telling someone that she's got unexplored potential, that she deserves someone more sensitive than the husband she's already got. I get paid £100 for two hours and if there's sex involved it's another £50. I never see more than one client a day because it saps me − mentally as much as physically. So it's a myth to think there's anything glamorous about being a gigolo. There's not. I dropped a couple of clients recently..They were paying me well, driving me around in open-backed sports cars. But they were the women I had to lie most to. I just got sick of slipping my hand into theirs, giving a squeeze and saying "You're a really special person, Lucinda" or "I understand your pain, Belinda". Their fragility wore me down. They began to cling to me, they wanted something intimate from me. They were getting too personal you know, they were stepping over the limits of our professional arrangement.'

'What are the other women like?' I asked.

'Well I have eight regulars now which is about right. I like something about each of them. They're all different. I have one woman who mostly wants what she calls "great cunt-stretching sex" while the others want their pussy-demands balanced with other kinds of attention. We'll go to a French movie or to an exhibition at the National Gallery or to the theatre. The women who like me are into being "arty". They like to do these kinds of things and they like to make intelligent conversation about what they've seen over coffee afterwards. I listen to them and I tell them what I think and they like that. If they're in the mood, which they usually are, we then go off and have sex. But things are different every week. Maybe one week they want to be tied down and fucked from behind and then the next week they'll want to see some painting by Turner.'

From Docherty's description it appeared as if female consumers of prostitution were more eclectic than their male counterparts. Yet if the services he offered to them were often more social than sexual what did that say about their 'real lives'?

'They might be comforted by their husbands' wealth but some of them seem devastated by loneliness — by the fact that they have nothing in common with their husbands apart from the kids and the house and the habit of being together. They also all seem unfulfilled and unappreciated. So they want some stimulation, something a little dangerous. And what could be more different and slightly *risqué* — but still safe and discreet than a gigolo?'

Docherty's professionalism paid off. He worked amongst

the liberal rich in palatial homes in Knightsbridge, Chelsea, St John's Wood, Hampstead and further afield in Surrey, in Ascot and Virginia Water. Six of his clients were married women with ostentatiously wealthy husbands, privately educated children, barking dogs, housefuls of servants and their own separate bank accounts. Their public lives exuded a veneer of domestic bliss. Meeting them for the first time, Docherty implied, was like stepping into a pastel-shaded *Garden And Home* world brought to mellifluously vowelled life.

But that dream life was set strictly apart from their private liaisons with Docherty. Their covert gigolo-game was kept secret from all but a tight-knit circle of best friends. There were two exceptions to this set of married women: Molly, the thirty-six-year-old company director, who preferred to retain her anonymity for professional reasons; and Kitty, a fifty-three-year-old widow, who lived alone in a plush Knightsbridge flat and claimed pleasantly to have driven her husband to a premature death ten years ago when he left her with an estate, she said, as massive as the coronary which killed him. Whenever Docherty and Kitty were out on the town, whether at the opera or a restaurant, she delighted in introducing him as her *'gigolo par excellence'*. That gushing description, delivered in a fake French accent, inevitably induced uncomfortably forced laughter from those who then had to shake Docherty's hand, unsure whether the joke was on them or on him.

Still being held back from my potentially problematic interview with Alistair, I was especially interested in meeting some of these well-heeled women clients. However, I didn't hold out much hope that this would happen. Docherty's women risked public disdain for even seeing him – let alone talking to me about their sexual consumption. Docherty, as surprising as ever, was more optimistic that he could 'arrange something' for me. There was one pre-condition.

Assuming I already knew what he meant I assured Docherty of my discretion.

'You know that I'll turn a chainsaw on you if you're not discreet,' Docherty stressed. 'But that's not the condition I'm talking about. If you set up a meeting between me and Mandy Kavanagh then we've got a deal. I'll arrange something for you in return then . . .' Docherty had been yearning to meet Mandy ever since I told him that her favourite book was Dostoevsky's *Notes From The Underground*; for Pauline Kael had once written that '*Taxi Driver* is a movie on heat, a raw tabloid version of *Notes From The Underground*'. As far as Docherty was concerned, that sealed his spiritual link with Mandy.

The interest Mandy evoked wherever I spoke about her was such that I had to constantly field requests from people wanting to meet her. Inevitably, she turned down more invitations than she accepted. But Docherty was different and, following some unscrupulous sales talk from me, she at last agreed to a meeting. Apart from keeping my end of the bargain with Docherty I was keen to see how the two of them got along, particularly as their 'self-invention' and the 'professionalism' of their respective kinds of prostitution were not that dissimilar.

Having grown unused to such uncommercial 'blind dates' they both, I thought poignantly, insisted that I accompany them to the tasteful restaurant Mandy had chosen for their rendezvous. Similarly unsuited to the role of chaperon I suggested to Docherty that we also invite Lesley, who had introduced us after all. He must have been more nervous than I thought because he readily agreed.

When Mandy and I walked into the restaurant a minute past the scheduled time of meeting we found a scrubbed and newly-shorn Docherty having his just-pressed suit smoothed once more for luck by Lesley. She revelled in her role as the trusted ex-girlfriend. I was thankful that Lesley was there for without her the first half of the evening would have been disastrous. Mandy was strangely cool, if always polite, to

the increasingly sheepish Docherty. It was as if his charm
had been worn down by excessive use and, faced with a
woman who was never going to be a client of his, he
appeared uncertain what to say or how to act. He sat there
glumly while Lesley entertained Mandy and me with stories
of her and Docherty's drug-taking escapades and, also, what
it was like to be an American living in England.

As Lesley and Mandy swapped further witty stories about
life in New York, Docherty suddenly switched from polite
glasses of Perrier to double-Scotch tumblers. The change
did him good because with each drink he looked a little
lighter and by the time he was on to his third he was more
like his old self. After he had whipped out a few of his Texas
back-wood anecdotes he even had the courage to admit that
he had been more frightened at the prospect of this evening
than when sitting through any number of 'Leatherface'
triple-bills.

'Well thanks a lot! Am I really *that* bad?' laughed Mandy.

'Oh no!' enthused Docherty. 'It's just that I'd heard a
bit about you and you're even more beautiful than I
imagined.' Lesley raised a tipsy brow in my direction as if
to say 'Uh-oh!' 'Well, I mean more intimidating in a way,
if you know what I mean.'

'I think I know what you mean, Lee,' said Mandy sweetly,
'but I'm not sure if I like it!'

'What I really mean is that you're even more impressive
than I thought you would be!'

Trying to bale Lee out of his verbal quagmire, Lesley
helpfully shifted the conversation on to a less personal setting
by asking Mandy if she thought there were any similarities
between her and Lee's prostitution.

'Well, I'm not really sure what Lee does with his clients!'

'Oh I'm very kind to them!' Docherty said bashfully.

'But what we all want to know,' Lesley responded with
drunken fervour, 'is how you manage to keep it up day after
day?'

At this point Docherty asked, with as much dignity as he

could muster, if Lesley would mind getting another couple
of drinks from the bar as service appeared to have ground
to a halt. Dragging me along behind her so that, in her
words, Docherty could 'make his big play', Lesley said that
she had never seen him acting so unconfidently. Although
she claimed to be fully supportive of Docherty's work as
a gigolo — seeing it as only right that women should also
have the choice of turning to a male prostitute if that's what
they wanted — Lesley was troubled by his awkwardness.
'I guess it must be difficult for him just to relax now. He
must be so used to performing that when it's an evening off
from work he gets all wound up. He should've stuck with
me as his girlfriend, hey?'

When we returned to the table, Docherty and Mandy were
more amiably comparing sexual services and prices. Back
on professional ground his confidence returned and there
followed an intriguing exchange between London's hippest
male and female prostitutes.

But when the evening ended and they swapped telephone
numbers it was clear that he did so with more serious intent.
In the weeks that followed, Docherty increasingly cancelled
appointments with his clients. He said to me that he was
so smitten with Mandy that he couldn't possibly think about
working as a gigolo. As Mandy only wanted to see him as
a very casual, and definitely platonic, acquaintance, I felt
unhappily responsible for the drastic decline of Docherty's
once steadily lucrative business. Even a rare screening of
Basket Case at The Scala only deepened his unrequited
gloom by convincing him that his own life was heading the
way of the film's repulsive and perpetually basketed hero.
For a few maudlin moments it looked as if he was close to
dropping his 'Docherty' pseudonym for what he considered
to be a more fitting '*Basket Case*' alias.

Despite his depression Docherty insisted on fulfilling his
promise to help me meet some of his clients. 'It'll take my
mind off Mandy,' he mumbled bleakly. His sudden

cancellation of appointments had also startled Arlene and Rachel, his two most regular clients. Sensing his sadness, they were perhaps in an even more agreeable mood than usual to hear Docherty's request that they meet me. Nevertheless, he must have momentarily escaped from his *Basket Case* mood for he set up an interview and morning tea for me at Arlene's house in Ascot one cold Friday in January.

Realizing the enormity of the gesture they were making on his behalf, Docherty provided me with a few lessons in gigolo etiquette. I was to act with scrupulous discretion at all times. I was expected to be punctual and polite and sensitive to the significance of any stray visitors. If needed, I should even be prepared to impersonate a washing machine mechanic. The latter tip, especially, worried me as spin-dryer repairs were not my forte.

However, I needn't have worried. Arlene and Rachel had worked out an alternative back-up plan. In the unlikely event that Arlene's husband arrived home a day early from his business trip to Chicago, I was to act as a freelance journalist writing an article about 'life in Ascot' for one of the quality papers. I had my tape-recorder ready, after all, as ample proof. On the subject of this recorder, Arlene and Rachel had also given the matter some considered thought. While they would be willing for our interview to be taped I would have to transcribe the cassette before I left Ascot. This meant that they could dispose of the recorded 'evidence'.

'I hope you don't mind all this cloak-and-dagger stuff,' Arlene said, 'but you can appreciate our positions. It's not that we don't trust you but we just can't afford to take any chances.' Arlene was an elegant woman in her early forties who obviously knew how to play the part of the 'executive wife'. Rachel, her best friend and in her late thirties, was no less stylishly dressed in a 'little jazzy number I picked up from Nicole Farhi'. I said, rather crassly, that that was where Mandy and Simone also shopped. Rachel let this slip

130

by with a demure 'I expect all sorts of women shop there' remark.

Not wanting to take up too much of their time and feeling conscious of the strangeness of our purpose in meeting, I soon had the tape-recorder rolling. It took a while to get into the swing of the conversation. Arlene finally decided to confront the crux of the problem head-on. 'It's very difficult to talk about this at first. I've known Docherty for more than three years now but I wouldn't dream of telling anyone else but this one mutual friend Rachel and I have. What do I call him even?'

' "Gigolo" is such a horrible word,' Rachel interrupted.

'Well, women are meant to recoil from the idea of prostitution. Most people we know would be shocked that Rachel and I both pay Docherty for sex. And I'd be lying if I said it didn't sometimes bother me.'

'We're lucky we've got each other to talk to,' Rachel continued. 'Although I know that there are many more women than you'd ever imagine doing the same thing as us, it's a relief not to have to hide it from your best friend. There's such a stigma attached to the whole subject that I don't think I would ever have dared meet Docherty if it hadn't been for Arlene.'

I knew that Arlene had been Docherty's first client — a fact which she not only confirmed but then emphasized. 'I gave him the idea my sweet! He used to work for my husband and I met him at a barbecue we had here. I thought he was irresistible. He was very different to all the other young bucks. I never gave any of them a second glance. He was just glowering in a corner all evening, literally burning with intensity!'

'That's our Docherty all right!' chuckled Rachel.

'He was very interesting. Instead of wanting to talk about how well he was doing at work or what kind of fancy car he was buying, he just started talking to me about movies and photography. I asked him what he photographed and he said he'd just started taking photos of the prostitutes who worked in King's Cross, near where he lived. I was intrigued and I made some off-the-cuff remark that that was a line of business he could do quite well in himself. He asked me what I meant and I said that some women would be willing to pay for a night of fun with such a hunky guy like him. I was a little loaded and I guess I was just coming on to him.

'Anyway nothing happened until about nine months later when he phoned me right out of the blue. He said he had been out of work for a year and he needed to earn some money. Did I have any suggestions? He was very forthright. I'd just started this little pottery business and I said I could do with some help getting the books in order. So he came over — to be truthful I was angling for an affair with him but he just came out with it. He said that affairs were messy and instead of going through the charade of him being paid on the pretext of doing my accounting we should do a more straightforward sexual deal. I was shocked. I asked him who he thought he was, speaking to me like that? He just stayed very cool. As he started to leave, for some reason, I called him back. I must have wanted him very badly. And I knew he was right. Affairs turn sour — there's jealousy and heartache. I didn't want to fall in love with him. I had a husband and two children and I wasn't going to give them up. So I said, "OK — we'll do it your way once and see how it goes." I gave him £100 and I didn't feel cheap or anything. I felt incredibly turned on. It was a wild thing to do. And he was very, very good in bed — as I knew he would be — and I've seen him a couple of times a month ever since without any problems. No confusion, no pain — just great sex and rock-solid discretion.'

'Well, no problems until recently!' said Rachel. 'He's gone a bit weird this last week or two. Blew both of us out. Do you know what's the matter with him?'

With both women looking searchingly at me I felt that this was not an opportune moment to tell them about their gigolo falling for another Nicole Farhi dresser. 'Oh you know Docherty,' I answered shiftily, 'he gets a bit moody sometimes . . .'

'Never before with us!' said Rachel sadly.

'He's not paid to be moody anyway!' Arlene moaned indignantly. 'I think I'd better have a word with our temperamental stallion!'

'So how did you meet the "stallion", Rachel?' I asked curiously.

'Don't you two call him that — he's a very sensitive guy!'

'I'll give him something to be "sensitive" about if he doesn't watch out,' Arlene muttered darkly.

Ignoring her friend, Rachel explained, 'Arlene told me about him. I had guessed something was in the air but it still came as a surprise. Anyway I was curious to meet him. And boy, am I glad I did! Docherty is the sexiest guy I've ever met. He's a real hunk but there's something else about him that arouses me. It's his sense of mystery. As much as I've talked to him over the last two-and-a-half years I feel I've never quite got to the bottom of him. That's curiously liberating because he's like no-one else I've met. I find it erotic that he's so different.'

'Do you think it's difficult to get to know him precisely because he's a prostitute?' I asked.

'Well, you'd be better qualified to answer that question,' said Arlene, turning towards me. 'You're not one of his clients — have you got to know him?'

'I think we understand each other. But there's a line that always separates us — I'm writing about him so there are obviously some things that he prefers me not to know. And at the same time I tend to talk more to him about the things I want to write. So I'd say that what I do know about him I know well — but that doesn't mean I really know the "Docherty" you see . . .'

'Yeah,' sighed Rachel, 'he's very good at keeping up his professional persona. There's this wall around him which gives him real strength but, at the same time, you sense that deep inside he's carrying some terrible pain. Perhaps it's just me imagining this vulnerability but he fascinates me because of it; and interesting people are always the sexiest.'

'So he's not just an archetypal "gigolo" — someone merely to have sex with?'

'I often think he is — for me at least,' Arlene answered.

'No, he's more than that to me,' Rachel said. 'But I also have to say that he does some amazing things to me in bed. He sets me on fire sometimes. He does things to me I can hardly believe. When I'm with him I feel so uninhibited which is strange for me because normally I'm very shy, I'm almost awkward about my sexuality with other men, even with my own husband. That's sad but true. Lee unleashes something in me, something that is almost overwhelming at times. I don't know whether I should really tell you this . . .'

'But you will anyway, Rach . . .' Arlene chuckled.

'Oh all right! Lee's fucked me in almost every imaginable position, in every possible way, and I still want more. I also want other things from him — but I don't push him because I know you can't get too intimate with him, you have to keep the most deeply personal facets of your personality to yourself. That's the way he works and I accept it. This is not a normal relationship, after all, is it?'

'But how does it affect the relationship with your husband?' I asked tentatively.

After a long pause as they exchanged one of those best friends' looks which are inscrutable to the outsider, Rachel spoke again: 'I love my husband but this marriage hasn't turned out the way I'd hoped. The same thing goes for Arlene. I suppose that's why we both see Docherty — because we feel something is missing from our respective marriages. But then we also get on with our husbands and we both have children and homes . . .'

'So we keep on as if everything's hunky-dory,' continued Arlene. 'And, you know, with Docherty around to fill in the gaps, it just about always is . . .'

'It's not a case that we want to leave our husbands, which must sound weird to you,' said Rachel.

'Well, married men who visit prostitutes tend to say exactly the same thing about their wives,' I replied.

'It's a frightening thought that,' said Rachel after a long silence. 'I sometimes wonder if my husband visits prostitutes . . .'

'Never!' scoffed Arlene. 'Money and power matters most to them . . .'

I decided not to mention Alistair at that explicit moment. Rachel continued dreamily, 'Not to Docherty though. That's odd, considering that he does this for money. But it's why we both feel completely safe with him. He has a real core of integrity. He would never put either of us in a compromising position with our husbands. And that's the advantage of seeing him instead of opting for the traditional route of an affair. Maybe the emotion's kept at bay but that can be a good thing. Affairs always end with hurt. That's why I'm sticking with our guy. I dunno, if things were different and I was ten years younger maybe I could have fallen headlong in love with him.'

'You already are, Rachel — at least a little,' said Arlene lightly.

'No I'm not! Too much has happened to him. I don't know if you can live with a man like Docherty, I don't know if you can love a man who is a prostitute. It's a very strange thing to do — as it is to be one of his clients, I guess. We live such different lives and maybe that's part of the excitement — that sense of doing something dark, something forbidden and forever secret with someone from another world . . .'

The more time Docherty spent in his clients' places of plenty the less comfortable he felt whenever he left King's Cross. Yet he had always known that the Cross was an area of dark tumult. When he walked down those streets late at night he sometimes felt engulfed by the promise of violence. There were times when he heard it in a rancorous pimp's threat to one of his prostitutes and there were times when he saw its embodiment in a slap or a punch on a street corner. And Docherty could always imagine violence in the blurred faces of the men slowly circling the Cross in search of a girl.

Some of the sunken-faced and tight-skirted women who worked this beat recognized him whenever he passed. They'd sing out words like 'Hiya love!' and 'How're things, darlin'?'. Docherty, in his singularly private way, usually did little more than answer them with a polite nod. But particular women stood out for him and, to them, he was more forthcoming. He'd stop for a while and share some words with them.

Docherty never asked them questions like 'How's business?' When he spoke he was strangely direct. He'd ask a prostitute if he could photograph the shoes she was wearing because he liked the way they shone in the rain or else he kept the camera in his bag and told her to leave her pimp because he was pumping her full of junk.

As for the women, they were never quite sure how to take Docherty. When he first derided their pimps they wondered if he saw himself as some kind of replacement. But Docherty's scorn for pimping never translated itself into any form of alternative. He never made any promises; he never offered to take anyone away from the Cross. The pared-down language he used was not that of a pimp.

Neither did he come across as a potential client, no matter how often they tried to test him. He was not like any of their other voyeurs who trawled the streets, watching all the while but never quite managing to summon the courage to actually see through a proposition. Almost every prostitute knew a man who'd go far enough to pick her up on a street corner and drive her to a deserted warehouse site where, in the silvery dark, they'd talk about sex until it got to the point where he had to slide back the car seat and hand over his £20. Then, the sweat began to glisten and he'd back out of the deal on the slimmest of excuses;

only to reappear a few nights later in the hope of repeating the charade.

Docherty was different. He always refused their proposals at the very outset, but he did so in a way where his cordiality matched his conviction. His resolute refusal to enter any form of sexual banter also convinced them that he was not a policeman or any kind of Vice Squad undercover man.

If it hadn't been for his camera bag they would have quickly accepted him as merely being an affable neighbour. It took them a long while to grow used to his wanting to photograph them. But it was the very fact that he always asked for their permission before he aimed the camera their way that slowly convinced his favourite prostitutes that he meant them no harm.

When the mood took them – and Docherty somehow always seemed able to pick the right night and mood to come out on to the streets – they even liked being photographed. He was at his quietest then for he could never ask any of the women to assume an expression for his camera's benefit. Instead he just moved a little, shifting his position slightly so that a close-up, square-on shot of a face might follow one taken in angled profile.

It was after such a late night of intense photography that I visited Docherty again in his King's Cross room. He was still hurting with a love for Mandy Kavanagh which I thought, as he had only met her once, was more mythological than real. But he was also preparing to return to work again – his photography that night was a sign to himself, he said, that he'd answer Arlene's and Rachel's increasingly frantic calls the next morning. And, whatever the reason, he spoke to me that night like he had never done before.

'When I look round this room,' he said, 'at all these photographs I see my sister too. Look how alive she is in that photo. Sometimes I think it's my best – even though I took it when I was so young. But the prostitute prints matter a lot to me too. They come from me and, being a prostitute, they say something about me too. They belong in this room. I'd hate to see them hanging in a gallery because I don't know how much they could mean to anyone else.

'The Cross is a hard place to be a prostitute. I could smell the desperation tonight. I could see it in the hatchet-faces and stained skirts. I could see it in the yellow bruises running down their bare legs. It was cold out there too. I felt something special for them tonight. They made me realize how lucky I am as a prostitute. I make a lot of money and I work in elegant places with some intelligent women. It's different out in the street.

'But they're alive, you know, these King's Cross prostitutes. They're women. That's why I photograph them — because they look incredibly beautiful together on the wall. Look . . . with my sister. I haven't told you this before but when I was twelve years old, not more than a few months after I took that photograph of her dancing on our front lawn, she started crying softly one night. We were at the dining-room table, with our parents, eating my mother's fish-pie. I got sent to my room when she began to sob. But even up there I could hear my father's voice, shouting "Whore, whore, you bloody whore!" She was sixteen years old and about to do her A-levels. She was also three months pregnant. She hardly knew what hit her. My parents were devastated. They felt swallowed up by shame.

'By the time they had pulled themselves together it was too late. She hanged herself on a Monday afternoon. She was wearing her favourite dress, the one in that photograph. I came home and found her, hanging in her room. This blue chair was lying upside down on the floor. I can never forget that. It was a week after my father called her a whore. I hardly knew her, being so young, but she was just a girl. She was my sister.

'It's strange, I know. I'm working as a prostitute and

I know as well as anyone what "whore" is supposed to mean. But when I'm out at the Cross, like tonight, I don't see whores. I see women I share something with. I see them here at the Cross walking with pain — but they still keep on walking, dreaming of something else, something better than the past. Just like the rest of us, I guess . . .'

Chapter Five

Kinky Ms Whiplash and the Chancellor

It seemed to me then that pain, even more than pound coins and notes, had to be considered the sex business's prevailing currency. Professional sexual encounters may ooze with the gloss of cash and desire but the prostitute and the client are essentially playing off one ache against another bruise. The success of prostitutes like Lee Docherty, as much as his less fortunate King's Cross counterparts, depends on the extent to which they control these ever-shifting parameters of pain.

But around the time I was getting to know him through the slow process of *Deranged*-type film outings, I met a different kind of woman. Considerably older than the 'Terminator Angel'/'Bitch Of Pain'/'Docherty' triumvirate, Sara Dale presented a further distinct contrast. She had begun sex-therapy work more through the pursuit of sensual pleasure than either monetary gain or the burial of pain. By the time I was formally introduced to her I had already heard much about Sara Dale. In interviews with male clients she had been spoken of in glowing terms, as someone who was not only compassionate but also remarkably skilful in massage and domination techniques.

A woman called Melissa, who was forty-five years old and a single parent of two teenage boys, was especially emphatic that I should meet Sara Dale. Melissa, who topped up her meagre income support allowance with afternoon massage, including some joint work with Sara, stressed that she had never met anyone else 'as committed to sex-therapy as a fundamentally healing experience'.

I thought back to Kyle's cynical use of 'therapy' as a euphemistic way of softening the fact that his lover was working for him as a prostitute. 'But this is completely different,' insisted Melissa, 'because Sara Dale really *does* help her clients, she *does* offer them an unusual kind of catharsis, a way of putting them back in touch with feelings which make them glow. She deals in pleasure much more than pain – she gives and receives enjoyment with equal grace.' Well, what could I do in the face of such incandescent PR but take the short walk from my home to Campden Hill where Sara Dale then lived, with her lover, David.

Her small house, covered in ivy and climbing roses, was as pretty as any seen on the gleaming lid of a biscuit-tin. Bicycles, used for early morning and weekend rides, were slung casually against the wooden fence and whenever I walked through their front gate a beautifully fat grey cat reclined on the lawn with a massive yawn and an outstretched paw in welcome. Perhaps because he was such an unusual feline – a seal-point tabby – he answered to the obvious name of 'Cat'. If the neighbours noticed the male clients streaming up and down the short pathway every day, they must surely have concluded that 'Cat's' well-spoken owners were indeed respectable psychotherapists. It was hard to believe that anything remotely deviant could unfold in such a setting.

During my numerous visits to this particular house I passed a couple of clients on their way out and, instead of skulking guiltily past as I expected, they greeted me enthusiastically. It was then that I began to wonder if there was some substance to the assertions I had heard that Sara Dale was fast becoming London's 'Queen Of Pleasure'. From a more personal perspective, I was most intrigued by her because she too was a South African. Although she had left the country more than twenty-eight years before, when

142

she was just into her twenties, Sara Dale retained a faint trace of a Cape Town accent. Most people assumed that she was English but my South African vowels soon had her flattening out her own in apparent empathy. We even spoke a little Afrikaans for old time's sake and I found it curious that she should have ended up working as a 'new-age sensualist', as she then described herself.

But strangeness was at the source of Sara Dale's eclectic heritage. She was the Cape Town-born daughter of a Lithuanian Jewish mother and an aristocratic French Catholic father. Branching away from this volatile mix she eventually veered towards 'Hindu and Indian Tantra spirituality – mixed with a sensual philosophy of open, limitless sexuality'. She would reel off statements like this with a flashing smile, a toss of her curly auburn locks and a husky stress on a word like 'sensual'.

'I understand the significance of sensuality,' she sighed, 'because I came from a very repressed background. You don't need me to tell you the extent to which South African suburbia is a dangerously inhibited environment. There was incredible sexual repression when I was growing up there. That obviously tied in with the political conservatism which, all in all, made it an oppressive place to live. Those hang-ups seemed to carry over into my first marriage. My ex-husband had a very fixed idea of the role that should be played by a "wife". I felt incredibly hemmed-in and stultified – not unlike some of those women who are clients of your friend Docherty.

But I wasn't content just to let things drift along. To cut a long story short, as our marriage began to fall apart I started to go out on my own. I also started to study and practise sexual psycho-therapy, as a result of which I had to research the whole subject of submission and domination. I was incredibly lucky to meet a man who acted as my "master" in a very safe S&M relationship. He opened me up to the power of touch and of role-playing. Eventually I graduated from being a slave to being a mistress and so

I am able to understand both the submissive and dominant sides of sexuality. I continued to study and practise sexual psycho-therapy, and wrote a thesis on the importance of touch at Dr Michael Perring's London Institute for the Study of Human Sexuality.'

Sara also told me how she had posed for a magazine called, evocatively, *Shiny Housewife International*. 'As a student of sexuality,' she suggested, 'I felt it was important to understand what it felt like to be photographed in such a magazine.'

'What sort of magazine is *Shiny Housewife International*?' I asked, with my voice sounding huskier than it should have done.

'Oh, it's just a fantasy magazine,' Sara replied airily. 'A glossy rubber and leather domination mag. It's nothing serious. But it was part of the process I undertook to change myself, to liberate myself from past shackles. And all through this time of transformation and of learning, during the last five years, I have been working as Sara Dale and living with David, who has been incredibly supportive of my work . . .'

'How would you describe your work?'

'In the simplest terms I offer two kinds of massage. For £60 I use my hands to massage all parts of the client's body for forty minutes. For £90 I also use my mouth and tongue and hair in a full hour massage. Although I have had intercourse with some of my clients this is a very rare occurrence. It happens in exceptional circumstances, when I feel that the therapy requires something more personal to overcome a particular psychological blockage. I believe that intercourse requires intimacy and such intimacy only really grows out of the trust developed in a relationship. My massage technique gives the clients, so they tell me, more pure pleasure than intercourse often does. It is a stylized form of sex, appropriate between strangers precisely because it is stylized. If I have known a client for a long time then occasionally intercourse might be suitable — perhaps if it is someone with low self-esteem or a man who has just suffered a terrible loss or someone who is disabled . . .'

This streak of seeming philanthropy had also drawn me towards Sara Dale. I had been told that if the 'extremely rare event' occurred between her and a client then it was considered to be a natural part of the massage service. She would not, I had been assured, request any further remuneration.

'Of course I wouldn't!' she smiled. 'If it happens it does so either spontaneously or because there is a need on the part of the client. I don't offer intercourse and when people ask for it I say "no". I consider myself to be primarily a touch-therapist. You see, I am so in tune with touch that even if I put my hand on yours I can uncover what's going on deep inside you — I find then that we can soul-talk . . .'

As Sara Dale's hand lightly touched mine she discovered that my own soul-talk is based on the assumption that I am actually the ghost of Franz Kafka. This, surprisingly, is not always an advantage for it leaves one a little bereft of soul-kissing idealism. But the fundamental aim of her service has always been to release clients from their sexual hang-ups. Eventually, she suggested, they will be so in touch with their own 'inner beauty' that no further soulful £90 tastes of heaven will be required.

But, despite my hopefully Kafkaesque pessimism, I was still struck by the significance Sara Dale placed on 'healing' and 'curing' her clientele. This attitude, whatever the depths of its idealism, runs contrary to the mercenary backdrop of prostitution. None of the prostitutes I had met shared this desire. They were more concerned with maintaining their own emotional and financial stability in the face of often traumatic circumstances.

'Aaah, but this is precisely why Sara's service is so exceptional,' smiled David her erudite partner. 'You're quite right in what you say about prostitution. The prime purpose of the prostitute is often to indulge her client's fantasies, not to cure him of them. Indeed, to attempt a cure would be bad for business. But the therapist's purpose is to free her client of his underlying trauma. A therapist like Sara educates a client in women's expectations and then teaches him how to satisfy them. This can help the client get his relationship with his wife or girlfriend on to such a satisfactory footing that he no longer needs to go looking outside for either escape or stimulation. He has no need of Sara then and she can feel the satisfaction of having positively changed someone.

'Now the typical client of an upmarket prostitute tends to look for a young woman with a fantasy figure. He usually pays her £200 a time for a form of indulgence which more often heightens rather than satiates his needs. If the service is poor he will emerge from a session with a prostitute feeling not only dissatisfied but also cheated and angry. Now a client who comes to Sara, a sexual therapist rather than a prostitute, is looking for someone who will listen to and understand him, someone who will be able to draw out what he has never been able to tell anyone else. In doing this through touch and psychodrama the client is slowly freed from repression and, soon, he has no need of the therapist. That's the point Sara is always working towards. You've seen some of her clients leaving the house after an appointment — their faces are wreathed in smiles. And I say all of this not only with feeling but with some authority because I too work as a Sara-trained masseur.'

He said these last few words with such pride that any thoughts I had been harbouring about a parallel Simone-Kyle relationship were immediately banished. Although his foray into the world of massage had so far been only on a part-time basis, David was not unduly troubled. He was more concerned with developing the AIDS education charity he was in the process of setting up. The book which he and Sara had just finished writing — *The Taste Of Heaven* — had its source in the AIDS education work he had been engaged in before their meeting. Unlike Kyle, his own work ambitions and interests echoed those of his lover. It was this

146

symmetry which led David and Sara Dale to work together, even though she was essentially carrying out the practical elements of the 'touch-therapy theory' they were both still refining.

Despite my scepticism towards their more romantically vague *Taste Of Heaven* concepts, I did not doubt the integrity of their harmony — how could I when David presented me with a Keatsian poem he had written in celebration of Sara Dale's work as a sensual therapist? Perhaps sensing my bewilderment, they then offered me a copy of their sex manual from which Sara initially read aloud a representative extract while David looked on lovingly.

'When your lover has reached a high state of arousal,' she began to read, 'it's your turn to be masturbated. Invite your lover to do whatsoever pleases you most. Or leave it to them to choose. Just allow yourself to sink into the pleasure. Allow yourself to be aroused and excited, set aquiver and penetrated. Just bask in these varied and, perhaps, new sensations. And, above all, enjoy! Enjoy! Enjoy!'

Apparently a devout student of such 'senzzual' enjoyment, 'Cat' chose this heart-stopping moment to jump on to my lap. David and Sara smiled encouragingly at me as I hesitantly began to stroke 'Cat', not wanting to appear too repressed in such expansive company. 'Cat' accepted the gesture in the way it was intended and purred with light-hearted friendliness. I listened more carefully from then on so as not to emulate exactly the *Taste Of Heaven* instructions, whatever change might emerge in 'Cat's' inclinations.

'However perfect your play and however exquisite its pleasures,' Sara continued as she glanced once more at the undoubtedly sweet sight made by 'Cat' and me, 'you should not fail to try fucking your lover with your hand — whether you're fucking her cunt by putting your fingers into it, or whether you're fucking his cock by curling your fingers around it — and bringing them to peak orgasm. Whomever you are hand-pleasuring or being hand-pleasured by — man or woman, of the same sex or the opposite — the best thing of all is to masturbate each other to orgasm at the same time, perhaps kissing each other continuously as your arousal increases. In fucking, it's very difficult to maintain continuous kissing while both lovers reach their climax. The bucking movements of their bodies are almost certain to carry them apart. But when you bring each other to orgasm with your hands, you can sometimes keep your mouths kissing together as passionately as you like through the foothills of pleasure and mountains of ecstasy right up to and through the peaks of pure bliss and, indeed, down the other side. The energy flow which this will produce between you is a quite literally mind-blowing experience. Once you have experienced this particular intermingling of energy, nothing will ever seem quite the same again.'

Both 'Cat' and I were already mind-blown by the purple prose. A dazed pause ensued as we tried to fathom whether we were up in the mountains or still down in the foothills of ecstasy. Finally deciding that we hadn't even ventured out of the parched flatlands of my practical interviewing technique, 'Cat' fell asleep and allowed me to ask Sara if she carried such sensuality into her everyday massage work.

'The concept of pleasure is absolutely crucial to my work! Even when someone requires domination therapy I always ensure that the "punishment" is followed by a show of affection and pleasure-giving. This is the theme to all my work — the giving of pleasure!'

'We wish to restore the glow in people's eyes that they have when they are in love,' David murmured as a way of explanation. In case such romance could not touch my Kafka-encircled heart, Sara added more pithily that 'we call it the freshly fucked look'.

It was a look she worked at. Whenever I bumped into her in the Europa supermarket in Bayswater Road, invariably over a sexy bunch of bananas at the crowded fruit

stall, Sara would greet me and ask when I was next coming
to have a massage myself. She could tell that I was writing
too hard and interviewing too many bleak people for my
own good. A massage would loosen the angst from my
slouching body. Although she was undoubtedly right my
supposed writerly detachment prevented me from taking up
her kind offer of finger-kneading nirvana.

Meeting Sara Dale there was always a surreal experience.
While we chatted pleasantly about the escalating price of
bananas or about the best type of hummus tub to use, I
would play an absurd secret game. How many other people
in the store with us were involved in the sex industry? Did
the bald man who was debating the comparative merits of
black and green olives with the caped Nigerian woman
behind the delicatessen counter look like a potential Sara
Dale client? What would the young woman in her new Next
suit think as she leaned over to pick out a couple of bananas
and heard Sara Dale croon those *Taste Of Heaven* words
again?

Whatever the banality of such thoughts I realized I'd miss
not seeing her in the same supermarket when she told me
that she and David were finally moving to a bigger house
in Kensington Park Road. This would enable her son and
daughter, both in their early twenties, to move in with them.
She could also, from then on, conduct her therapy in a
proper basement. Despite the fact that we'd bump into each
other less often she insisted that, at least metaphorically,
we stay in close touch. 'You must come and have dinner
with us soon in the new house. You'll see, it's *perfect*!'
Neither of us could have guessed then, as we lingered one
last time over the hummus counter, that their lives were
about to be turned upside down in that apparently perfect
home. In the middle of April that year − 1991 − at the
outset of a wet spring, catastrophe struck.

Then, at their weekend retreat in leafy Woodbridge, Suffolk,
David and Sara Dale were enjoying a drink and deciding

whether to venture out for a meal at the local Indian restaurant. Her work for another week in London was over and she was luxuriating in the bliss of a quiet Saturday evening. Suddenly the phone rang — breaking their serenity for months rather than minutes. A senior journalist from *The Sunday Times* asked David for a quote on the front page story that the *News Of The World* were running on the couple, and especially Sara Dale's use of Norman Lamont's Kensington home as a 'vice den', in the next morning's edition.

'It was a complete shock,' David emphasized when I saw them a few weeks later. 'We had absolutely no idea that the tabloids were even aware of our existence. It was one of those terrible moments when you have to say, in disbelief, "Could you run that past me again?" So I listened in stunned silence for the next fifteen minutes while the story on both the front and inside pages was read over the phone to me. The pictures they had used were also described to me and I quickly realized that they had been taken from the *Shiny Housewife International* shoot we had told you about. They were three years old and being used completely out of context, as was the fantasy text the *News Of The World* had quoted liberally from. One thought that kept running through my head was that this story was a complete travesty, a cruel caricature of the healing therapy Sara has perfected over the years. It took us some time to gather ourselves and prepare a short statement in reply to this cheap smear.

'Within an hour the phone was ringing whenever we put it down and the normally discreet streets of Woodbridge were teeming with journalists. Their portable phones were ringing and their flash-guns popping as if we were celebrities caught *in flagrante*. We managed to dodge our way to the local Indian restaurant where the friendly owner barricaded his door against the press. This didn't stop one journalist getting through. Then, much to our astonishment, she turned out to be a representative of the *News Of The World*, of all papers! "You must already know," she said, "that the press from all over the world are about to descend on you tomorrow. It's going to be hell for you. Wouldn't you like to get away from it all and spend the next ten days in a five-star hotel in the country where nobody can get to you? All expenses paid, of course!" We were flabbergasted at her audacity! She just ploughed on. She said that this would give us a chance to collaborate with them on the much wider story they were hoping to write. Of course, we would be very well compensated for our co-operation. Sara and I were enraged. "Thank you," we said quietly, "but the only place we will talk with your employers will be in court." Feeling anger and indignation helped but I was still overwhelmed by shock that night . . .'

Sara Dale was jolted even harder although she reflected that 'I had an inkling that something was wrong on the Friday night. Mercedes, our Brazilian helper, let this man into the house even though he didn't have an appointment. She shouldn't have done that as I *never* see anyone from off the street. But he was in deep distress. He'd been told that I was an excellent psychotherapist and that if anyone could help him it would be me. He begged me to see him for at least a short while. He was unshaven and untidily dressed. It seemed as if his life was crumbling around him. An essential part of my work is dealing with damaged people and I felt that this man had been broken up by destructive emotions. He was brilliantly convincing.

'So I said to him, "Look, I'm exhausted, it's eight-thirty. There's no way I can give you an adequate therapy session right now. But I'll interview you and we'll see about an appointment next week." Despite the fact that I was so tired after a long day I felt that I couldn't merely run him out of the house. I decided to use that half-hour interview to try and get some feel for him, to gauge what seemed to have gone so terribly wrong in his life. Then, when I saw him for a formal session the following week, I would be able to move straight to the core of his difficulties. So we sat

151

down and talked, Chris Blythe and I, in the home of the Chancellor of the Exchequer.

'He told me all his problems. I thought that there was a dark trail of negativity and self-loathing in much of what he confessed. I tried to be as sympathetic as I could towards him but by showing him compassion I provided the openings he was looking for.

'He said he wanted to use psychodrama because he felt that he needed therapy which would enable him to move outside the strict confines of his everyday life. He wanted to place his trust in me and psychodrama was one of the ways in which he could deal with the issues of responsibility, repression, guilt and despair which shadowed his life. I agreed that psychodrama can often be an extremely effective form of therapy. He was leading me on very cleverly. He then asked if he could expect some kind of sexual satisfaction from our session. I looked at this rather dishevelled man and I thought that there is someone else inside this person, someone who is not so beaten down by harmful emotions. So I replied, "If sexual relief is appropriate, then sure, whatever is necessary to help you realize your own integral beauty."

'This must have given him confidence because he became much more straightforward. I started to feel a little uncomfortable about the way our conversation was heading. In hindsight, he was trying to put specific, quotable words into my mouth. "Would we have sex?" he asked. "Well if by 'sex' you mean intercourse then the answer is 'no'," I replied. "How about caning? Would you cane me?" he asked. "If you need to be caned then you must have done something really naughty," I answered. "You'd better send me a letter written by someone in authority, say a parent or a teacher, telling me exactly what you've done, you naughty boy." You see, a letter like this tells me something about a person's creativity, where someone's thoughts are mingled with their soul-self. I told Chris Blythe that I knew exactly how to use the cane when it was really necessary because I know exactly how to use it to open up a person. I explained to him that usually a person doesn't even need to be caned because even the swish it makes through the air can break down barriers. But he wouldn't leave it at that. He kept on and on about how he needed to be punished. When he asked me if I did spanking I knew he was just fishing for something salacious. I terminated our interview and I remember telling David how distraught this man had appeared. But I never guessed who he was or the type of damage he was about to inflict on me and my family.'

The surprise of this story is not so much that Sara Dale was hooked by a relentless *News Of The World* reporter, but that she and David had even contemplated moving into the Chancellor of the Exchequer's house in the first place. Knowing the extent of this country's preoccupation with sex, it was perplexing that they made such a move. The only doubt was always going to centre around the *when*, rather than the if, of their being rumbled by the media. They looked devastated when I said that there had even been speculation that they actually chose to move into the Lamonts' home with the certainty that voluminous publicity, and eventual fortune, awaited.

'That's crazy,' said Sara Dale. 'We never thought about the media for one minute. As for the so-called financial benefits! We've lost an incredible amount of money. David's business has been ruined. My work has been severely affected. I lost many of my most valued clients who were scared off by the publicity. The number of time-wasting crank telephone calls went up a hundred-fold. As a result of all this economic turmoil it also looks like we're losing our home in Woodbridge. Anyway, as for this cynical theory, I have to say that we were only told it was the Lamonts' home after we'd confirmed our desire to rent it. We were also far from being the only people considered as prospective tenants by the Lamonts. There were supposedly lots of other people who viewed the house and this meant that the whole process was exceptionally protracted. The

Lamonts also insisted on personally filtering through every application in thorough detail. Even though we knew that the checking routine would be very strict we welcomed this because it meant that there would be no room for misunderstanding about the work I did. As Norman Lamont finally said, our application and references were "impeccable".'

According to Sara Dale, the Lamonts apparently knew that she was going to use their basement for 'therapy'. Presumably they were not aware of the sexual background to this therapy service for it should not have been too obscure a thought to them either that the tabloids could sniff out a trashy story from these bare details.

'She wasn't interested in anything I said about my work,' observed Ms Whiplash of Mrs Lamont. 'She was much more concerned about coming back to prune the roses, which I found odd. But we did explain to the Lamonts that we'd use the basement for therapy — so it was puzzling that they tried to evict us on the grounds that they hadn't known we were going to use their house for work.'

Chris Blythe and the rest of the tabloid pack gave both couples a conspicuous run-around for the next six weeks. They filled their pages with stories linking the Chancellor and Ms Whiplash in a lurid tryst. The *News Of The World*, the connoisseurs of this form of journalism, ran the story on their front pages for successive weeks, only breaking the momentum in week three when Sara Dale was relegated to the inside pages in favour of a 'Maniac Fights Dog' headlined-story which detailed the exploits of a man who fought pit-bull terriers for money.

'What really hurt,' murmured Sara Dale, 'was the involvement of Mercedes. David had initially employed her as a cleaner and we quickly realized that she was a very intelligent woman. However, she was also very frustrated by work permit problems. When we moved into the Lamonts' home she literally implored us to take her on as a type of Girl-Friday. She said she would answer the telephone while I was working, she would take on any number of administrative chores. In exchange, all she wanted was to live with us. Eventually we agreed that she could stay. But the problems were only beginning. Even when I said I would train her in massage techniques I found that she did not share any of my philosophies. But we did try to help her — and look what happened. The last time we saw Mercedes she was being escorted by Chris Blythe. She had been whisked off to one of their country retreats and she came back with him to collect the last of her things from us. He looked terrible because he'd had a week of Mercedes screaming at him. That was the type of thing she did and I thought that they probably deserved each other. It was clear that she had been deeply involved in setting us up, probably right from the start.'

The precise role played by the ubiquitous Mercedes in blowing the lid off Sara Dale's work in the Lamonts' basement was initially clouded in confusion. But, with or without her help, the *News Of The World*'s 'Kinky Miss Whiplash & The Chancellor' campaign reached fever pitch when the paper published recent photographs of a commitment ceremony in Suffolk where David and Sara had invited their guests to strip them naked prior to their exchange of 'free love' and wedding vows and plants like Pussy-Willows and Raspberry-Canes.

'The publication of those deeply private photographs,' remembered David, 'left us reeling. We were losing money fast and the tabloids and the Lamonts' solicitors knew we didn't have the financial clout to take them on. When the scandal first broke we felt that Norman Lamont was, like us, a hapless victim of scurrilous journalism. But Peter Carter-Ruck, his libel lawyers, made sure that they were seen to be doing something every single day by the thirty-odd reporters camped outside our front door. It was like *LA Law*! Eight of them would arrive at the door — Christopher Smith, who was a Carter-Ruck partner, was accompanied by a barrister, two assistant solicitors, a surveyor, an estate agent and two embarrassed senior policemen.

'It was around then,' Sara Dale continued, 'that we began to think that this might be something more than just a *News Of The World* sleaze-piece. Christopher Smith asked us about "the disabled man" — this was a reference to a friend of ours who had come for dinner a few weeks before and stayed the night. This meant that, long before the *News Of The World* story, someone had been watching us.

'When we viewed the Lamonts' house we saw these suspicious men parked across the street. They were earnestly eating apples. We thought then that they must be security men, for the house was fortified with complex alarm-systems, shatter-proof windows, even a bullet-proof cat-flap! But we soon realized that someone more shadowy was watching the house. Even now we're not sure exactly what we're getting into . . .'

Amidst the uncertainty of a then vaguely imagined conspiracy theory, Norman Lamont was the one bulky constant. As David repeated, 'In the beginning we also felt that Mr Lamont had been set up along with us. But the way he called on Peter Carter-Ruck made us wonder. They are merciless libel litigators. Instead of allowing us to defend ourselves against the *News Of The World* he attacked us. 'Some of his cabinet colleagues were with me at Cambridge — but instead of turning to them for a first-hand assessment he chose to follow the *News Of The World*'s character-assassination. Although that newspaper had been careful not to call Sara a prostitute, Lamont accused us of carrying out "the business of prostitution and the purveying of sexual or quasi-sexual therapy services" — whatever "quasi-sexual" means! But he spoilt the moral tenor by claiming that, by way of compensation, he wanted as large a share of Sara's earnings as the courts would award. This, essentially, would have meant that the Chancellor of the Exchequer could have been held to be living off immoral earnings!'

'Imagine that!' chortles Sara Dale. 'Having Norman Lamont as your pimp! Of course it never came to that —

we issued subpoenas for Mr and Mrs Lamont and Christopher Smith to appear as our witnesses. After that he agreed to withdraw his actions and we agreed to leave the house.'

The chunky weight of the tabloids, Norman Lamont and Peter Carter-Ruck finally forced the family out of the Chancellor's home. They moved into the four-storey house in Chelsea where they now live, next door to George Best and in the same street as Lord Reay, a Tory whip in the House Of Lords, Viscount Windsor and Bruce Gyngell, managing director of the fast-sinking TV-AM. I first visited them there on a humid, drizzly summer morning — supposedly perfect weather for wearing a red hot-pants suit round the house rather than down the King's Road. Sara indicated as much by bouncing down the stairs in that infamous outfit. She and I exchanged our ritual 'South Africans in London' salutations — 'Howzit long time no see, hey?' — and reminisced that the last time we had actually seen each other had been over that tub of hummus the week before they moved into the Lamontville badlands.

For all Sara and Daniel's affable chit-chat we were soon re-running the saga of Chris Blythe's 'expose'. As he shredded the 'legal inconsistencies and moral hypocrisy' of the Chancellor's attitude to their erstwhile tenancy of his home, she described the hounding meted out by the tabloids as being 'the closest thing you can get to sustained, emotional rape'.

But, and this is what is most curious about this particular story, the eventual themes were already turning out to be less ruination and shame than re-manipulation of the tabloids and a celebration of, in the sultry voice of Sara Dale, 'senzzuality'. She included ironic, ringing tabloid endorsements of her massage service in the personal columns of the local newspapers. The *Daily Mirror* claimed that a massage from Sara was 'unbelievably relaxing' while the *Sun* described it as 'bliss'.

157

Having had notoriety thrust upon them, there was an admirable defiance about their decision to manipulate the media for their own purposes.

Apart from her continuing *Taste Of Heaven* daily work, the couple had decided to branch out into a variety of business activities — including the launching of The Sara Dale Foundation, 'concerned with the role of pleasure in the maintenance of stable relationships'. To this end they endeavoured to produce more books, videos and sensuality courses for couples to overcome what they described as an Orwellian mind-fuck 'controlling people in this country so that,' as Sara Dale said, 'Britain is like a wasteland of sexual repression'.

Sara and David were not rejoicing, however, in the fact that their taste of conspiracy was being sharpened by the visit of a stray American — sounding like a haunted refugee from a Don deLillo novel. He had warned Sara to leave the Lamont home quietly a few weeks after Chris Blythe's visit. He returned again just before I saw them in their Chelsea home, after the preceding weeks had proven that they were determined to continue speaking to the media because, in Sara's words, 'we wanted to articulate our position so that people could judge for themselves whether the work I did was squalid or essential therapy'.

Taking on the tabloids at their own game, David and Sara Dale would follow up one paper's sensational account by running a 'spoiler' in a rival publication. Whenever the *News Of The World* were set to run another story on them they would phone up the *People* or the *Daily Mirror* and offer them an alternative account. It's a dangerous game to play and the American took Sara Dale out for what he called 'a pancake and some friendly advice'.

'I was interested to hear what he had to say. He took me with him to the Old Dutch pancake house in the King's Road. He must be some kind of tacky undercover man — I would've preferred somewhere more chic for the unfolding of this conspiracy theory. It was a crazy night. He said, with an election coming up, it was imperative for me to keep a low profile. If I continued to speak to the media I'd be asking for trouble. He stressed that what I said to the newspapers could be very damaging for some important people. He wouldn't say who he worked for — just that I was treading along a precarious edge.'

'Mr X' assumed a foreboding bearing. For David, 'It's become — apparent that there's something more ominous at work here than just a couple of unscrupulous tabloid journalists. It was put to us that the Lamont saga was instigated by members of the Conservative far right, angry at the role our friend Norman had played in the downfall of Mrs Thatcher. This seemed vaguely plausible. But there are also people who are not in favour of our sexual openness, who seem set on bringing us down . . .'

I was similarly puzzled by the enigmatic appearances of Sara's American pancake-agent. It was indisputable that Sara Dale had been closely watched — and not always by apple-munching men sitting in darkened cars. These other identities remained elusive.

Yet the real conspiracy, as they readily acknowledged, was that unspoken pact of deceit and hypocrisy existing between politicians, the legal establishment and the tabloids in their refusal to accept the imperative decriminalisation of the sex industry. Instead of confronting the contradictions of prevailing sex legislation it's more comfortable for 'family newspapers' like the *News Of The World* to deal with someone like Sara Dale as if she is merely a 'scandalous tart'.

Although she steadfastly gave Chris Blythe the 'integral beauty' line when he tried to probe her links with prostitution, I wondered where she subsequently placed herself in the context of the age-old vocation. 'Well it hurts when they call me "tart" for it cheapens the work and it hurts my children. But we realize that people are going to call me all sorts of names, that there might well be some kind of vendetta against us — but *I know* that my work is healing, whatever they might say. I also know that being called names matters nothing when it is set against the violence and the exploitation and the hypocrisy of much of the sex industry.

'But if I allowed them to warp my thinking I might as well pack up now! Whether or not it's a campaign against us, there are people who want me to cave in. That's not going to happen, even though they've caused us terrible hurt. The worst thing about the entire saga is that it even put my own libido on hold.'

As Sara Dale and I looked pensively at each other, David made us suddenly laugh. 'Listening to the two of you talk I suddenly had the grotesque image that the next time I touch Sara she'll think it's the fingers of Norman Lamont!'

But, for all the irony of that thought, I was more chilled by the knowledge that, the following evening, I would be meeting Alistair. Like both David and Norman Lamont, Alistair had made his way in the world as a Cambridge graduate. He, however, had moved on, into territory far darker than that traced by Sara Dale's sensual fingers. My mood was clouded further by the death of 'Cat', my soul-talking pal, who had been knocked down by a car during the most convoluted stages of the *News Of The World* scandal. I wondered if this was some sort of grim omen that, unlike 'Cat', I was moving away from heavenly heights and heading down towards a place touched by a more personal hell.

Chapter Six

The Connoisseur

As darkness spread across Soho Square, at the tail-end of one of those long London summer evenings, I saw him at the bottom of Sutton Row. He climbed from the back of a black cab and rolled a note from his inside pocket into the driver's waiting hand. He was already walking quickly down the cement path before the taxi had begun to move again. This slick flourish, this middle-aged financier's spry step, clearly fuelled his perception of himself as a powerful city go-getter, as an ardent 'go-get-her'.

Sweeping past the square's chipped statue of Charles II, he stepped over a drunk wearing a string vest and a soiled sailor's cap and walked right up to the bench where I sat. He looked down at me with the measured evaluation he prided himself on at his board meetings. When he said my name, with a sense of conviction rather than enquiry, I got to my feet and offered my hand. He replied with a crunching shake and an assertion that I could call him 'Alistair'.

He led the way down Greek Street, wasting no time with the frivolities of small talk or of our keeping in companionable step together. We marched past the Georgian House of St Barnabas in Soho, for battered and 'fallen' women, The Gay Hussar and L'Escargot. Crossing over into Old Compton Street we strode into Wheelers, a restaurant known for its refined presentation of fish dishes since its establishment in 1856.

We were seated at a corner table, breath regained, menus

perused and orders placed before he looked at me again with
a glance which said 'So?' or 'Well?' I answered him at first
with a copious emphasis on my liking for fish but he sighed
a little, as if he had no time to burn on my opinion of his
restaurant choice. So I followed this with a blazingly earnest
explanation of my intentions in writing about the buying
and selling of sex in London.

The longer I talked, the deeper his silence grew. It assumed
a life of its own, descending over us with brooding disquiet,
growing thicker with each passing minute of my one-sided
talk. After five such protracted minutes his silence appeared
impenetrable. My few questions, asking why he had chosen
to meet me and whether he'd consider discussing the subject,
were answered with a shrug and a wry smile.

It was only when my words had faded and the last curled
medallion of lemon sole had disappeared from his plate that
he opened his mouth for a different reason. He spoke with
a voice rich in rounded vowels and clipped inflections about
the 'absolutely crucial necessity for complete
confidentiality', the absence of which would result in
punishing law-suits administered by the city's most rigorous
and, if they so chose, 'downright vicious' solicitors. I
thought how ironic it would be if, like Norman Lamont,
Alistair felt compelled to call upon the abrasive talents of
Peter Carter-Ruck. It would not be worth my while, he said,
for whatever reason, to breach his confidence.

His sharply fanged legal team would have no compunction
whatsoever in tearing me apart in a court of law, in
shredding me to the bone, in more than a manner of
speaking, so that I would no longer ever wish to write again.
Alistair himself, moreover, would personally see to it that
the inevitable regret incurred by such action would seep into
every facet of my life. He asked, more than once, if he had
made himself clear to me.

I nodded a few times. My silence was now a subdued echo
of his earlier reticence. Yet they still rained down on me,
these warnings of legal menace and dire personal

162

consequence, through three cups of decaffeinated coffee and matching glasses of port until he at last sank into his high-backed chair.

So there we sat, banker and writer, full of fish and mutual doubt, waiting and wondering who would be the first to make a move, either for the door or the other's throat. A small goldfish circled its bowl on the bar's marble surface, as if it too was awaiting the outcome of our surly exchange. I was the one to give in, the wordless void between us becoming unbearable.

I outlined the argument that the identity of a prostitute's client is, by definition, obscured. The shame a man is supposed to feel should it be discovered that he has paid money for sex necessitates the ring of secrecy surrounding prostitution. I understood his desire for facelessness, for it is this very sense of disgrace which is one of prostitution's most enduring themes. Then again, I also realized that any dosh to be derived from selling his kinky tale to Sara Dale's soaraway chums at the *News Of The World* would be, as he had been thoughtful enough to point out, nothing compared with the hefty sum of retribution he'd dole out.

Just as I warmed to this topic he slid a bridge across the fish-flecked chasm separating us. It was a pale grey envelope, with my name typed on the front and its flap unstuck at the back. The crux of any discussion between us lay within the envelope's enclosed two pages. They too were typed, the double spacing and the justified borders making the black words stand out clearly against the white backing. But, this being a legal letter, the meaning behind the words was shrouded in the pedantic rhetoric so admired by solicitors. Alistair claimed that it was 'a watertight document', binding me to silence should I sign it. It was irrelevant that we both knew this to be untrue. If I wanted to spend some time with him, 'discussing the history of Soho', I would have to sign the document that night. I signed it as soon as he handed over his gold pen.

We might have been in Iceland, playing the old roles of

Gorby an' Ronnie, such was the impact of my putting pen to paper. The atmosphere positively crackled with heady change; this presumably signified the cracking of our own private cold war. Alistair called for more port, a couple of Irish Whiskeys and two large cigars. Even at the risk of chilling the thaw, I passed on the cigar and concentrated instead on chasing down the drink.

We reeled out into the night an hour later. Alistair was ready to roll. This, he crooned, was going to be a time I wouldn't forget in a hurry. We purled past the Soho Brasserie, only slowing briefly when Alistair brushed against a red-haired girl wearing a small pill-box hat and a black cocktail dress. He bowed ostentatiously and murmured an apology which did not convince her that the contact was completely unintentional.

But Alistair had another target in mind. He crossed over to the other side of the street, jostling his way past the Andrew Lloyd-Webber and Tim Rice fans swilling their interval G 'n' Ts outside the Prince Edward Theatre. It didn't take long to work out where he was headed.

The shop window, framed in red, was painted black. A neon 'Electric Blue' sign provided the only indication of activity inside. Above the window there was just one word — Janus. On the outside, to the uninitiated, it could have conceivably been mistaken for one of those hip wine bars where designer alienation goes with expensive drinks. A couple of curious Japanese businessmen were pondering the exact nature of the Janus myth as Alistair bowled past them with serious intent and a 'Sex shop, boys, sex shop' aside. This sent them a few steps back into the road and incurred the hooting indignation of a passing BMW. The Japanese men followed me into the shop.

Alistair was already ensconced at the back, flipping expertly through the shiny copies of *Rope And Burn, Dominatrix, Blushes, Knotty* and *New Uniform*. I looked lucklessly for a copy of Sara Dale's *Shiny Housewife*

164

International. Alistair appeared unmoved by most of the others, only stopping occasionally to tilt a page my way. Without exception the photographs he lingered over were those which disturbed most. One showed a young girl splayed against a pitch fork in a muddy field while a masked older woman streaked dirt down the right side of her face; another had a bespectacled man being branded with a thick poker by a leather-clad woman called 'the bitch burner'. She had none of Simone Maillard's elegance. Yet this picture made me wonder how much of Simone's personal grace could filter through the sieve of the *Chienne de Souffrance* professional mask she used whenever called on to do this kind of work. Alistair's attention had already drifted to the walls above, where ropes, spikes, chains and whips were pinned with refined austerity. Once more his glance flicked coolly over the display, perhaps comparing them to the more limited offerings on Mandy's wooden rack.

He felt at home here, unlike most of the other men filling the shop. Apart from Alistair and me, and the bemused Japanese, all the others were on their own and showing signs of furtive embarrassment as they scanned the shelves of pornography. I thought back to the comparative mirth of my afternoon in the cellar of pain with Mandy and Alice. Despite the dark undertow of their discussion they had shown a deft touch when deconstructing the language and imagery of S&M. Dragged down by the soiled seriousness of the Janus clientele I wished Alice would burst through the red door with a 'Kinky Karate Kat' yelp to shake up all these shifty 'sniffy-tasties' and 'dressie-feelies'. She would have sent them scuttling away in shame for they seemed to be pretending that they were inspecting plywood in B&Q rather than *Rope And Burn*. In a way I felt more comfortable confronting big Al's candour. He was happy to confirm that this was his own patch and he showed as much by calling out to the sallow-faced man at the front desk: 'Have those new German videos arrived yet, Dave?'

Dave, more circumspect about the Janus etiquette, silently

motioned us to join him. He spoke in a hushed, whistling sort of voice which sounded all the stranger when he mentioned bullwhip-wielding Bavarian nuns and 'foreskin crucifixion'. But all of this was positively old bondage hood to Alistair, or 'Mr Bates' as he was mysteriously referred to by Dave, and it was finally established that he was only interested in 'brand spanking new' videos. Alistair smiled a little at his play on words before introducing me to Dave, as 'young Don here, a pornographic writer'.

Dave had heard it all before and he gave me a cursory nod which made me understand that there was no way he wished to speak to me unless it entailed my spending money on his more expensive sex items. He quickly sussed me as an 'FTW', a fucking time-waster who'd rather ponce around than spend a pound or three on a Janus product. There was something cruel in Dave's long sunken-in face, some indefinable sense of malice behind the way he curled his near whitened lips into his thin mouth when Alistair was not looking, only for him to suddenly purse them in fake supplication when promising delivery of hardcore German bondage videos 'any day now, Mr Bates sir, any day now'.

But perhaps if he had been selling sprouts down the road in Berwick Street market I might have imagined him as one of the dying breed of cheery Cockney chappies. I wasn't sure whether it was the drink or the fetid smell of lubricated rubber, but Janus was starting to gnaw at me, to get under my skin like a splinter under a nail. Surrounded by those illustrations and instruments of pain and subjugation, he sent a chill through me — as Alistair did when he picked out what he called a 'right big brute' of a heavily studded belt.

I remembered Mandy Kavanagh looking away when she'd first spoken about Alistair; about the way he liked to be pinned down in that dead butterfly way. She would then have to pick out one of the belts he'd bought for her that week at Janus. Then she'd have to beat him until it felt as if her arm was about to unhinge itself from its socket; and then he would tell her to lash into him some more, until the thick leather crinkled with use.

Even Mandy, with her rigorous detachment from the pain of prostitution, had flinched when she told me that sometimes, on rare occasions, Alistair hinted that one day he would like to flip the tables of flagellation. Then he would be the one who did the beating. She hoped that this was mere face-saving talk, an attempt to redress the imbalance of his masochistic relationship with her. Mandy said that it was not unknown for a masochist to also develop a sadistic desire; but such was the depth of Alistair's masochism that she rarely tried to imagine the wasteland his sadism would inhabit.

I turned away to look at the others in the shop, only for my eye to fall once more on the magazine cover of the teenage girl having her face lined with filth. I couldn't help but wonder whether the Janus belt Alistair bought was meant for his, or someone else's, pain.

Then we were off again, with a wave of the hand for Dave, and a 'Cheerio chaps' farewell to the increasingly flabbergasted Japanese. Across the road, on the corner of Dean Street, there was another sex shop. As he dodged his way through the Friday night traffic, Alistair spoke over his shoulder to me about the 'decline of Soho'. It was only when we were once more faced with plastic-lined sheafs of glossy magazines – these, for the 'straight sex' market, bearing titles like *New Cunts* and *Teenage Anal Sex* – that I realized that Alistair associated 'decline' with the decreased availability of hardcore pornography in Soho.

He remembered a time, not so long ago, in the early Eighties, when there were around a dozen decent sex shops in London. 'Decent' in the sense that if you were on first-name terms with the owner you could choose from a whole stash of specialist, first-rate pornography. Scandinavian, French, German, Thai, American; bondage, bestiality, paedophilia, transvestism, transsexuality, housewives' group sex — you name it, reminisced Alistair, you could find it then in Greek or Frith or Old Compton streets.

It was not the issue, he stressed, that he might draw a personal line on some of these forms of deviant sexuality. Rather, he celebrated the availability of choice as well as the fact that, just like in Amsterdam or Hamburg or Paris or Copenhagen, this gamut of human sexuality had been self-contained in a single sector. But the Soho of today, he mourned, is no longer the Soho of then, which he knew and loved so well. While 'these media types' continued their relentless gentrification of the area, Alistair had to resort to dubious mail-order purchases from darkest Essex. Apart from stripping Soho of its 'sexual distinctiveness', this mid-1980s clean-up severely limited his choice of pornography. He now had to buy most of his goods 'blind' and the product varied alarmingly in quality.

The man behind this sex-shop counter appeared more genial than Dave. No doubt attracted by the rich plumminess of Alistair's voice, and scenting a possible killing of sorts, he shuffled over to our corner. 'Couldn't help over-hearing you gents,' he sniffed affably. 'I've got some special under-the-counter material which might be more up your street.' He sniffed again and then winked conspiratorially at me. Alistair had switched back to his imposing trick of silence. For perhaps ten seconds he stared at the man with an unsettling sense of disquiet.

His 'would you like a quick look then?' question remained unanswered. This was Alistair's territory and I too stayed silent. He hobbled back to his perch. It was then I noticed his club-foot.

Alistair had seen it some time before. It was as if he had been waiting for this particular moment for a long time. 'Have you any interesting material on disabled sex, friend?' he asked. The last word jerked the man's head back but he recovered quickly by turning this involuntary movement into an elaborately snorting sniff. He then resorted to what must be the pornographic salesmen's standard ploy by emulating

168

Dave's restrained motion for us to join him at the front where we would discuss the matter in more secretive tones.

In the ensuing charade the mag-seller muttered that he could cater for all tastes as long as the money was right. Alistair, meanwhile, rumbled forth on his supposed interest in young girl amputees and club-footed men 'in action together'. This was one of his little jokes but it took a moment or two to strike home. Behind the counter, the man's mouth popped lightly as bubbles of saliva spluttered finally into a slurred 'Piss off!'

Alistair rocked back on his heels. This was turning out to be his idea of a night of fun. With a sigh of regret he followed me through the coloured strands of plastic screening the shop's doorway.

Old Compton Street was still sticky with heat and people, most of them drifting in and out of bars and restaurants with the sort of leisurely bonhomie that does not attach itself to most Friday nights in other parts of London. There was no discernible rush to wash away the week's work with frantically legless drinking. Alistair described the people here as 'the dreaded young liberals, *The Guardian* set' and then, after another couple of shots of Scotch, as 'lifestyle layabouts'. They were the ones who 'trumpeted and whined' the loudest about subjects like pornography and prostitution even though they, he said, were also from the social milieu least able to confront the secret truths of sexual craving.

We were jammed in a pub alongside Janus, drinking iced, triple Scotches ordered and paid for by Alistair before I'd had even a chance to decide what I might like. It was the right choice. I needed something with a kick to keep me going through whatever lay ahead. All around us, said Alistair, you could hear the air thickening with the braying chatter of these people in search of an honourable reason to feel good about themselves. They rejoiced in the restyling of Soho. The replacement of sex shops and peep show parlours by wine bars and brasseries allowed them to believe that they were eradicating the prostitutes and the punters.

And there is nothing a liberal likes more, he continued, than 'to try to wish something away, to pretend it doesn't exist just because it's been removed from eye-level'.

Yet in reducing Soho to a thin shadow of its former self, nothing had been done to alter the darker course of human sexuality. 'These trendy types', he gestured grandly towards the throng of drinkers around us, were precisely the people who refused to stare into the unknown blackness of their own desire, preferring instead to draw fuzzed-over links between pornography and rape, prostitution and exploitation.

By now I wanted to ask him about the disguise he himself used as a respectable executive. Did he not adhere even more closely to 'fuzzed-over' concepts of bourgeois deception? But I knew enough of Alistair to realize that this sort of monologue was his only real way of conversing and so I left him to it, hoping for a time later that night, at the formal 'interview' he stressed we would conduct at his men's club in Pall Mall, when he would actually answer a question. But we still had some way to go before then.

Leaving his liberal favourites to 'their Canadian lagers and Nicaraguan coffees', we walked back down Old Compton Street until we hit the Charing Cross Road. A block beyond this, we strolled past the first series of windows lit by the age-old sign of a bleak red light. There were two here, illuminating the second and third floor windows of an old red-brick building. The doorway, right next to the Man Fu Kung Chinese takeaway with its 'cheapest food in London' boast, was always open between noon and midnight. There, the message of the red light was fleshed-out by frayed scraps of paper Sellotaped to the thin passage walls. Alistair pointed these out with particular relish; he loved their shambling attempts at colourful creativity.

You could find them down selected streets in Soho. Bright crayons decorated their otherwise grubby pages. All of them feature the word 'model', Soho's traditional euphemism for a prostitute. Words like 'new', 'teenage', 'exotic', 'leggy', 'friendly', 'bouncy', 'busty' and 'dusky' featured prominently and were coloured in painstakingly. The more innovative were sketched out on blue or yellow pieces of cardboard, their model messages being framed by pretty patterns of hand-drawn flowers or shaky artistic impressions of the young beauties waiting upstairs. Alistair literally chortled at the thought of these colouring-book type ads being designed by the ageing maids who let in the clients, kept the money safe and cooked at least one balanced meat-and-two-veg meal a day for their working girls.

At times it sounded as if he knew the name of every model and maid filling Soho's remaining buildings of prostitution. Alistair denied this, pointing out that the turnover of women was so rapid that he did not have the time to keep up to date with the occupiers of every building. He had, however, paid for sex in most of them and he still tried to spend an evening every month going from one to another, across the breadth of Soho, to ensure that few newcomers were left unseen by him.

He had not visited this Charing Cross building for some months, so up the narrow staircase we climbed to, first, the top floor and, then, back down to the middle flat. Both flats were smaller than an average household front room and they were divided into two by a thin partition wall. In each, the space where the prostitute worked was so cramped that, apart from a single-bed, there was barely enough room for two people. Both prostitutes were waiting for their next client − a sure sign on an otherwise busy Friday night, intimated Alistair, that this particular house had hit a slump.

The two women − 'Sarah', a 'new English Rose', and 'Maxine', a 'friendly model' − both knew Alistair, although they referred to him as 'Robert'. He soon let them know that ours were courtesy, rather than business, visits undertaken for my 'book research'. 'Maxine' feigned a polite interest but made it plain that, this being a lean time of the night for her, she would prefer to finish the remains of her bread and butter pudding instead of chattering away to us. 'Sarah', however, appeared genuinely interested and said that she had once dreamt of being a writer, some time before she met a man called 'Gordy' who first introduced her to prostitution. She spoke a little about the writers she liked most, an unlikely combination of Ed McBain and Jilly Cooper.

I found it difficult to look straight into her face for her red-rimmed eyes were sunken into black rings of exhaustion or what I thought might also be despair. Alistair chipped in anyway, saying that we couldn't linger but had to get back on the streets because it was near ten-thirty and, this being London, we only had a few hours left before Soho began to shut down for the night. The door had hardly closed behind us when Alistair launched into his typically flagrant prediction that 'Sarah' would struggle to keep her room going if she couldn't 'pull herself together'. 'Maxine', in his opinion, was little better. But later that night, he promised, he would show me a more inventive side to prostitution in Soho.

Not unexpectedly, Alistair suggested that we have another drink at The Cambridge pub, on the curved corner of Charing Cross Road and Moor Street. I was still sufficiently sober to realize that if I had one more quick triple Scotch I would be well on my way to indisputable drunkenness. Alistair, oblivious to the idea of refusal, had soon shouldered his way back from the bursting bar to the street outside where I stood next to a group of riotous young professionals who all looked like they had enjoyed a successful money-making week in computing or share-dealing. Alistair was more at ease here, alongside the packs of drinkers breathing in the passing car-exhaust fumes while they lined this dirty street corner. Although he looked more frayed than he had done in Wheelers, he still stood apart from this younger crowd of city workers. Even against such a squalid backdrop he exuded the authoritative arrogance and self-absorption that prolific financial success often evokes. He was momentarily lost in his own world and, as

The Connoisseur

he stared silently at some point in the distance, I had my chance to stay a step or two behind him. I took most of the triple scotch into my mouth and made the short walk to the pub toilet where I deposited it down the nearest grimy sink.

This was not a night to be sentimental about wasting good drink for I knew that to lose control with Alistair would be to hit a deadly artery of danger. Once my own senses began to slip towards a filmy haziness I knew he would ram home his advantage mercilessly. He would use drink to screen the otherwise visible darkness seeping through his Soho dream. If reality became blurred by the more desolate textures of imagination, Alistair would be less a besuited banking executive than the black-hooded man arcing that 'big brute' of a studded belt.

I rejoined him outside with a burning mouth but a clearer head. He had decided on the itinerary for the rest of the night. We would take in a peep-show and then set up an appointment to see a prostitute in the early hours of the morning, after we had conducted our promised 'chat' at his club. He drank what remained of his own Scotch and then, wordlessly, led the way round the corner.

Moor Street is one of the shortest in Soho, more a bricked walkway than an actual road, but it has a full increment of sex establishments. Apart from the Adult Entertainment And Live Show Centre and its accompanying video and book shop, three passages were filled with the now familiar model adverts. At the door to the Centre we were greeted cheerfully by a young woman sporting a Sisters Of Mercy goth-rock wig and a bright red leather mini-dress. Her face was whitened with foundation and her lips and eyes were shaded with a violet tint accentuating the skin-jutting prominence of her cheekbones. She raised a lazy arc of a smile our way and enquired whether we'd like to step inside for a real treat of a live show.

Alistair sauntered into the glaringly white foyer. The Goth-girl, who couldn't have been long out of her teens, was sitting on a high stool. Her black-stockinged legs swung

casually back and forth, with her Doc Martens making a
quiet dragging sound against the brown carpet every other
swing. She smiled again when Alistair removed a £10 note
from his wallet.

'Two for the live show, sir?' the girl asked demurely. She
raised a pencil-thin eyebrow when Alistair shook his head
and asked for change in single pound coins. Earlier, during
his initial tirade against the dilution of Soho's 'traditional'
sexual character', he had lamented the erosion of the 'live
show' in London as a prime example of censorship getting
it wrong yet again.

In the early 1980s six Soho venues had offered a variety
of live sex shows, at reasonable prices, to a select market
of people. These exhibitions usually featured five or six
naked men and women acting out the barest bones of a plot
before they ended up on a grubby stage floor in diverse
positions of copulation. Alistair realized that these Soho
shows could never match the more gymnastically imaginative
versions seen in Amsterdam, Berlin and Paris but he liked
their distinctly London flavour. Moreover, they had been
good for the balance of trade for they were extremely
popular with Japanese businessmen.

With the government clampdown on Soho between 1983
and 1984, the authentic sex show had been banished and
replaced by a series of cheap fakes. Although the signs on
the windows outside were still the same, pledging
fantastically steamy 'live bed-show action', the interior
reality was radically different. Instead of the promised show,
deluded customers were presented with a mockery where
tame simulation was shrouded in an atmosphere thick with
menace. Although only a few pounds were required to gain
access to the showroom, visitors were then expected to buy
a drink not only for themselves but for one of the 'hostesses'.
This would incur a bill of between £80 and £100 and if the
client refused to pay the money he would be threatened by
a couple of thick set bouncers. Alistair railed against the
logic which shut down Soho's past centres of sexual

entertainment and replaced them with these exploitative establishments run by 'a squalid ring of Cockney thugs'.

Yet he still felt a distinct weakness for peep-shows. Even though he realized that each pound coin he spent went straight into the pockets of these entrepreneurs he continued to frequent their peep-show booths. The violet-tinted girl counted out the ten coins methodically and lined them up in two vertical rows of five. Alistair slid the first from her desk and handed it to me. Pocketing his own five coins he scoffed at my mortified protestations that none of this was really necessary, that I would wait for him outside, that I had no wish to use his pounds to attend a peep-show. The girl let slip a low laugh for we were plainly an odd pair. Alistair made a jibe about me 'going all liberal' on him and guided me firmly towards the first booth where he shut the door behind me. I heard him slip into the stall next to mine.

A fat man would have seen the booth as a hell-hole. It was probably no more than three feet long, a foot wide and five feet high. So, boxed-in, I struggled to find one of Alistair's five coins. It was murky and stinking and the coins remained elusively lost in the lining of my trouser pocket. After a minute of futile scrambling I backed out of the booth and, straightening myself out, glared accusingly at the podgy bodyguard seated behind a glass-caged counter at the other end of the parlour from the smiley Gothic Brontë sister. The fat man's eyes stayed glued to his tabloid for he knew that if *he* tried to enter one of the five peeping booths he would find himself interminably jammed between the four narrow walls.

A coin popped up immediately and, with a deep breath, I returned to my booth. It was like being lowered back into one of those hot-boxes Alec Guinness whistlingly endured in *Bridge Over The River Kwai*. Alistair told me that the peep-show business had sadly dwindled to the point of primarily catering for the nervous Japanese businessmen who had yet to learn of the Soho bed-show scam. No doubt the size of each minuscule, uncomfortable booth was some contemporary smart-alec's way of 'paying back the Japs' for past war-crimes against the Empire.

I pushed my coin glumly into its groove and, like technology at its slickest, the light at the back of my peeping mechanism went out. By dropping my head down sharply and lifting my eyes as high they would rise, as though I was rolling them back for the benefit of a tiny torch-shining optician, I had a perfect view of the bed-show.

A tall girl, wearing nothing but black stockings and a suspender belt, stood unsteadily on a double-bed. She attempted a sensual dance of some sort in time to Chic's late-1970s *Good Times* disco-smash. Occasionally she would smooth her hands tiredly over her body but, more often, she used them to flick the blonde ringlets of hair from her eyes. Few people can ever have seen a girl more bored than this. And, in its way, this terminal tedium exuded a disturbingly hypnotic fascination for the first forty-five seconds of money.

But at that point the window was once more filled with stark white light. I slipped another coin into the slot. The girl slid back into view. It appeared that she had lifted herself from her trance-like reverie and noticed both Alistair and I peering up at her. She climbed off the bed and began to walk across the bare wooden floorboards directly in front of our window-slits. Like the archetype of a cat in a glassed cage she paced briskly up and down, even though at every fourth or fifth pace she had to swing around to avoid hitting one of the walls. Homing in on Alistair as her more likely benefactor she eventually came to rest in front of his booth and lent back to remove a ribbed vibrator from beneath the bed. After a few seconds of watching her fondle the dildo I made my exit when the light flooded back into the booth.

I stood inside the foyer while the goth-girl whistled coyly at a handful of men peering into the centre as they drifted by. She shrugged amiably a few times, as if in emphasis of the fact that it was no skin off her nose whether or not her banter enticed a few more punters. Eventually a middle-aged man wearing a polka dot tie and a striped short-sleeve shirt ducked in and made for the booth I had just vacated. The girl rolled her eyes in mock outrage at the man's sartorial style before settling on a witty variation of the 'phew, what a scorcher!' theme that echoed around Soho as the temperature continued to rise even though we were already deep into the night.

Five minutes later, Alistair emerged from his booth looking flushed around the jowls. When I handed over his remaining three coins he asked brusquely if I planned to loosen up at any point in the evening. This tickled the Doc Martened girl's overworked sense of sarcasm and she emitted a series of staccato sniggers and asked whether I was Alistair's son. As it was difficult to guess who was more offended by the idea, Alistair and I left in silence with the girl's request that we come back soon gurgling in our ears.

We were aiming for 'Josie', near the middle of the street, on the left-hand side, on the last stop of our tour before we would sit down and begin, hopefully, to talk to each other. It was a more upmarket building than that around the Charing Cross corner. The door was painted a rich, olive green and the stairway was both wider and cleaner than usual in Soho. Written in gold against a black backdrop, 'Josie's' card proclaimed her to be an 'Interesting And Versatile Model'. The first floor of the building housed a film and video production company and it was only on the second flight of stairs that the adverts began to feature heavily underlined 'DB' initials. As if he could read my unspoken query Alistair said, 'Dominant Bitch,' when he rang the bell to her room.

After a short delay the door swung open to reveal a short, grey-haired Italian woman in her late-fifties. Her hair was screwed back in a bun and she wore a blue apron over her grey dress. She greeted Alistair effusively with a kiss on both cheeks. He wrinkled his nose in reply. The tang of cooked onion drifted from her hands and through the flat. It appeared to be wafting in accompaniment with the strains of Cole Porter lilting on her portable cassette desk. *Night And Day* was playing, as if in suggestion that this covered the expanse of time when the maid was frying and boiling and stewing her onions.

Alistair drew her into the adjoining tiny kitchen where, presumably, the smell was at its most pungent. They whispered together for a few minutes before she let loose a chuckle and said, 'Of course, Roberto, for you, of course!' A minute later she left Alistair in the kitchen and motioned me to follow her. Alistair, still smarting from our minor brush at the peep-show, refused to meet my eye. I walked across the room and through two doorways leading to a chamber encased in leather. In the middle there was an impressive, black wood frame and a shining metal pulley similar to Mandy's engineered version. The walls were covered by the then familiar hoods and uniforms, whips and belts, manacles and ropes. She motioned me to sit down on a long couch and intimated that they would be back for me.

After ten minutes, more than time enough for me to make myself acquainted with the variety of contraptions on display, I heard Alistair and a younger woman laughing loudly together. Through their laughter, the Cole Porter songs rolled on. Eventually there was a quiet knock on my door and the maid said that 'Roberto' was ready for me. Alistair was on the first-floor landing, jangling some loose coins in the pocket of his elegantly light Paul Smith suit. The onion scent slipped down the stairs and it was only when we were back in Moor Street that it finally faded.

In a trice Alistair had hailed a taxi where, in the back, he confirmed that we were at last on the way to our interview rendezvous. But, more significantly, he said, 'Josie' was expecting us back in Moor Street in three hours, at 2.30 a.m. when, with her doors shut to ordinary trade, we would round off the evening in 'outrageous style'. Thinking of those manacles and whips I felt the sweat congeal coldly on the back of the cab's leather seat as we moved through Piccadilly and then into the stretch of Pall Mall where Alistair's

178

gentlemen's club was located in its hundred-and-fifty-year-old splendour.

In the long, book-lined portals of the club's 'smoking chamber', and directly beneath an imposing portrait of a former Tory Prime Minister, Alistair spoke for nearly three hours. We had the space to ourselves, with only a blue-coated barman for company whenever Alistair rang the small bell resting on the mahogany reading table. The surrounding stillness seemed to encourage his unbroken flow of words.

Initially, he had eyed the tape-recorder with considerable suspicion. I decided not to tell him about the innovative interview security system devised by Docherty's clients, Arlene and Rachel. Yet he soon appeared oblivious to the recorder's whirring, barely noticing when tapes clicked to completion and had to be turned over or replaced. He would only stop if forcibly interrupted by a question or by his own request for more Scotch and cigars; otherwise Alistair liked to talk in huge slabs of speech as if he needed to clear something acrid from his chest.

'You must realize,' he began, 'that we're dealing with a subject which is distorted by secrecy. This isn't my choice. I always think that things should be brought out into the open. That's my way. And, on paper, it's the way of capitalism, the way of a free-market economy, the way of democracy, the way of a free press, the way of the Western world.

'But, you see, we have a problem. And that problem is truth. It's a simple but much-abused word, truth. If we could live according to truth then we would obviously have discovered some form of paradise. But before we can get to truth we have to get past fear. And the fear that most people suffer from is the fear that the truth about themselves will be uncovered. One of the most basic truths is that almost everyone, without exception, lies. We lie out of fear, fear of being judged for the truth of what or who we are.

179

'And for better or worse we live in a society — and it *is* the best type of society existing today — where fundamental truths are often replaced by what I call "convenient" truths. Let me give you some clearer examples here. It's a fundamental truth that since time became history there has been prostitution. It's a fundamental truth that there will always be women who will sell their bodies in exchange for something they want. It's fundamental truth that men, most men, are sometimes in need of this kind of sex. It's a fundamental truth that even if there was no poverty, even if there was excellent education right across the world, there would still be prostitution. One need only look at Mandy Kavanagh — a beautiful, rich, eloquent, indeed brilliant woman — to realize this. It's a fundamental truth that we all have a "dark" side to our sexuality. I know this to be true, you know this to be true . . .'

Alistair allowed me to ponder my own sexual darkness as he peeled the cellophane wrapping from a new cigar. While it was true that my 'anthropological' interest in his consumption of prostitution was bound up in a darker kind of voyeurism, it took me a little longer to recognize that the effectiveness of his language enabled him to blur the difference between truth and assumption. Rather than stripping away everything obscuring the core of truth, Alistair's words only seemed to deepen the mystery of prostitution. His assertion of prostitution's inexorable inevitability was meant to be so persuasive that it would be reduced to a banal mystery — like the fact that, every day, the sun rises and sets across earth. In his terms all women were, instinctively, prostitutes and all men helplessly prone to uncontrollable sexual cravings.

More interesting than this, Alistair's authoritative vignette rang with the supposed resonance of the definitive expert. While we had trawled across Soho I kept thinking of him as a connoisseur. Whenever he bemoaned the fact that his space of specialist consumption had been eroded, ironically enough by the rise of his otherwise beloved Margaret

180

Thatcher's rampant free market economics, he was staking his claim as a connoisseur. It was this 'expert' knowledge of Soho's original and apparently more authentic past which made Alistair stand out from the 'lazily flippant' Friday night crowd. Is this how he saw himself, I asked, as 'a connoisseur'?

'A "connoisseur"? Well, well, well! *That's* an interesting word, my friend,' Alistair chortled as he puffed on his newly-lit cigar. 'Mmmmm, "connoisseur"? Yes, I like it. I like it a lot! Of course I am a connoisseur. I'm a connoisseur of truth . . .'

Before he could move back onto his track of truth I interrupted. 'I meant "connoisseur" in less abstract terms. I was thinking more of you as a connoisseur of pornography and prostitution.'

'Mmmmm, those are your words but hell . . .' he said as he swivelled his chair round to make sure that we were alone, '. . . I'm not going to argue with you there. But tell me, son, why did you use that word in particular?'

Unsettled by this 'son' interjection, which would surely have got the Goth-girl from the Adult Entertainment Centre rocking in delight on her stool, I cautiously replied, 'You seem to think of yourself as an expert on Soho. You gave me a guided tour of the area and compared it with your more historical knowledge of the Soho that's virtually disappeared. I thought that was interesting, but . . .'

'Forget the "buts!" Frankly, I'm flattered, old boy! Glad to be of service!'

'But I found it strange that you even agreed to be seen in public, in the places we visited, with me.'

'I've already told you. I'll crush you if you cross me,' he said evenly.

Trying to stay calm beneath both the fire of Scotch burning through me and the icy chill of his stare, I said, 'It made me wonder if, rather than trying to shock me, you were wanting to make prostitution and pornography appear more respectable. It was like the consciousness of the

historian brushing up against the leer of the pornographer
– if you don't mind me saying . . .' I trailed off tamely
into silence.

'How so?' said Alistair, his Arctic glare remaining intact.

'When you talk about pornography – whether it's about
Thai lesbian mags or German bondage films or Dutch
pictures of disabled women – you give it a gloss. You move
it away from the traditional moral arena where people
debate its harmful effects. You move into a more aesthetic
arena . . .'

'Exactly! Because it is about aesthetics! It all comes down
to taste in the end. Maybe this is not to some people's public
taste but it is *my* taste and I resent having my arena invaded.
These are specialist, informed tastes. They might try to ban
it but they cannot stop it. It's a negation of freedom. This
is one mistake the British are making. And, as a very proud
Britisher, I am at liberty to say this. They are trying to sweep
the truth under the carpet. But it will not stay there, it rises
to the surface . . .'

'Yet in a way,' I asked as I tried to keep my increasingly
drink-fuddled head clear, 'aren't you doing exactly the same
thing? Rather than confronting any moral truth about
exploitative pornography you're pushing it under the smooth
surface of your connoisseurship? Doesn't your concept of
truth get lost in all these "freedoms" of taste?'

'No, no, my friend, you're stepping into murky waters
there. Freedom is truth! I think you're thinking more of our
"Terminator Angel" here. She's the one who is looking to
obscure the truth of who she is behind all these false devices
of tastefulness and control. She comes across all high and
mighty, holier than thou. Yet what is she? She's *a mere
prostitute*, a *whore*!'

'She never seems to deny the fact of her prostitution.'

'Oh she's much too smart for *that*! No, no, no, my friend,
what she prefers to do is to try and obscure the truth in a
more complicated way. All this talk of five-year
experiments! I mean it's pathetic. She'll never stop. She's

always been a prostitute, she always will be. I find her pretensions quite insufferable at times!'

'Why do you see her every Tuesday then?'

'Well, that's an interesting question. It's *the* important question! On the surface you might say it's because, in terms of pure looks and figure, she is devastating! That's certainly what drew me towards her. I also admired her at first because she had the courage to come out as a prostitute. But then I began to see that she thought she was pulling off a much more magnificent conceit. She's trying to turn the meaning of the word "prostitute" inside out. She's trying to control her life to such a degree of perfection that she finds some strange source of power in being a prostitute. It's quite ridiculous! She thinks she's stronger than me — and this is why she is so fascinating, if insufferable. I don't know any other woman who would take the liberties she does with me . . .'

'Well you do seem to pay her an awful lot of money to take severe "liberties" with you . . .'

'I'm not talking about *that*! That is a private affair between me and her! What has she been saying about me?'

'It's not what she's said about you. It's just that I know the type of work she sometimes does . . .' I answered vaguely.

'This is typical of her! She always tries to cut me down. What happens on a Tuesday afternoon is my "experiment", if you like . . .'

'What sort of experiment? To be dominated without receiving any kind of sexual relief?'

'Never you mind. All that is important is that I'm wise to her. She wants to outwit me, to stand up to me, to prove herself the stronger. She is not — I'm merely toying with her. Everything will crumble when her five-year date passes and she comes crawling back to me. Then the whip will be in the other hand . . .'

'What do you mean by that? That you'll be the one doing the beating?'

'My, my, all this drinking obviously doesn't agree with you. It's making you very inquisitive. I'm not sure if I approve of that . . .'

'Was it a difficult decision to agree to meet me?'

'Not at all. You know the score.'

'But aren't you bothered by the risk you take in visiting these Soho prostitutes? Couldn't a man in your position be easily identified? Isn't it safer to stick to a more discreet prostitute like Mandy?'

'The thing with Mandy is that she's terribly austere. In a way she is the one who has driven me to look elsewhere. Trying to get into her heart is like trying to chip away at an iceberg. Sometimes I prefer to have some brash, raw, sluttish sex instead . . .'

'And that's when you go down to Soho?'

'Precisely.'

'Do you worry that this secret might be discovered?'

'Is this a threat?'

'Not at all.'

'Because if it is, my friend . . .'

'I know, you've told me.'

'Do *not*, on any account, forget it.'

'So,' I persevered, 'do you worry about someone spotting you coming out of a Soho room?'

'Look, I'm a realist, a pragmatist. I know that I am, despite my considerable success, not indispensable in the world of business. I had to fight damned hard to get where I am today. And yet there are always competitors waiting to take your place should you slip a little. It's jungle-law. I accept that. I came up this route and if someone can outwit me then they jump above me. That's why capitalism works because, generally, the strong rise to the top and they have the strength to drag the rest of society along with them. So I accept these laws. I am precise in my efforts to ensure that no rope is given to those who would wish to hang me. While I'll follow the true course of my sexuality, at the same time I'll choke off any threat to my career. I'm not going to lose everything because of some sex scandal. You see, my public profile is very low-key. If it was what I wanted I could have found myself regularly on television or in the newspapers' society pages. But I'm not in this for fame. I don't need to be known to feel strong. I'm strong anyway. I know this. So I can move wherever I like, whether it's in the homes of the Mandys of this world or in the rooms of Soho. Mandy Kavanagh is the only one who really knows who I am but, then, I also know her. I know how she works, how her mind operates. She is far too proud to reveal me as I am to some scurrilous hack. She wants to beat me on my own terms . . .'

'Is that why you sometimes feel such rage towards her — because she knows you like no-one else does? She knows you better than your own wife does . . .'

'Well she is much more interesting, not to mention younger and better-looking, than my wife . . .'

'And doesn't that affect your marriage?'

'What do you mean?'

'The fact that you're more interested in your struggle for power with a prostitute than in your own wife?'

'On the contrary — it maintains the equilibrium of my marriage. And you might not believe it but a loyal, middle-aged wife is a considerable asset at certain business functions.'

'Mandy seems to think that you're consumed with guilt.'

'Does she now? That's interesting.'

'Are you guilty about the way you treat your wife?'

'And how would you know how I treat my wife?'

'Well, I do know about your Tuesday afternoon sessions. Isn't there perhaps some shame and guilt in your need to be punished by "The Terminator Angel"?'

Alistair quietly considered the wrapping on a new cigar. I wondered if he was capable of murder, such was the depth of venom he struggled to contain. After a minute of silence, during which time his face flipped through a variety of strangulated expressions, he finally swallowed phlegm from the back of the throat. 'Perhaps . . .' he at last said in a strange voice, 'perhaps she is right. I feel many different emotions with her. Lust, anger . . . shame, grief, relief.'

'Why relief?'

'Because I don't have to lie with her. I am what I am when I'm in that cellar. As she is too — "The Terminator Angel". She is what all women would like to be . . .'

'I don't know too many women who aspire to be prostitutes . . .' I said slowly.

'You know well what I mean. She is strong. She is formidable.'

The impact of these sudden confessions appeared to have exhausted Alistair. He sank back into his chair, looking confused and tormented. We sat there silently for many minutes before he finally asked, wearily I thought, 'Should we adjourn to Moor Street? To "Josie" — she is much lighter of heart than "The Terminator Angel" . . .'

'No, I think I'd better get going . . .'

'Why? It's not even two yet!'

'It's best if I leave now.'

'Yes, you're probably right. You've probably got to check in with "The Terminator".'

'No, I just need to get home.'

'Before you go, there's just one thing . . .' he said with a determined show of renewed vigour, '. . . when you do see our friend Amanda again, you might tell her that she's now got a rival for my affections . . .'

I kept silent, until he had to prompt me with a 'Don't you want to know who it is?' For a scarifying moment I wondered if he was playing some kind of trick on me for, confused by his brazen insistence on our tour through Soho, I had struggled to identify his motivation. Was he actually yearning to have his 'personal' truth uncovered? Or did he find a mysterious sexual thrill in having another man 'bear witness' to him as a connoisseur? Alistair, however, had 'prettier prey' in mind.

'She's a strange young thing. A dirty-faced little pixie. Name of "Jackie". I found her in Lisle Street a while ago.

In a place with green walls. I gave her a terrible thrashing. I beat her 'til the screaming dried up from her. I enjoyed the change. It gave me more feelings of release than Mandy Kavanagh ever gave to me. I'm going to go back there, down to Chinatown next week, and I'm going to colour in the face of that dirty little pixie. You tell "The Terminator Angel" that, you tell her that I am about to wreak my revenge. And then I'm coming for her. But in between those two lovelies I can tell that I'm going to have to gun for you. I know now this whole evening has been a terrible waste, a tragic mistake. I'm going to break you, my friend. You just wait, I'm going to break you . . .'

The fury breaking up Alistair's voice into a series of hoarse, savage cries forced him out of his chair and he lunged towards me, trying to scoop up the tape recorder in the process. He swore and stumbled drunkenly, cracking his leg against the table with a sickening thud. He crashed to the floor in agony, his melodramatic screams echoing through the club. With visions of him laying an assault charge against me, I decided to make my move. I gathered up the tapes and the recorder which Alistair had knocked to the floor. His 'Fuck you, I'm going to break you, break you' mantra resumed in full throaty swing as he clutched his leg on the thickly carpeted floor. I turned away from him and ran down the long passage and out into the night where the air still felt thick and clammy.

187

Chapter Seven

Chinatown Whore and the Dream of Casablanca

Alistair's words ran through my head for the rest of that
night and most of the next day. Again and again his grisliest
images slipped down the cavernous sides of my hangover.

Mandy called me in the middle of that hazed-over day
to find out if I had 'survived' the previous night. My
description of our ranging through Soho kept returning to
the set of words which had slid from his mouth near the
end of the night. They were heard just before the last tape
hissed to a stop; and because I could not recreate the chill
I had felt when he spoke those words, I spun the cassette
back a few reels. Alistair's voice flooded from the small
speaker and along the telephone line to where Mandy
listened in troubled silence. I clicked the tape off after less
than a minute, for that was all the time one needed to
imagine the worst for his 'dirty-faced little pixie', his £15
Chinatown whore, the girl he called 'Jackie'.

Mandy had not known that the inverse of Alistair's
masochism already entailed something more tangible than
mere fantasies of degradation. She had not known that when
he visited prostitutes other than her he played a part much
closer to his own heart; a part where he was the one wielding
the belt with an intent at which we could only fearfully guess.
We made mutually disturbed and supportive noises but,
essentially, there was little comfort to be found. The further
we peeled away the layers of Alistair's professional self, the
darker he seemed to grow.

Yet even as we said we would both be more careful I knew that Mandy would see Alistair again that following Tuesday; and that later that night I would be back in Soho, on its fringes, around the crowded restaurants and shops of Chinatown. There, somewhere, in a small room at the top of a green-walled staircase, Jackie worked.

I knew too that as Mandy's days as a prostitute moved ever closer to their five-year culmination she would endure those Tuesday afternoons — no matter how dizzying it became to look down into their depths. At the very least this would be an internal act of solidarity with those prostitutes, suddenly given shape by the image and name of Jackie, working in more dangerous worlds than her own.

My own reasons for returning to Soho that night were more ambiguous. I felt something like despair in the dry, metallic taste in my mouth whenever I thought of this faceless prostitute left to Alistair's remote mercy. Perhaps a bad headache pumped additional swirls of melodrama into my mood but, then, it appeared as if I had no choice but to warn this girl, to tell her what Mandy and I already knew of Alistair, who paid money to beat her. With less nobility, I knew as well that I wanted to see her face so that her image would become less drunkenly enshrined with sweeping suffering. Maybe if I could just see what she looked like I would be able to think of her less.

The sky above Chinatown turned a glorious purple as the last of the day's light drifted away. It was nine o' clock and a pale moon slivered across the top right hand corner of this thick mauve canvas — the colour briefly reminding me of one of Kyle Johannsen's better post-pepperoni pizza paintings. I passed the first of the scrawled, hand-written 'Busty Model' adverts pinned to the side of a narrow doorway. The night when I had sat in Simone's front room, lined with paintings and Gourmet Salmon-fed cats as Kyle warbled on about Jackson Pollock, seemed a long time ago. I was on my way down into a different, more desperate world of prostitution with Alistair as my dreaded linkman.

The streets thronged with an early Saturday night crowd. An American family still talking about the performance of *Les Miserables* they had just seen jostled with hand-holding couples on their way to a West End movie and with a bigger group of twenty-year-olds apparently aiming for The Spice Of Life pub in Cambridge Circus. Chinatown, for all of them, was a vibrant place to pass through. This view shone, too, from the faces glowing inside the stream of Chinese restaurants. Outside each of these restaurants, bordering both sides of the street, still more couples peered intently at the old rain and grease-splattered menus. 'Yes, look,' I heard one woman say, 'they have Singapore noodles *and* prawn crackers,' as if this should be a surprise in Chinatown.

Only the Chinese themselves appeared less self-consciously aware that it was a fun Saturday night out. Behind the steaming bowls of food they carried from table to table, waiters bawled tetchily at each other. Meanwhile, inside the almost exclusively Chinese-patronised grocery stores and Cantonese book shops business clicked over with a similarly brisk rhythm.

I caught sight of a red light glowing softly in a third-floor window a block away. A bare light bulb hung from the top corner of the lace-covered window. There were no Chinese lanterns swinging gently in the breeze, no wafting images of exotic romance to divert attention from the fact that this was a '£15-a-go whore' room. I wondered if this was where I would find Jackie.

But there were at least six separate lights, and therefore rooms, at this end of Lisle Street. I crossed over to inspect the modelling adverts at the bottom of each grim stairway, trying as hard as I could to look like a diligent writer in search of truth rather than the hard-up letch I more probably appeared to the passing parade of respectable lovers.

There was none of the glamorous *frisson* of words like 'Terminator Angel' or *La Chienne de Souffrance* in these home-made adverts. Rather, they searched for an earthier

191

inspiration. If Mandy and Simone, with their psychological domination of masochistic clients, were the seriously classical actresses of prostitution, these coyly-named Soho 'models' belonged to the seamier skin and splatter side of the sex market. Only 'Kiki – Experienced French Model, 2nd Floor' passed herself off as a mildly different kind of prostitute. Her advert had been carved into a thick piece of slate which had then been screwed into the wall. She had obviously been there for some time; the 'experienced' adjective being another coded hint that she was perhaps an old prostitute. Alistair, I thought, would have zipped by her plaque with a derisive sneer. Despite his own age and looks, he 'liked them young and pretty'.

At the third and last doorway I finally saw the advert I was searching for. There were more adjectives on this thin blue sheet of paper than in any other along the street. 'New, busty, leggy, pretty young model – 3rd Floor'. The walls were also painted green. This was the place. I walked slowly up the winding stairs noticing the stern warnings not to give money to anyone until inside either the second or third floor rooms. How many nervous men had been ripped off in the past by a stray hustler demanding bogus entry money at every landing? And then, in turn, how many prostitutes had suffered the ensuing kickback – violently rather than just financially?

Seeing these notes and smelling the piss clinging to the frayed carpet was like having one's face pressed into the rank hypocrisy of British law on prostitution. In another classic piece of legislative fudging these Chinatown and Soho 'houses' are effectively allowed to operate as one-woman fucking rooms with the police looking the other way, as long as the adverts maintain their 'modelling' euphemisms and the rent is paid on time to eager landlords. There is no wonder that someone like Alistair can methodically club a helpless prostitute in a place such as this where safety and hygiene are only cursorily considered. If the 'model' signs were torn down and replaced by a properly run brothel, owned and organised by the prostitutes themselves, the environment would be different. There are, after all, brothels in some parts of Holland and America where women do not automatically feel like cheap slabs of meat nor their clients like furtive miscreants. Yet that would mean a public denunciation of hypocrisy in favour of decriminalised prostitution and that's not the way things are going in this country; and so those other low and dirty feelings clung to the core of this dump, oozing out from its green Chinatown walls.

With some relief I found the stairwell to be empty as I continued my climb. The adverts for both second and third floor models were even looking sweeter up every flight. The one I aimed for had little rings of flowers drawn along the edges. Outside one of the two second floor doors I heard muffled voices. 'Beautiful Leggy Alex' was obviously entertaining a gentleman caller.

Eventually, I stood uncertainly on the cramped third floor where there were two adjoining doors. The adverts on the first finally gave name to the room's 'new and busty young model — pretty Jackie'. Above this door's small white bell there was another message — 'Please Ring'. Feeling abruptly foolish, I hovered around the landing. At last, sufficiently psyched up to talk to Alistair's 'dirty-faced little pixie', I rang the bell. After a long pause full of the sound of a television being turned down and the scraping of numerous chairs, the door opened a crack and a perspiring pug-faced woman, with a cigarette in one hand and her glasses lost in a stiffly permed bush of hair, peered round at me. 'Sorry love,' she said kindly, 'she's busy and there're two waiting.' I must have looked at her dully, attempting to absorb the fact that there were three men crammed into these tiny rooms, for she suggested, 'I'd come back in about half an hour if I was you, after ten, before the pubs shut — it's usually a little quieter round then.'

I nodded dumbly and stumbled down into the glistening street outside. I brushed past a group of sniggering teenage girls who guessed where I had just been. They proceeded to describe each other in the advertising jargon of Chinatown prostitution. 'I just have to be called "versatile!" ' shouted the loudest girl to a chorus of uproarious laughter from the others. If Jackie was as young as Alistair intimated then she could hardly have been more than a few years older than any of these supposedly carefree girls, their thick lip-stick rimming the cigarettes they waved in the air.

I felt empty wandering down Old Compton Street. Memories of the night before made me turn sharply away into first Frith and then Greek Street. There were more adverts, ciphered in crayon, for models along these streets. They promised a similar type of prostitute to those working in the rooms of Chinatown and so, almost on a whim, I entered an open doorway where yellow and white cards were stuck against the walls.

The first two doors I knocked at were also 'busy'. Then in a building on Greek Street, on the first floor, I found myself being ushered in by a small, smiling Italian woman who must have been well past pensionable age. 'Come in, come in – you not wait long,' she assured me. I could smell cabbage cooking in the small kitchen where her portable black and white television set was tuned to ITV's Saturday night movie. Burt Reynolds, looking suave, was driving a fast car down a big wide road.

Veering me away from the kitchen, where I also noticed her knitting resting on a chair in front of the television, she showed me into another minute room. 'Wait here – she come soon,' she said, shutting the door behind me and no doubt feeling eager to return to her knitting and Burt. I looked around this room. There were tatty piles of old soft-porn magazines on the long table in front of me – *Penthouse '89 Xmas Issue, Mayfair Letters Of The Year 1987, New Directions, Knave* and a coffee-ringed copy of *Big And Bouncy*. There was a small bookcase across the room – some of the books weren't that bad. I spotted copies of Jane Austen and Graham Greene on the second shelf. Greene, I thought, would have been pleased; Austen less so.

But I tried to focus on more pressing matters. I picked up a magazine and cocked an eyebrow at the dubious pleasures of the flesh offered by Beryl — one of the 'Readers' Wives Of The Month'. Beryl was defiantly blatant in the three snaps shot by 'husband, Ray, from Huddersfield'. Her legs were opened wide to reveal her naked glory while, in a more symbolic gesture, Beryl licked an unpeeled banana. Just as I was about to move onto a perusal of the pornographic parody exhibited by Helen, from Catford, I heard another set of doors opening and closing as a woman said, 'Take care, love.' A short while later the side door leading into my room opened.

A thin, tired-looking woman stuck her head round the door. 'Come through love,' she said with a wan smile. She must have been in her mid-thirties with her long black hair pulled back into a pony-tail. She was wearing a skimpy white bodysuit. 'What can I do for you, my love?' she asked gently as she buttoned down the suit at crotch level. 'They're awfully tricky buttons down there,' she laughed as my eyes inevitably flew down to her fingers. 'Button up, button down all day long — aaah, there we are!' she exclaimed as there was a sudden click. 'Right — sorry about that! Where were we?' I wasn't sure about anything any more except for the fact that, as the doorbell rang, this was probably not an appropriate moment to say that I was writing a book and on the scrounge for an interview.

Sensing my awkwardness she continued readily, 'I'll tell you some of my services first, should I?' I nodded as I heard the Italian maid opening the door to the next client. 'Well it's £15 for straight sex with a condom, £20 for French and sex and from £60 for any of my more specialist services,' she said, gesturing to the uniforms and canes hanging from the wall behind her. 'How much is it to stay a little longer — perhaps for half an hour to an hour?' I asked, gauging the possible price one might have to pay for a decent interview. A little too hopefully, perhaps, with the idea that maybe I was going to be more of a big-spender than she was used to, she replied that it was '£50 for half an hour and £75 for an hour — as many times as you can manage in as many positions as you like, love. I'm really good!' It made me strangely sad to have to disappoint her and tell her that I did not have enough money with me to stay for an hour. With another client waiting she wasn't overly shattered by my leaving and suggested I have 'a bit of a look round and come back later — there're a couple of cash-points down the road'.

I saw that she called herself 'Emma' and wondered if she really was a Jane Austen fan in disguise. I climbed up the next flight of stairs to where 'Helga' was sure to keep me waiting. Yet, to my surprise, a well-built German girl opened the door — naked but for a small pair of bikini briefs. Apparently the maid had gone to get Chinese takeaways as a special Saturday night treat. This was 'Helga' herself welcoming me into her velvety boudoir. She was an unexpectedly attractive woman, in her late-twenties, and I listened a little more closely as she flipped through her range of prices. She was £5 more expensive than 'Emma' on every service.

Her friendliness appeared genuine and so, a little more confidently, I told her the truth about my visit. She seemed to believe me — 'I would very much like to read this book when it comes out!' she whispered huskily — but pointed out that this was neither the time nor place to talk. She recommended I leave my number so that she could contact me the following week. I did so, even though I knew she would not call. But as she waited for her maid to return, and for her next caller to arrive, she suggested I sit with her.

She told me she was planning to go back to her home town near Dusseldorf and that she was easing out of prostitution. She only worked two days a week now — on Saturdays and Sundays — and was planning to find work as a beautician once she returned to Germany. This kind of prostitution was too hard on the body and she shuddered to remember the times when she worked for fifteen consecutive days — from noon to midnight in this box of a room. She was just working out how many hundreds of men she must have 'serviced' in a fifteen-day stretch when the maid turned the key in the adjoining lock. With her nose twitching in anticipation 'Helga', or 'Inge' as she told me to call her, slipped on a robe and showed me out with a smile and the promise that she'd be in touch soon.

By the time I was halfway back towards Lisle Street and she was deep in her bowl of chop-suey, I was sure that she had already crumpled and flipped my telephone number into the wastepaper basket brimming with semen-filled condoms and tissues from her initial ten-hour stretch of the day's work. I couldn't blame her. She had already shown me sufficient favour without any monetary reward and, as she stressed, this kind of prostitution was too hard for any 'model' to waste her time on anything but the back-aching work in hand.

This briefest of opening tours around the sex rooms of both Chinatown and Soho had driven home the point that prostitution in these confined quarters is defined most by the mundane opening and closing of doors. There were many more doors than rooms; and often those rooms were hardly larger than the doorways themselves. Space was at a premium and to separate the waiting men from each other, more doors had to be introduced. By shutting one door and opening another, the clients could be assured of anonymity as they moved alone from one room to another — for there were few men who would wish to be seen buying sex in these depressing places. Ultimately, the cost of all these doors fell on the prostitute. Her space was pinched back to the point where she worked in a quarter-sized room with barely enough space for a bed and a mirror. This was battery-hen type prostitution. I found myself hoping that 'Helga', or 'Inge', would escape from her Greek Street coop on schedule.

Business appeared to have slackened a little in Lisle Street for the maid let me in with a 'She'll only be about ten minutes, love' greeting. I was motioned to sit in a plastic bucket chair next to the front door. A curtain was drawn across the hallway. Apparently the budget didn't extend to real doors in this house; so curtains separated one client from another. After about five minutes of sitting in this gloomy passage there was a flurry of activity and I was moved into the next section. Things were considerably brighter here. Between two sets of curtains a table lamp shone down on the obligatory collection of skin-mags. These were a little more up to date than those in 'Emma's' lounge; but it was still a consolation after a couple of minutes when the routine resumed. Either business was exceedingly brisk or else clients were getting cold feet at the last moment.

Whatever, I had moved another notch up the clientele ladder. I had reached the kitchen at last. The maid and I exchanged pleasantries about the weather before the door to Jackie's room opened and a thin white hand stretched out, holding two £10 notes. As the door closed again the maid put one of the notes in a drawer and shoved the other down the front of her dress. Either she had one breast considerably larger than the other or else there were an awful lot of £10 notes stuffed in her brassiere. I wanted to ask if it wasn't both uncomfortable and unsafe to use your bra as a bank but she was deeply ensconced in the TV film's climactic car-chase. Burt Reynolds was still driving that car, although its one side had been badly dented by a huge container truck. His moustache, however, appeared unruffled by the chase. 'Oh, isn't Burt just a hunk of man?' she suddenly said. I mumbled in a non-committal way, before realizing that this had been a rhetorical question.

There were more magazines on the kitchen table and, figuring that the maid was too bound up in Burt to mind, I picked up one idly and coincidentally turned to another 'Readers' Wives' section. This particular page featured Meryl, shot in the buff by 'boyfriend Bill in Leeds'. It seemed that the 'Readers' Wives' nude Polaroid slot was particularly popular in Yorkshire. Meanwhile, in these Chinatown rooms the obvious intention of displaying all these magazines was to coax the client to a pitch of such arousal that by the time he entered the prostitute's bedroom his own ejaculation would not be a long way off.

As I heard the door on the other side of Jackie's room open and close in quick succession I put Meryl and Bill to one side and took a deep breath. A minute later the door opened onto a dingy red room and the maid said, encouragingly I thought, 'Go on love — it's your turn at last!' Jackie was standing behind the door so it was only when I was actually inside the room that I saw her face to face.

In this box-room, against the red illuminations and folded-back mirrors, Jackie showed a kind of bruised beauty. I thought this not only because I knew what Alistair had done to her but because her very prettiness seemed to be mocked by the tiredness seeping through her lightly made-up face. There was a momentarily eerie sensation that I was looking at two faces simultaneously, with one struggling to rise up and destroy the other. The surface face belonged to a nineteen-year-old girl but then, looking deeper, I thought I could already see the face she would wear a few years from now when she would be old both inside and out. She tried to reach for a smile but it hardly even touched the corners of her mouth. Instead she just rested against the window-sill and said, softly, 'Hello.' I said 'Hello' back and we looked at each other for the most fleeting of moments.

She had big wide eyes and the spiky look of her blonde hair was accentuated by her studded bracelets and earrings. She wore a black bra, red panties and a matching polka dot suspender belt. On her right arm there was an elastoplast. She noticed me looking at the plaster and, then, she did smile.

'I'm not supposed to tell any of the punters but come have a look,' she said in a stagy whisper. 'I only had this done a month ago.' Jackie motioned me over to the window where she drew the curtains back slightly. The yellow street light fell across the top part of her arm, making it look even paler. She pulled the elastoplast gently away from her skin.

'The maid says I have to keep it hidden. She says the punters don't like to know a girl here has a boyfriend.' Jackie pointed to the thin tattoo which had been covered by the plaster — 'I did this for *my* boyfriend, look.'

I looked. Two words were written in black and red ink — '*TYRONE FOREVER*'.

'What'cher think?' she asked.

'It looks pretty in this light. Did it hurt?'

' 'Course it fucking hurt! Love hurts, baby! You never had a tattoo then?'

'Not so far.'

'Naaah, I don't think you'll ever get one. Not the type.'

'Maybe not,' I admitted.

'You been here before?'

'No.'

'So what do you fancy? Sex for fifteen? With a rubber of course. Or what about some horny French and sex for twenty? I suck like a dream . . .'

It was disconcerting having to break into her sales pitch but I no longer knew what else to say than that I was writing this book. She looked at me silently as I told her that the night before Alistair had bragged to me about what he had done to her. I felt I had to tell her what he was like so that she steered clear of him when he returned.

It must have sounded wretched and laughable at the same time because she listened with a smile which then broke out into an infectious laugh. She came over to placate me, telling me that she was all right — that she knew the punter I was talking about and, yes, I was right, he was dangerous, but she'd never let him in again. Anyway, who did I think she was? Some stupid tart who didn't know how to deal with the crazies who came in and out of the door every ten minutes? She'd been in this game long enough now to look after herself, boy. I was the crazy one but that was OK because it made her laugh and she'd had a crappy day and she was exhausted and in need of something to laugh about. But, more important than that, it made her think that someone out there had cared and, soppy as that was, it was still kinda nice in this fucked-up world.

Hearing this murmuring rush of words from her working girl and wondering why Jackie's hand hadn't stretched through the door yet, the maid knocked sharply on the wall. 'What's going on in there?' she asked caustically.

'It's all right, Molly — he's just deciding.'

As if organised by the maid herself, the front door bell rang. Jackie stood up from the window sill and, in a way she meant to be tender, put her hand on my face and said, 'Thank you — but look I've gotta get going.'

She moved languidly towards the mirror, looking over her shoulder at me. 'Do you want some French and sex before you go — I'll do it for fifteen, just for you. You'll like it . . .'

I asked her if we could meet some time instead, if she felt like talking to me about working here.

Jackie stood in front of the mirror playing with her hair, running her fingers through it with mock sensuality as she pursed and then licked her lips. It looked as if she had suddenly remembered it was Saturday night and she could imagine she was home somewhere a few years ago, sixteen again, and getting ready to go out on the back of her favourite boy's motorbike.

But she had been listening to me all the time. As she whirled away from the mirror she said, 'Sure, come by tomorrow — round eleven, just before I start working. We can go for a coffee or something. See you then, sweetheart!'

She pressed her eye to the door's peephole and turned back to me with a wink. 'All clear — bye for now — and thanks again, hey!'

As I made my way down the stairs she asked me my name. I told her and she replied, 'And mine *really* is Jackie!'

The next morning Jackie forgot our appointment — only arriving at work at ten past twelve. The maid had already sent me packing an hour earlier with a curt 'We only open at twelve on a Sunday, dear!' dismissal. I saw Jackie running up the stairs and just caught up with her on the first floor landing. She was out of breath and took a moment to recognize me. 'Oh Christ, I forgot — sorry, sweetheart — Tyrone had to kick me out of bed, I was so knackered after yesterday. Look, I'm late, but I'll meet you tomorrow — it's my day off — round one, outside the Hippodrome? OK? Gotta dash!' And off she raced up the second flight. I left with a slight shrug — not expecting her to be there the following day.

I arrived ten minutes late that Monday afternoon with my mind already made up that I'd only wait another twenty before moving on elsewhere. Yet Jackie was already there, looking at her watch, wearing a short, candy-striped summer dress and Roman sandals. Her hair was slicked back and held down by an Alice-band. She looked about fourteen.

My apologies for arriving late were accepted with a soft 'I didn't think you were coming then!' rebuke. Jackie looked uncertain when I asked her if she wanted to go somewhere for lunch. She said, after a long while, that even though she'd worked in Chinatown for two months she'd never eaten in a Chinese restaurant — 'Never — not in my *whole* life!'

It must have looked like I was taking my country cousin, rather than Chinatown's most adjectively advertised prostitute, out for a day on the town as she studied each menu haphazardly before finally forcing me to choose a restaurant.

We sat in the furthest corner of one of the quieter Chinatown restaurants, for Jackie had said, 'I don't want nothing to do with opening and shutting doors on my day off!' She negotiated the menu successfully even though it took nearly twenty minutes to decide which dishes to choose.

Although she concentrated mostly on the new surroundings and her food, during the meal she told me that she had come down from Hull with Tyrone three months ago. She had grown up in Humberside and, after school and a deathly boring spell first as a packer in a fish factory and then as a check-out girl, she had eventually slipped into doing massage parlour work with an ex-hairdressing apprentice friend of hers. They found the work to be 'not much cop really. Ten quid to give some greasy guy the old how's your father hand-job!'

The friend soon moved down to London, not long after Jackie had 'discovered' Tyrone at the parlour's neighbourhood pub. It was the old 'lust at first sight' chestnut and, within a couple of days, Tyrone had moved in with Jackie. Before she knew it he had convinced her that the real money was to be made in London. She found her friend and they walked the beat together at King's Cross where she had once bumped into Docherty, 'that weird guy with the camera bag'. They moved on to Stamford Hill for a couple of weeks before Jackie was told about the opening at her current room in Chinatown. She was already sick of standing on corners in high heels and being forced to lift her skirt up while lying down in the folded-back front seats of motor cars — '*That's* the most degrading kind of paid fuck, looking up at the holes in some punter's upholstery.' The thought of walking the streets in winter was also enough to make her jump at the chance of a slot in a heated Chinatown room.

Yet more pressing than any of this was the need to earn double the amount of money she made on the beat for, as she said, 'Tyrone's habit went bad not long after we came down here. He needed to shoot up more and more every day. I had to get a steady job to help him.'

I asked Jackie how much money she gave every day to Tyrone to buy heroin.

She wiped her mouth diffidently with a serviette. 'At least a hundred, I reckon,' she said thoughtfully.

'£100, every day, just for heroin?'

'Some days, I guess . . . but I'm trying to get him to cut down, 'cos it's not right, is it? It's a terrible thing, smack.'

'Have you tried it?'

'I've only snorted it − I hate needles! I won't ever let anyone near me with a needle so there's no chance of me spiking up.'

'And what about Tyrone − does he want to come off?'

'Course he does! He's just a little sick now − he can't quit it yet. That's why I'm working so hard, so I can take us away, for a long holiday or something. If I can just get him out of this poxy country for a while I know he'll go straight.'

'Where would you want to go on holiday?' I asked.

'Just somewhere warm and cheap. Spain probably. But when I'm in my room with all these men breathing over me I often think I'd like us to escape to somewhere more exotic-like!'

'Like where?'

'I dunno, Egypt? Morocco, maybe. You're not supposed to want to go somewhere really foreign like Morocco if you're from Hull − you know what I mean?'

I did and I couldn't help laughing with her as she ordered us another couple of beers in an attempted 'Moroccan' accent.

'I know that there're probably plenty of drugs in Morocco too but I'd just dump me and Tyrone in a hotel near the edge of a desert somewhere. As long as there's a swimming pool for me we could straighten him out in no time.'

She made a happy little burping sound, her eyes shining with imagination. 'It's my dream, you see − a few months away, cleaning him out − in Spain or Egypt or, best of all, *Morocco!*'

Would this dream really happen?

'Like now, I have to say, "Yes, definitely yes!" I can see it. One day I'm just going to take the money I put away in my building society account and I'm going to book us a flight. I'm gonna drag him on that plane with me, without any of his fucking needles, and we'll be gone from here. No-one'll know 'cept us. And I'll come back with Tyrone one day and we'll be real sun-people and all the girls will say, "And where've you been then? You look fuckin' fanta-stic!" An' I'll say, "Oh we've just been to Morocco, for our summer hols, just fuckin' *Morocco*."

'But then, when I'm in that fuckin' hole up there,' she jerked her head back in the direction of Lisle Street, 'sometimes I just wanna break down, you know. It feels like I'm stuck there for good. That I'm just gonna be a £15 Chinatown whore forever and that Tyrone's gonna die with the smack. I dunno — what do you think?'

'I think you should go to Morocco.'

'Yeah, you're right. Fly to Casablanca; Tyrone and me, like in the movies, like what's their names, you know those black and white movie stars.'

'Humphrey Bogart and Ingrid Bergman?'

'Yeah, baby, Tyrone as Humphrey Bogart! Is Bogart the guy who wore a patch over his eye? — 'cos Tyrone once had to wear a black patch on his eye, after a fight . . .'

'You should go to Morocco soon — with or without Tyrone.'

'Shit, I couldn't leave Tyrone — look, it's *forever* baby!'

Jackie started to stroke and kiss her tattoo, making gentle cooing noises which the Chinese waiter sensibly took as a sign to bring us the bill.

We stepped out into the scalding mid-afternoon heat and I bought Jackie an ice-cream, like she was my country cousin again. Still talking about her dream of mythical Morocco we ambled up to Soho Square, where I had met Alistair the Friday before. We found a spot in the shade, underneath a tree which Jackie leaned against. The tramp whom Alistair had walked over without a glance was sprawled across the same stretch of grass.

When I listen back to the tape we made that afternoon her words are interspersed with the incongruous sound of birds singing in Soho. Her own voice, however, lowered in tone as she told me about her life as a 'Chinatown whore'. When she seemed too sad to speak further she looked away from the tramp and down at her tattoo, as if in search of courage to go on − whoring rather than just talking. But she spoke for more than an hour in her own moving, breathless way.

'I miss the sun when I work, you know,' she began. 'I miss seeing the day go by most of all. 'Cos it's always fucking dark in that room. They like it that way. You don't know what it means − to wake up and not to have to go to that room. You don't know what it means to me to go to a real Chinese restaurant and to sit here, like stretched out, all warm and happy in the sunshine. Unless you work there you can't ever know what it really means.

'Like now, look, it's three o'clock. By now, on a day in my room, I've already had maybe ten men shove their stinking cocks up me. Small cocks and big cocks, all sorts. Pricks all veiny or floppy. Dicks that smell like fucking cheese or onions. Maybe both − if I'm lucky!

'I won't have felt no sunshine. Not since I started working at eleven or twelve. I'll have just had ringing bells and doors opening and shutting and one man after another coming in and me saying, smiley-wiley, "Hello, love, it's fifteen for sex with a rubber, twenty for French and sex, fifty for half an hour, seventy-five for uniforms or bondage, hundred for an hour, hundred and fifty if you want to beat me . . ."

'And if they stay, and most of them do, it's usually just for a fifteen or a twenty job. They give me the money first − that's rule number one. I give it to Molly to hold on to. I tell them to get changed and, if there's no-one waiting, I go into the kitchen with Molly and I have me half a smoke. When I go back they're naked and they're looking at the porno mags or else they're standing in a corner, all frightened like. I feel sorry for them then. They look pathetic, like. Most of them are OK, to tell the truth. They just want a fuck and to get out of there as fast as they can.

'So I break open a rubber and I roll it on — "Always with a rubber," I say and I mean it. That's rule number two. Then I go down and I think of Tyrone or us in Morocco and I bob my head up and down a little. Not much but I still get the fucking taste of the rubber in my mouth. Then I wank them more, then I bob the head a little again and if I'm lucky they're hard and I lie back and I'm still greased from the time before. They slide it in, groaning and grunting some of them, asking if I like it. Others are quiet — the nicer ones even say, "I hope it's not hurting." Sometimes it does but I settle them in and off we go.

'Christ, it's just so boring. That's the worst thing. I hate it when they breathe all over me. I just turn away, even if they don't like it. But then I reach down and I hold their balls and I say, "It feels good, man — you've got such a big prick" or anything else like that. They believe it and they come soon then, jamming away at me. It takes a minute or two and they roll off and I feel, "Phew, another one down." I give them a tissue and they rip their rubber off and I dump it in the bin. They're all shy and quiet then. They're dressed and out of there before you know it. I fix my hair, fluff my knickers up and then I see the next one.

'I'm feeling horrible round this time — in the afternoon. It seems such a long way to go. But then Molly makes me a stew or something and after I eat, around five, I get a second wind. Just as well 'cos it gets busy then — all the punters fancy a quick screw after work, just before they go home to the missus. Most of them are married, I can tell. All my regulars are 'cept for one or two who're too shy to get an ordinary girl. I like them ones the best — they don't try to show off or nothing. It's them creeps just out the pub who think they can turn me on I hate — like I'm doing this for pleasure or something. Like they can show me a trick or two when that's just my job — turning fucking tricks like them, one after another. Them and weirdos like your mate — Alistair? They're the pits.

'It's busy on and off all night — but it can go quite quickly

207

until about ten. Then I'm knackered. On a regular day I can have forty men easily — hardly worth a blink. But it hits me when I get home. I just slump in the bath, I tell you. Tyrone's good sometimes — he makes me tea and stuff and puts me to bed. Tell you something else tho', there's no chance of a sex-life then — I'm fucked, forty times over, and the smack's got a hold of Tyrone. Maybe we'll catch up on sex when we get to Morocco — I hope so. I miss it sometimes, you know, fucking for love, fucking 'cos it's what *I want* . . .'

In the ceaselessness of this work, in its grinding inexorability, the mindless magnitude of being fucked daily by forty men inevitably overwhelms everything else — except for the dream, 'Morocco' in Jackie's mind, which still foams around the edges of each twelve-hour stretch of emptiness in this meagre Chinatown room. Even the horror of visitors like Alistair 'turning crazy' is nothing compared to the work's otherwise unremitting tedium and the accompanying, mythic reverie of moving elsewhere.

'That was a bad one, for sure,' Jackie said later in reference to Alistair's flogging of her, 'but to be honest I just shut stuff like that out. Otherwise it'd just drive me completely loopy. Maybe a hundred men walk through that door some days, a lot of them just to have a look, you know, time-wasters. But I still have to talk to every one of them. And how's it gonna be if each time I open the door to a man I think he's gonna beat me up? Nah, in this game you gotta have a bit of faith 'cos, as I said, most of them are fine, nervous as fucking kittens actually. But, yeah, I learnt something from that prick, that fucking Alistair. I'll watch out from now on.

'See, he caught me off guard. It was around nine and I was real tired. I wanted to pack up but that old bitch Molly always squeals if I shut up shop early. Then this Alistair guy comes in — real smooth like. Tells me his name, straight off. I remember that 'cos most of them never give their names, even false ones. He spoke real nice — he was different to most of them. He took out about five crisp twenties, said he really liked the look of me but that he felt I needed a spank on my bottom, what did I think? I said, "Put down another three twenties and you'll probably find you're right." I'd done that sort of thing before, you know, pull on the old gym-slip, bend over his knee, take a bit of hand on the old butt. I don't care − let them do it if they pay me. Then I can make what it normally takes to fuck ten punters. So I tell ol' Molly not to let anyone else in − this is a big one, the last of the night.

So we go through the old schoolgirl thing − piece of piss really. I'm even having a bit of a lark to tell the truth. Then suddenly he goes crazy. He bends me over and he starts clubbing me with this cane. Fucking like he wants to knock my bleeding block off. Lucky he broke the cane when I started screaming. Gave him such a fright he caught the end of the bed and it cracked. Poor old Molly was having hysterics. She was sure I was a goner 'cos I was screaming blue murder. He'd already eased off by the time Alex from downstairs was banging on the door with her fucking shoe. He was all red and purple in the face like he was some kind of dog. I was just screaming, "What the fuck do yer think you're doing? Are you some kind of maniac?"

'He cooled down fast then. Started to smooth things over. I think he knew he'd gone too far. He took out more money from his trouser pocket − he'd kept them on − and he gives me another twenty and he goes out and gives Alex and Molly twenty each. Smooth as fucking butter. That's what scared me the most, you know − that they thought I had gone over the top, that no-one who dressed and spoke as well as him would go as far as I said he did. They told me to go home − I was just tired. They said it was nothing, to forget it. I dunno how he got away with it − you would have thought that they would've got the police out but no, to them, I'm just going over the top.

'Fuck it, you should've seen the bruises I carried home that night. I could hardly get into the fucking bath. Oh no, boy, *I* won't forget him in a hurry — he's never coming through my door again and if I were you, mate, I'd steer well clear of him too. He's a dangerous one all right.'

The real danger, though, is always to the prostitute; for in the eyes of the police and the public, by the very nature of her vocation, she has invariably been 'asking for it'. Knowing this, Alistair can lay into a 'Chinatown whore' like Jackie, wave a few £20 notes debonairly and get away with grievous bodily harm.

I told Jackie about Alistair's Tuesday afternoon visits to Mandy Kavanagh, about the way in which roles were switched then and how she, 'The Terminator Angel', punished him.

'Oh yeah, great stuff baby!' she laughed. 'Tell your angel to give him a couple of biffs from me. Yeah, I love it!'

The problem, I pointed out, was that Alistair also liked it. Moreover, Mandy's hope that her beatings were keeping his hatred of women in check had been shattered by the news of his attack on Jackie.

'Ah, she sounds a bit of a love. I'd like to meet her some day and tell her not to worry. Creeps like that Alistair just keep rolling on — she shouldn't give her whole life up to worrying about what he'll do to other whores. She don't sound much like the girls round here.'

'Would you really like to meet her?'

'Yeah, she sounds amazing . . . but she wouldn't want to meet *me*, would she?'

It was difficult to tell whether Jackie's fascination was more intense than the compassion felt for her by Mandy and Simone. For an entire Monday afternoon there was an affinity between the three which stretched to their insisting that I stay with them, as their token male, in Mandy's blue room while they swapped stories about their very different modes of prostitution.

Apart from each other, this was the first time either Mandy or Simone had spoken to another working prostitute; Jackie, in contrast, said she 'shot the breeze with a whole bunch of Chinatown whores almost every fucking day'. The difference showed. Mandy and Simone were astonished at the number of men Jackie fucked every day and kept asking if she felt her body was withstanding such punishment. Jackie, however, was less interested in discussing the humdrum elements of day-to-day intercourse than she was in telling the others about Tyrone and stressing to Mandy how she loved this 'fucking house' and that the two of them, 'The Terminator Angel' and *La Chienne de Souffrance* were 'way too fucking brainy and beautiful to be on the game'.

This was a cutting irony as both Mandy and Simone had wanted to meet Jackie so that they could encourage her to opt out of her kind of prostitution. Instead, they listened quietly while Jackie gave them some mildly reproachful stick for 'not using [their] brains more' — only to suddenly burst out in laughter at the supposed absurdity of her, 'just a tattooed Chinatown whore' as she kept calling herself, telling off two of London's most expensive and specialized 'postgrad' prostitutes.

It had only taken Jackie a few minutes to overcome her initial shyness at meeting Mandy and Simone in these comparatively lavish surroundings — from then on she literally ran the afternoon, to the extent of deciding what cakes I should go out and buy from Mandy's local patisserie. When I returned, Mandy and Simone had finally moved into a higher gear and were persuading Jackie that there were infinitely easier and more lucrative ways of making money as a prostitute than in her room downtown. After the caramel and cheese-cakes and a guided tour of Mandy's basement, Jackie, having produced a searing demonstration of what she'd do to Alistair on his favourite convex couch, promised that she'd think about everything they'd said. Basically, she admitted, she was sick to death of working in Chinatown. She wondered how much longer she would last there. Jackie was near tears when she'd said she'd keep in touch and come visit the two of them again 'sometime soon'.

As Jackie and I walked towards the South Kensington tube she was filled with excitement, saying that 'I could even be friends with those two — even if that Simone's a bit rich telling me to leave Tyrone when it sounds like she's got the same sort of dead-beat bloke round her neck.' But by the time we had reached the underground our laughter died for there was the dead weight around her own neck. Her breath caught sharply at the back of her throat when she saw Tyrone watching us from the opposite end of the street. It was only when she called his name that I realized that it was him. He walked towards us angrily, calling her a 'fucking bitch'. He looked painfully thin and ill but, clearly, there was still a wiry strength in him as he held her tightly by the wrist.

He turned on me, his black eyes burning and staring angrily. All I could see were crude tear marks tattooed down each of his cheeks, the tears which Jackie said they were going to have removed once they returned from Morocco. 'Please leave,' she said quietly to me, and then more urgently, 'Go, just go, will you?' So I left for the underground, only looking back once to where they stood on the opposite corner, holding each other. I could see that her tears were real.

I never saw Jackie again after that strange afternoon. When I next went to Chinatown and passed by her room, her adverts had been taken down. In their place there were others, without flowers around their borders, endorsing a 'friendly, versatile honey-blonde model'. When I knocked at her old third-floor door, the maid immediately started her 'Sorry love, she's busy' routine. When she heard I was looking for Jackie she said, simply, 'There's a new girl working here — she's very nice.' I asked her if she knew where Jackie had gone but closing the door, she said sourly, 'Naaah, she just disappeared. Good riddance — she never was good enough for this room, I'm telling you.'

On my way down, I stopped off to see Alex who was similarly uninterested in Jackie's whereabouts. 'Ah, fuck her,' she said as she shook her curly hair in front of the mirror, 'she'll be all right. Off with that junkie boyfriend somewhere; they're hopeless, the pair of them.' She turned to face me, thrusting her large breasts out and pulling the front of her silvery body-suit away from her crotch as if to give herself a needed breath of air. 'Do you fancy fucking me instead of talking about her — I'll suck you first, for fifteen, just for you. I've got a hot mouth, I promise.'

As I shook my head and said 'bye' instead, a shutter of hardness seemed to drop down the length of Alex's face. 'Well, fuck you too,' she called faintly after me as I walked down the stairs, hoping that Jackie had finally made it to Casablanca.

Chapter Eight

Benoni-boy and the Bed-show Girls

He had seen me walking towards the narrow doorway.
Setting his espresso to one side and lighting a small cigar,
he watched me through the filmy flare of smoke. He was
always interested in the type of man who went to those rooms.

Then, he said later, I surprised him. I just stood at the
entrance for a minute or two, seemingly lost in some
meandering thought. This made me look shameless to him.
He knew then, right off, that I had not just been at the
receiving end of a fifteen, or even a twenty, pound fucking.
If that *had* been the case, he laughed, I would have walked
briskly out of there like everyone else. My head would have
been down and my hands sunk deep into any pockets they
could find. If I was married, as most of them were, I would
also have checked to see who, if anyone, was monitoring
the leaving of the clientele through that dark blue door.

As he watched me looking casually at the strips of paper
adverts lining the black and white panelled wall he wondered
if I was perhaps the landlord. Who else, apart from the
landlord or an utter fool, would loiter so intently round
those whore-rooms? And then, he grinned, he saw what I
was wearing and he was sure that no pimping entrepreneur
had ever looked that dishevelled.

Tagged his fool then, I had finally left the doorway and
made the short walk towards the pavement table where he
was sitting. For a crazy moment he thought I was about to
join him. Yet I brushed by without even noticing him and

sat instead at a table on the other side of the entrance to the Italia café. He saw me peering through the doorway at some silent, year-old footage of AC Milan running on the big screen at the end of the bar. He turned around in his seat, too, and saw Ruud Gullitt, dreadlocks flying, flick a ball through to Van Basten who checked once, twice, before side-footing home in the bottom left-hand corner.

He forgot everything for a while then as he drew on his cigar and stared at the flickering Italian league football unfolding before him. It had always been his only sport from way back, long before he and his mother had returned to Europe. And then, in one of those curious coincidences that still made his life worth living, he heard that accent again. It was maybe a little softer than he had remembered but, still, it was unmistakable. He looked round with a feeling close to amazement; for his fool was speaking to the smiling Italian girl who had brought him his espresso.

'And so where in South Africa are you from then?' he called across the tables to me in his own distinctive London accent.

I looked at him with a deep, inward sigh. Why do I always get them? 'Johannesburg,' I replied with what was meant to be an edge of finality in my voice.

'You know Benoni then?' he said, all smiles now.

I knew Benoni all right. Benoni is a dull little town about twenty miles outside of my own hometown, Germiston, the South African equivalent of Luton, just east of Johannesburg. But it still gave me a perverse kind of thrill to meet someone in London who had even heard of Benoni.

'Well, I'm actually from Germiston,' I called back, even smiling myself now.

'Ah, Germiston! Sure, Germiston! The biggest railway junction in South Africa!' he enthused.

That was one of its charms, I agreed, pulling up a chair for this definitively swarthy man with the North London accent, who had come over to my table in delight at our supposed Benoni bond. It was debatable quite what the

Italian waitress made of this parochial exchange but she kept
on smiling and soon returned with another espresso for the
Benoni-boy, who actually looked well-entrenched in middle
age, and a cappuccino for me. Pumping my hand excitedly,
he told me to call him 'Michel', or 'Michael' if I felt more
comfortable, or even 'Mickey' if I must. I told him my name
and said he could call me anything he liked, except 'Donny'.

For some reason this tickled him. He rocked back and
forth with laughter, so much so that the coffee cups shook
as if we were travelling on a train. From then on he always
called me 'Donny-boy'.

As we sat at our rickety table, soaking up the nostalgia
of Benoni and Germiston which felt as tangible again as the
late-afternoon autumn sunlight screening Frith Street, he
told me about his fleeting South African past. His father
was from Cyprus and soon after the Second World War he
had travelled to London where he met Michel's mother —
an Islington girl of Cypriot stock. They married a few
months after meeting and travelled down to Southampton
one Sunday morning. The next night they sailed to South
Africa — where one of Michel's uncles had emigrated a few
years previously and found plenty of sunshine and work as
a white emigrant. Michel's parents settled in Benoni, in a
small house across the road from his uncle. Six months later
he was born, a 'Benoni baby', he laughed, having been
conceived at sea which, he said wryly, possibly explained
why his mother always said he had such 'stormy good looks'.
He would have preferred it, he exclaimed, puffing on a new
cigar, if this had been the way the girls, rather than his
mother, had described him.

But he only started noticing girls long after he and his
mother left Benoni, when his father died. Michel was ten
then and they returned to Islington, where they moved in
with his maternal grandparents. He had lived in North
London ever since, even though his mother died too before
he was twenty. A week before his birthday she was killed
in a car accident.

When his grandparents died in quick succession a few years later, he was bereft of any family in London. That had been a hard time for him and he even considered returning to Benoni. Instead, he sold his grandparents' house and with the proceeds bought himself a flat just off Upper Street. To fill his spare time, when he wasn't working as an apprentice carpenter, he began to redecorate his flat. When he decided to sell it a few years later his handiwork had trebled its value. He bought another flat and the same process was almost inadvertently repeated. Before he knew it, he was able to buy two new flats — one of which he let out to tenants. Michel was in early on the London property boom in the late 1960s and, if he had been especially interested in money, he might have become a very rich man. But he fell in love and became less interested in buying up cheap properties and redoing them.

Michel told me this much of his life history in the time it takes to drink a couple of coffees and, as interesting a story-teller as he was, I must have glanced at my watch when he asked me to explain how I had ended up in London after starting out in Germiston. He looked strangely hurt that I was even thinking of terminating our brief meeting.

'How about a quick pint over the road?' he said almost forlornly. Perhaps it was the way he suddenly averted his eyes from mine which made me realize his essential aloneness. Considering this, as well as our South African past, it suddenly seemed churlish to do anything but agree to his suggestion.

'Fantastic, Donny-boy, fantastic,' Michel said with serious ebullience, 'and the first drinks are on me. The Benoni-boy always buys the first round.'

I wasn't sure how many rounds I was keen to stay for but, after the second, just when I was preparing to finally take my leave of Benoni-boy, Michel startled me. He told me then that he had seen me standing in the blue-doored passageway just before we met, that he had even thought I might be a landlord too.

218

For a second I thought he meant that he owned such rooms in Soho. Then, from his embarrassment, I gathered again that he was the landlord to more respectable properties elsewhere.

'You obviously know what happens in those rooms,' he said shyly.

'I think I do,' I said equally coyly.

'It's an interesting business,' he said and then as if not to offend me, 'in a way, I guess.'

The certainty with which he said those first words encouraged me to tell him the now familiar story of the book I was writing.

'Fantastic, Donny-boy, fantastic,' he enthused, thumping me on the back. After a pregnant pause, in which time he decided to temper his excitement in case I got the wrong idea about him, he murmured with more restraint, 'It's a world that's not that well-known is it? It's a British-type secret. That's why I'm a Cypriot first, a South African second and only a Brit third and last. How can I be British when they are so hung up about prostitution?'

It was tempting to point out that the Cypriot legislative record on prostitution was hardly unblemished but I stuck closer to home and berated the singularly South African style of official hypocrisy pertaining to sex — particularly when looked at over the course of apartheid during the retarded 'Immorality Act' decades when sex 'across the colour-line' was forbidden.

'Oh, but Donny-boy, Benoni is Benoni,' he argued with unimpeachable logic. 'This is fucking London — supposed to be one of the freest cities in the world and look how fucked-up it is! No-one gets to grips with what prostitution means. You expect that in Benoni maybe, but not in London.'

I knew what he meant and, also, I was intrigued by this burst of passion. What did prostitution mean to him, I wondered, as he went over to get us another couple of drinks. By the time it was my turn again I had still not asked him, thinking it only right that I should reveal to him first what I had found in my previous eight months.

So I told him who I had met, ending with a summation of Jackie's disappearance six weeks before; how it had been Jackie I had been thinking of, still wondering where she was, when he had seen me standing so pensively in the doorway earlier that afternoon. Her abrupt vanishing act had disturbed me and I could not even find a photograph of her on Docherty's wall. Despite my hope, I did not really believe she had made it to Morocco. I was sure she was working elsewhere as a prostitute — perhaps in conditions even worse than those she had endured in Chinatown. In disappearing, however, she had shown me how ephemeral the protagonists were in any one corner of prostitution. No matter how regular a face might appear to become, the substance of the work created a constant whirl of upheaval in a prostitute's life. This was especially so in a city like London where the law offered so little protection to prostitutes. For all I knew Jackie could have been beaten up badly again by Alistair or by Tyrone, or any of their equally brutal punter or pimping equivalents. What recourse then would she have to refuge from the law, with no safe 'house' from which to work as a prostitute?

Worn out by my own tirade I went back to the bar for some needed sustenance. Michel was so far into his next cigar that he was engulfed by the clouds of smoke. But his words were clear enough when I sat down again. 'I wouldn't be too worried about Jackie — she's a tough nut.'

'How would you know?' I asked Michel bemusedly.

'I visited her once in Lisle Street — not long after she started there.'

'You did?' I repeated.

'Yeah. I know quite a few of the girls from around here. I'm what they call a "punter". One of their regulars, if you like.'

Maybe it was the fact that we had started talking to each other because of Benoni, for I could not hide my surprise. 'So you really knew Jackie too?'

'Only once — to tell you the truth she wasn't a very good prostitute. A sweet girl, I'm sure, if you got to know her. But, as a hooker she was lousy. Very unprofessional. Not like Virna or Natasha, the older French women. Have you met them?'

They were based in Frith Street and I had seen their adverts; but on the one day when I'd paid their room a visit, their wheezing Italian maid shook her small head sadly and said, 'Very, very busy today!'

'Different class to a kid like Jackie, really, them two. But, you know Donny-boy, Jackie was lousy as a prostitute because her heart just wasn't in it. And who can blame her for that? Not me. But I could always tell she was thinking of moving on out of that room even before you gave me this Morocco story. Now I'm not saying she's made it to Casablanca but she'll be all right. She's a tough cookie, that one, junkie boyfriend or not.'

I was still unsure whether I'd developed a sentimental attachment to Jackie as my mythical 'country cousin' or if the others, the maid and Alex and now Michel, were right — and she was always going to land on her feet no matter what Tyrone or Alistair did to her. But Michel was already enraptured by another subject — the elusive, ultimately empty thrill embedded into the very core of both prostitution and pornography. He was crisply incisive and I found myself in that curiously anti-social mood of wanting to find another empty tape to record his words for posterity. But, instead, I switched off my saturated recorder and just listened. An hour later he said he'd repeat it all again, 'more clearly', on tape, if I really wanted 'to interview Benoni-boy again'. He'd cook me a 'real Benoni-Cypriot meal', in Holloway of all places, where he now lived. 'In the meantime,' he said as a way of parting, 'don't loiter in those Soho corridors unless you really do want to be a pimp from Germiston . . .'

He lived in a large house, in one of Holloway's less grim roads, not far from Highbury Fields where, whatever the weather, he would walk most evenings. The house was immaculate and it was obvious that he had not just tidied it for my benefit; rather, it had the feel of a home which was always kept clean and cared for.

'I once brought a prostitute home for the night,' he remembered as he showed me around the house, 'and she said that there are only two types of men who are able to keep a clean, decent home — a man who is gay and a man who is sorrowful. She meant, firstly, a homosexual and then, secondly, another kind of man, a man who has given up the idea of ever being in love with a woman again. She knew I wasn't gay, you know, a "poof", so I think she knew what she was talking about. And she was right about me in that way. When I was much younger, when I still thought that maybe I would marry one day, I was terrible. The house was like a pig-sty. Clothes unwashed, dirty dishes everywhere, socks lost in the fruit basket, dust all over . . . and being a normal Cypriot-South African bachelor living in North London I was waiting for a woman to arrive and sort me out. Terrible, isn't it? Then one day I just knew it was not going to happen and so I scrubbed the house from top to bottom, sorted everything out, and I've kept it that way ever since. I may be alone forever but because of that I'm not going to live in a dirty hole any more. So, it's tidy, hey — for a Benoni-boy, especially!'

Michel's constant allusions to his Benoni-boy status were less endearing than they were a lumbering cover-up of a hermetic kind of hurt. When he told me about the day he discarded his newly bought answerphone he made me understand that where I had initially thought he was just a man who lived alone he was, in reality, lost in a more corrosive kind of solitude. His house was neatly maintained and the meal he served me — Greek salad, home-cooked kebabs marinated in wine, followed by baklava, coffee and tumblers-full of ouzo — was a model of appetising efficiency. But as the evening wore on it felt like I was being gathered into the basic wilderness of the life he lived. Where some people, like Lee Docherty, can be sustained by an essential apartness, there are others who suffer from loneliness. Michel, as he knew only too well, for all his laughter and jokey Benoni-boy endurance, was such a casualty.

'I read in the newspaper once,' he said, 'that an answerphone can change your life. When you are out all kinds of people might phone. Your family, your friends, even your long-lost friends, maybe even some new people who could be your friends. You didn't know who you could be missing when you were out. So I went out and bought one of these machines. I got it working and the next time I went out I turned it on. I came in a few hours later and there were no messages. No problem, these things take time. I waited a whole two weeks, went out every day and most nights, often just to be out the house so someone would call. Nothing. Every time I came in the red light was still. The instructions said if someone called it would flash. I checked the machine — it was working. It wasn't the machine's fault, even though I hated it. I never had one message on that fucking machine. What is the point of me having an answerphone when no-one calls? So I gave it away to the people who live in the second flat I own. I said, "Take it, have it for free, it's no use to me." '

It's only right that silence should follow such a speech for what is there to say that would not sound either trite or dismissive of this hurt? So we drank our ouzo and I searched for a fire to look into, for it is at moments like these that you need flames to stare at — either in meditative contemplation or despair. But the evenings were still only cool outside and so the hearth was covered by a basket of dried flowers. I looked instead at the bottom of my glass. Then, clearing his throat slightly, Michel reached over and poured me another shot of fiery ouzo. He stoked his own chimney with another drink and tried to look more cheerful.

'But you get used to it. It's not as if I sit around and worry about it. I get out, I do have friends to see. It's just that most of them drink with me in the pub down the road. They have no reason to call me. They know they can always catch me at the pub. Sometimes we go to a game — at Arsenal or Spurs — or we play as a quiz-team against other pubs. It's not bad. And then, the times when the loneliness does get me, when I am not so good, I go out and I have sex and it makes me feel much better — for a while at least, until the next time.'

In the ensuing moment of savage intimacy, when I felt acutely the cheapness of my question, I asked him if he only had sex with prostitutes.

Ironically, he seemed to welcome the question. 'Oh yes, Donny-Boy, I can hardly remember the last time I had sex with any woman who was not a prostitute.'

I liked the fact that he could say this without even a trace of the self-pity that had filtered through his earlier comments.

'I see at least five or six prostitutes a month. All kinds of prostitutes. Mostly around Soho because it's easy then. I just walk up the stairs and I'm in — usually only with a little wait. But I also go to prostitutes who advertise in shop-windows and newspapers. Sometimes I even call an escort agency if I feel rich. Why not? I have nothing else to spend my money on.'

'When did you start visiting prostitutes so often?' I asked.

'Nine, ten years ago maybe. A long time now!'

'You must have met a lot of prostitutes!'

'Sure! Too many to count! But often I find a favourite one and I see only her. She's like my girlfriend then. But, always, I move on. It's only to some of them that I keep going back. Like to Virna in Soho. There is no better value in town: £20 and she gives you everything — a dignified prostitute too. First you go in and she talks to you a little while you undress and then she washes you gently in her bidet, talking all the time in that soft French voice. Then she moves over to the bed and there are mirrors all around and she massages you a little bit and when you are ready she rolls the condom on and then she sucks like magic. A beautiful blow job, every time. Then I slide gently, slowly into her. I can see us together in the mirrors and all the time she is playing this music on her cassette. It's very strange. Music like whales calling under the sea to each other. So, to Virna, I always go back. And, when she is away, to Natasha, who is much older but also very special. She is a healer of some sort. I'm not sure what sort but she knows many things. They are like my oldest girlfriends in town.'

'Do you sometimes yearn for a girlfriend you can call your own, someone who is not a prostitute?' I asked.

'I used to a lot. Now, only sometimes. Long ago, more than twenty years ago, I was in love with this woman. The one I told you about the other day, the one I fell for when I was doing up my first two flats. Sarah. That was her name. We were in love, we were going to be married. Or so I thought. Then one day, after about two years of us being together, she takes me for a walk in the park. She asks me if I remember Antony, the man she used to go out with before me. I say, "Sure, I know the guy, what about him?" She says, "Well I saw him the other day and I think I'm still in love with him. I think I want to marry him." I can't fucking believe it! "But you're going to marry me," I say. And she stands there, with tears rolling down her cheeks and she says, "You know I love you." And I shout, "Of course you fucking love me!" She just starts to shake her head and really cry and she says, "I'm sorry, Michel, I'm sorry . . ." Turns out she loves this fuckwit more than she loves me. Fuck, I really tried with her. I loved her. And then she did that to me. She says she didn't mean to hurt me, that's just the way she is, and so she's sorry. I told her, "Forget it, it's all right, go to him. I love you, but if that's what you want, you go to him." I never saw her again. She called for a while, she wrote to see if I was fine. I never answered. From then on I never really wanted a girlfriend, even the idea of a wife. How could I, after she hurt me like that? Look, I don't blame her — she was a good, decent woman. But she spoiled me for anyone else. Ever since then I've felt alone inside. Ever since then I've been on my own.'

Michel said it was difficult to talk about such things but he felt he could say them to me. It was not so much the formality of the recorder between us, acting as some kind of confessional spur, but the fact that I was a writer. Since he had met me the week before he had thought a lot about writing. Surely there was little work as lonely as a writer's? All those hours you had to spend at a desk, completely on your own, writing about feelings, writing about love and the loss of love. He thought it must be beautiful in a way — that kind of aloneness, when you were building something of your own, word by word, sentence by sentence. He felt it was very different to his own loneliness.

Michel's words had their own kind of grave beauty. But, as I said to him, with this book the problem was more one of being engulfed by people, by the magnitude of feelings they had shared with me, in all sorts of ways and different kinds of settings, about prostitution. Moments such as these were almost unbearably intimate — it was a sharing of something, of another's hurt. And because theirs was an intensely personal pain, the interviews inevitably forced real people into this book. Writing another sort of book, a fictional book, would be perhaps lonelier but certainly less fraught with the problem of trying to do justice to the words and feelings of all those who had been around me during the 'building' of such a book.

'Ah, but still,' he went on to remark with brutal precision, 'even with all these people, Donny-boy, you're still writing about the loneliest subject of all. I know the loneliness of it well, that's all I can say . . .'

Even though he could not immediately elucidate this theme I felt he had struck a curious seam of truth in that one line. For prostitution was almost always about separating one self from another, exchanging what Simone Maillard called one's 'real' self for another persona. There were few acts lonelier than abandoning the self you saw as your own for a repeatedly shifting set of identities.

In the very grain of the act, of selling sex, fundamental barriers separated the prostitute from the client. Money, more even than that detachment of self, reinforced prostitution's main support wall. It was the solidity of that wall, that professionalism, which made prostitution such an essential vocation in a broken-up world; for by giving up themselves both physically and emotionally, prostitutes allowed their clients the freedom to fill in their own raging needs or fantasies. Those walls protected the prostitutes but also created an inevitable isolation, leaving them exposed to an acute form of loneliness.

'There are many prostitutes I know who are lonely,' Michel said as he listened to these ideas, 'because they give up so much of themselves. They give up their bodies, their names, their hearts, themselves even to keep doing their work. That's why I admire so many of them so much, that's why many of the people I care most about are these women, these prostitutes. I understand that loneliness because I feel it too. Each time I see a new prostitute, a new woman, I am very excited. But as soon as I come, the thrill is gone. There is some emptiness there. I am alone again so quickly. But at least it's not pain I feel, it's a dull feeling. Then I forget all that a week later. I feel that thrill coming again and it starts all over — only it goes as soon as I come . . .'

Michel's loneliness lined his heart's most private recesses, stemming from his feeling of being deserted by those he had loved. But it came to me as a conspicuous kind of metaphor for the lonely, shifting thrill offered by both prostitution and pornography. Because they are both billion pound businesses — in which contrived themes of excitement and pleasure are produced, advertised and then consumed — there are fixed parameters for the 'thrill-seekers' as much as the 'thrill-givers'. Those boundaries are money-lined and the interaction between the sex-worker and the sex-consumer is usually less a relationship than a transaction.

For the consumer, the bringing of 'fantasy into reality' can only be a transient experience, a sexual encounter whose pretended intimacy is forever filtered through the barriers of cash, the separating glass in a peep-show booth, the erotic dance stage, the telephone, the glossy magazine page, the cinema and television screen. Inevitably it is, as Michel said just before I left his home that night, money which 'chills the thrill'.

For him this is not necessarily a bad thing, for it buffers his vulnerable heart against too deep an emotional involvement. Some might argue that Michel's loneliness is exacerbated by his consumption of both pornography and prostitution; if he did not have access to these 'crutches' of fantasy then perhaps he would force himself into more 'normal' relationships, even at the risk of emotionally hurting himself. But this argument has to be based on the reductive assumption that consumer sex can *only* be irredeemably alienating and isolating.

And, looking at Michel again, another perception emerged. Despite his acknowledgment of prostitution's intrinsic boundaries, Michel was still able to uncover and invest compassion in prostitution. Certainly his description of having sex with Virna in Soho had an almost lyrical tenderness. Perhaps I was tantalised by his melodramatic justifications, but in his attachment to prostitution I felt he was reaching out to others: to women, who happened to be prostitutes, willing to haul him out of his maudlin solitude. Consequently he was sentimental about prostitutes; but that was also because his feelings for these women penetrated the dividers which delineate the sex business.

This unspoken empathy between the prostitute and the client, against all odds, often adds a different dimension to what would otherwise be just a business arrangement. Many prostitutes stress this side of their work — where the selling and the consuming is still imbued with 'caring', with 'feeling'. Their attempted subversion of the 'chilled thrill' can only increase when the laws relating to prostitution change and other ways of selling sex are permitted — where safety, cleanliness and public openness replace the type of squalid and shame-ridden sex of back-streets and vhore-rooms.

For that to happen, for prostitutes to be sufficiently empowered to control their own working environments and create their own chosen styles of brothels, the 'ownership' of the sex industry will have to change as much as the law. In pornography, despite the dogmatic refusals to accept such truths from the blinkered likes of Andrea Dworkin, there has been a subtle shift — at least in America. The pornography of Candida Royale, the performed eroticism of Annie Sprinkle and the creation of organizations like the Prostitutes Of New York (PONY) have transformed the way in which sex is sold. Their pornography and prostitution have been extricated from male entrepreneurs and placed back into the hands of women sex workers themselves. So sex, in these rare American spaces, is consumed differently than it is here. There, the estrangement typically inherent to the sex trade is being clipped back as women also become consumers and owners in the business; here, however, that loneliness just seems to grow wider and deeper, as Michel confirmed.

Although his consumption had more to do with compassion than cruelty, Michel was not that dissimilar to Alistair. Quintessentially, they both prided themselves on being international connoisseurs of the sex industry. Michel, twice a year, 'rewarded' his solitary fortitude with a holiday in one of the sex capitals of the world — Amsterdam, Copenhagen, Hamburg, Paris, New York, Los Angeles, Bangkok or Rio. The last was his least favourite for although the prostitutes were amongst the most beautiful he had ever seen, they were invariably transvestites — and, as Michel stressed, he was more a sorrowful than a gay man.

During the course of these sex-trips he gives compassion a break in order to cast a more critical eye over the prostitution and pornographic wares on display. London lags behind and, moreover, dishes up the most despondent sex-for-sale scenarios he has ever witnessed in all his jaunts across the humping and grinding globe. There is no lonelier, more heartbreaking place to consume sex than in one of Soho's few remaining, rancid peep-show booths. He suggested strongly, as 'one loner to another', a phrase I was not quite sure how to take, that I subject myself to the ordeal. When he heard that I had already done the rounds with Alistair he told me that I should still meet two of the 'saddest but sweetest' girls who had ever worked a Soho bed-show.

Back in the dreaded booth again I saw a miserable-looking woman in her late-twenties lolling around a double bed. She wore a baby-blue suspender belt, flesh-coloured stockings and a pair of bright yellow high-heeled shoes. In haphazard time to Donna Summer's *I Feel Love* disco opus, she brushed her hands across her breasts and inner thighs. She looked desultorily round the circle of windows. By another trick of modern science she could see into each of the occupied booths — an opportunity which the peepers were fortunately spared.

Watching the way she licked her lips snidely in the direction of two windows — mine and another a little to my left — I reckoned there was only one other peeping fool wasting a pound coin at this time on a wet Friday afternoon. He may well have been one of Alistair's Japanese business associates for she seemed to be playing up to his booth rather than mine. As she turned more towards that window I noticed that while one buttock featured a small tattoo of a butterfly, the other was marked by a yellowish bruise. But she looked desperately bruised by boredom and after a minute I felt myself succumbing to the same tedium. As if in deference to this feeling, the light suddenly switched itself back on. My minute of peeping was over.

But I had come prepared. Michel had told me that he was a casual friend of this particular bed-show girl, the girl with the little butterfly tattoo. I wasn't sure exactly what he meant by 'casual' but he knew her sufficiently well to tell me that she was from Rotterdam and that she called herself Vicki. As he said, it was sometimes difficult to make personal contact with the bed-show girls when their hulking boss, 'Mort', was around the peeping premises, he suggested that I hold up a note to her saying that I was a friend of Michel and that I wanted to have a quick word with her in the pub across the road. Being an ingenious Benoni-born, peep-show connoisseur, he suggested that I write this note in Afrikaans seeing that it is a language which derives from Old Dutch. It would be a linguistic gesture of solidarity with Vicki, he argued, even though he himself couldn't speak a word of Afrikaans and she spoke perfect English.

So, feeling more ridiculous than ever, I slid another coin into the slot and held my already written message up against the screen. The other booth must have emptied because Vicki was sneaking in a quick lie-down. But as my booth light went out she went back to work, rubbing herself absently between her legs. She soon saw that I was holding paper in my hand and thinking it must be money she rolled quickly my way. Her subsequent puzzlement at seeing my note soon gave way to a burst of giggling and head-shaking. I had written, '*Verskoen my, Vicki. Ek is 'n vriend van Michel. Kan ek met u praat in die "pub" asseblief?*' (In English, this absurdly ungrammatical Afrikaans message basically read as follows: 'Excuse me, Vicki. I am a friend of Michel. Can I talk to you in the pub, please?')

I was mildly drunk when I first agreed that this might be a good idea, and in a similar state while holding up my Afrikaans card; but, even accounting for a few Guinnesses, it was still ludicrous. Yet it worked. Vicki, still laughing, pointed to her wrist and held up two fingers, in a polite 'V' sign. At first glance I took this to mean that she'd see me in two minutes' time but as she spun her hand around her wrist I gathered she was talking in terms of hours. She was still smiling and shaking her head as the light blazed on, separating us from peeping view.

She arrived in the pub bang on time and if it hadn't been for the fact that she was still laughing I wouldn't have recognized her with her butterfly covered up. She was tall and thin with her black hair falling around her face like a mop. That was the significant difference — apart from the boots, mini-skirt, tank-top and leather jacket she was now wearing — between her in the street and on the bed, where her hair had been tied back by a scarf.

Before we had exchanged greetings she exclaimed, 'Do you *really* know what you said on your card?'

'I think so,' I said with the certainty that I obviously did not.

'You said "Wash me, Vicki!" Why?'

'Wash you?'

'*Verskoen my!* It means "wash me" in Dutch!'

'And "excuse me" in Afrikaans . . .'

'Well, it made me laugh at least. If your Dutch had been perfect maybe I wouldn't be here. So, dirty boy, you're the writer?'

'How did you know that?' I asked.

'Michel told Toni — you know, my girlfriend — the other day. I was expecting you, but not that you'd be looking for a wash!'

A little tetchily, I felt the joke had nearly run its course so I bought Vicki a double Scotch to muffle her laugh. I was glad, however, that I'd given her some pleasure for her last two hours must have been grindingly dull on the bed and Michel had stressed that she was normally 'a very angry girl'.

Her anger flared sporadically later that night when we were joined by her lover Toni, a quiet waif of a London girl who shared bed-show duties with Vicki. We stumbled into the Passage To India restaurant round the corner and, much to the bewilderment of the waiters and surrounding Friday night diners, Vicki proceeded to loudly blitz her way through the despairing backdrop to Soho bed-show work. Toni and I stuck timidly instead to our onion bhajis, nans and chicken korma dishes.

'Look, I've been around,' Vicki began affirmatively. 'I worked for three years in Amsterdam in live-sex show bars. You know, the type of place where you quickly learn to physically pick up the guilders with your pussy-lips. It makes men laugh and so you do it. It's not the greatest work but I stuck it for three years. I did more than OK. They liked me. They said I had the tightest pussy in Amsterdam 'cos I held on to that money so well.

'Then I got itchy feet. I wanted to live somewhere other than the Netherlands. I could speak French not too badly, English quite well. I thought, well, Paris first, then London. After three weeks in Paris I got a job. A peep-show girl in Montparnasse, in rue de la Gaîté, this old street. Before it was a porno place it was a house where Trotsky once lived. I always found that sad, that a place where someone like Trotsky stayed should become a sex showroom.

'Anyway, in this place, I would do private shows for men. For five hundred francs they could jerk off in a booth with me while I played around with a vibrator. Of that money I'd get maybe two hundred francs for myself. But I was the lesbian-show specialist. Me and this other girl would put on a show for a thousand francs. But I didn't like her too much. I didn't think she was always clean so I left that job.

'Now I'm telling you all of this to show that Amsterdam-and Paris are not perfect. No way! But there is much more respect for the girls there than here, especially in Amsterdam. There you're a working woman. A professional. Here we are just meat to these peep-show owners. They care fuck-all for us. And the booths you guys stand in are so horrible that I don't blame any of the men for not coming. This is the way it works here. There is no respect − not for the girls, not for the johns. Fuck all! It makes me sick!

'But in Amsterdam, even in Montparnasse, we worked in almost civilised places. They were kept clean, they were warm, there was some money to be made for the girls. The men weren't frightened and so they were nicer to us − more generous, kinder even. Even to a lesbian like me. But here it's horrible. Here we make so little and the work is so boring it makes me miss using my pussy on those Amsterdam tables and my Montparnasse vibrators. That tells you how bad it is here! Soho is finished!'

The Passage To India patrons had gone ominously quiet, no doubt stunned by this scathing indictment of the very area in which they were seated. But Vicki could also be a sensitively polite girl. Suddenly realizing the loudness of her voice she called out, 'Sorry, I got carried away, forgive me!' From then on she spoke in a softer voice – ironically, I noticed, to the disappointment of more than one couple who were forced to return reluctantly to their comparatively mundane topics of conversation.

Why did she feel Soho had become such a bleak, exploitative peep-show setting?

'Well maybe it's much better in a way for other people. They don't have to see too many of these places. But what has happened is that only the worst rip-offs have stayed open. They are in league with the police maybe. The police know about these places but they don't do much. Instead they go around arresting poor street-girls just trying to do their work. Now I like the English very much – look at Toni, I love her – but they are very backward when it comes to this kind of sex. They try to push it under the carpet, to say it's not really there. But it's here and it stinks.'

'How much longer are the two of you going to stick it out in Soho, then?'

'We're already on our way out. I'm telling you. We're going to do telephone sex instead.'

'Hopefully that's less boring than the bed-show work,' I said.

'It is, thank the fuck!'

Trying to include Toni in our discussion I asked her if she had done any telephone sex work. She shook her head and said softly, 'Not yet. They said I must work on me accent. It's 'cos I'm from the East End. They don't think it's "posh" enough!'

Vicki's voice went up another few octaves as soon as Toni had finished her sentence. 'Can you believe it? They take me, with my Dutch accent, and yet they don't want her because her accent is too much like a London accent! Which fucking country are we living in? Christ, this class thing here makes me so angry. They think every English girl must speak like the Queen! But I've told Toni she should just stay as she is — she'll get some telephone work soon!'

'How've you been doing on the phone then, Vicki?' I asked.

'Oh not bad! But it's fucking hard work talking dirty to an Englishman! I can promise you that. You would be different — you're so fucking dirty you have to hold up cards saying "Clean me!" With the British it's different. I get given a number to call. The guys are always very nervous, giggling on the other end of the line. I used to start off in a husky voice: "Hi there, this is Tammi. I'm a very randy Dutch girl and I lurve to talk dirty!" Now if this was in Amsterdam the guy would be away. Not here. I have to drag it out of them. "What is your favourite fantasy?" I ask them. In Holland the guy would say something like "I like to eat pussy while a hot bitch sticks a dildo up my arse." Then you talk dirty to him for a minute or two and he comes. He's happy, you're happy.

'Here in England it's different. Ten minutes later the guy tells me his fantasy is talking dirty on the telephone. He's already doing it — except he won't talk dirty to me. I have to do all the work. I'm saying, "My pussy's so wet, my juice is running all the way into the crack of my arse. I'm so hot. I need some of your hard cock in me." I think I'm doing not too bad — but there's just silence on the other end of the line. "Don't you like the way I talk?" I ask the guy sadly. "Oh no, I love it," he says. "I've got an erection, really. Please go on." Fuck, it's one-way traffic, baby! After half an hour he sighs, "I'm going to come, I'm going to come," and I want to say, "I want to scream with happiness, I can put down this telephone, I can go and suck some throat sweets now!" But I want to keep this job. So I just moan, "Aaaaahhhhh, yes, shoot over me, baby!" So don't laugh, it's fucking hard work for me!'

Toni and I were virtually rolling off our chairs and it was only the frowning Indian head-waiter who kept us in check. Trying to get serious again was difficult. Had she always done this kind of 'non-contact' sex work rather than any more conventional form of prostitution?

'Well, look, I don't mind if you call me a prostitute. That's fine. I know I'm selling my sex. But I have a rule. No man touches me, not for any money. At most I'll give a peep-show guy a hand-job. But that doesn't happen much.'

'It must still be difficult, as a lesbian, selling stock male fantasies all the time.'

'Without there being any touching it's not too difficult. I don't hate men − well only "Mort" and the guys who run these peep-show places round here. I just find it boring. I'm a lesbian and I have a lover so there's no question of me having real sex with a man. So that has always made me a peep-show girl and a telephone girl rather than a straight prostitute. It would be nice to do some more erotic lesbian stuff for women but you don't get much chance to do that in London. New York is the place for that − so let's hit the Big Apple, Toni-baby!'

Toni, not a girl of many words and obviously well-accustomed to everything that Vicki had already said, merely replied, 'Anytime you like, baby' before returning to her Kulfi ice-cream. For a waif, she packed away an incredible amount of food. I asked Vicki how helpful, or perhaps damaging, it was working with a lover in the same bed-show parlour.

'We like it. We're inseparable, you know. A double-act, in every way. But for other girls it's maybe not so good. You're together a lot of the time. For us, it helps. Because

236

when the one gets down then the other lifts her a little. That's what I really think all prostitutes and porno girls need more than anything else — support. Support from each other of course, but also support from politicians to change the laws. We're not going away — so let them accept it and make things better for both the whores and the johns!'

'That's what Michel always says.'

'Ah Michel — he's sad, but very sweet!'

'Those are the exact words he said about you two,' I remembered.

'Shit, Michel always says everyone is sad! I'm just glad he thinks we're sweet.'

'He made us an ace meal at his place one night,' said the waif with a burp.

'Kebabs?' I asked, with interest.

'Oh no — more exotic than kebabs! Fucking calamari for us girls, hey Vic?'

'Yeah, it was calamari, I remember,' murmured Vicki. 'You know, Michel's the type of john who gives me hope. He respects us, we respect him. He takes down some of the walls there are between us at the beginning. If only the others were more like him, if only the owners of these bed-show booths had even a touch of his kindness in their hearts. Things would be very different for us then. He may be a lonely man. He may be a man who can only go with prostitutes. But he is a better man than almost any other man I know. Because to us he is . . . how should I say it . . .? Yeah, I know now. To us, he is always very tender . . .'

Chapter Nine

Sexual Healing in Surbiton

Across town, a long way from tenderness, the ruin of Marina Studzinski lay all around her. It emanated from the chaos of her Surbiton front room like the tang of grease rising from a stack of unwashed plates. For Marina, then, even that short walk to the kitchen sink appeared too formidable a journey to face; and so the plates heaped up as one despairing meal out of a tin followed another.

You could recognize ruin too in the piles of unopened bills and in the clutter of upturned chairs and half-filled boxes of faded possessions. It was even more obviously at home within the drunk emptiness of the nine wine bottles strewn like skittles across the stained carpet.

Yet all this was nothing when set against the ruin which turned Marina's face into a rippling blend of twitches, frowns and hapless smiles. It was as if her heart had cracked open, letting loose every conceivable emotion which came with the realization that everything was irretrievably lost. She sat in the middle of the room, on an old East India tea-chest. Her arms and legs were crossed. She drew intently on a cigarette wedged into the right side of her mouth. Seemingly handless then, she only allowed her lips to shift the cigarette's position an inch or so after every other drag. The smoke curled out of the opposite corner of her mouth and drifted down through her nose. Her body remained remarkably still, virtually statuesque.

But Marina's face, that curiously dancing face of tics and

distortions, appeared to rejoice in its abandoned movement. Only the dark circles of sleeplessness beneath her eyes stayed constant. The bruise on her throat, which had previously been a storm-cloud shade of black, was tinged with mauve and with yellow, with rainbow colours. In the sky, or on canvas, those colours would have looked pretty; on Marina's throat they rose and fell with every breath she took and spoke only of the savagery of a man she had loved, a man against whom her front and back doors had to be buttressed with steel bars.

'It's all over now, baby,' she said as the cigarette burned down to the butt. 'That maniac Frankie will surely kill me soon. Anyway, that doesn't matter — the bailiffs have already come and gone. The house gets repossessed tomorrow. The business, my delicious "Angels Of Love", is finished. There's gonna be no more sexual healing round Surbiton any more and that, my baby, more than anything else, makes me sadder than words could ever say . . .'

Six months earlier, Marina and I had also faced each other across the wide expanse of her front room. Everything else was different, except that she called me 'baby' a lot then too and her face was similarly mobile. But that afternoon, during our first meeting, Marina had been in firm control of her animated facial muscles as she strung together a remarkable sequence of pouting and winking gestures which appeared as ironic as they were seductive. Those were her favourite 'Angel Of Love' expressions and she exchanged them with subtle alacrity.

She winked a lot at me while the other men in the room were favoured more with the pout. Marina was dressed in an outrageously tight red boiler-suit, with the gold zip down the front only being pulled up to what she had laughingly called 'nipple level', so that her cleavage was amply accentuated. Consequently, I was not completely sure what meaning resided within her wink. It may well have been a hip deconstruction of the age-old 'Madame' persona, a kind of dazzling parody of how Marina was meant to act and look as both the founder and current proprietor of the 'Angels Of Love Escort Agency', located in the suburban surrealism of Surbiton. More probably, Marina was merely delighting in *The Observer*'s sympathetic interview with her the preceding Sunday. Apparently, my interest in 'Angels' underlined further her belief that widespread public recognition of her therapeutic sexual service was imminent. But deep down, I worried that Marina's thirst for publicity was encouraging her to actually give me the eye — in more ways than one. I wondered how the other men would feel, being deprived of the wink, especially when they were such long-standing 'Angels' clients and I was so obviously a non-paying newcomer.

But it didn't take long to realize that they, instead, were thrilled to be on the receiving end of her sultry pout. Even after who knows how many times they had visited this angelic house of love, the men around me exuded the personal certainty that she wanted each of their ambiguously hunky bodies, like she had never wanted anything before. Winking was clearly kids' stuff — the pout was the thing. The only problem was that none of the men seemed to notice the uniformity of Marina's pout. It was as if each man was thinking, 'She only has lips for *me*'.

And, boy, did those lips of hers move. When she wasn't pouting she was wetting her lips, purling them back into her teeth-gleaming smile and, more often than not, using them to talk — sometimes charmingly but, more usually, excitedly. It was only after some time that I realized her fevered activity indicated that she was as nervous as I was; for just as the experience of visiting an escort agency was strange to me, so this was only her second interview.

Yet Marina had gone to much trouble to make my first visit an illuminating one. Although I had been surprised when she had ushered me into a room full of men, of her most representative clients no less, I had also been heartened by this show of ingenuity. I'd gone to Surbiton expecting to find Marina alone or, otherwise, surrounded by a draped house-full of the women who worked for her as 'escorts', as her 'Angels Of Love'.

That she had somehow managed instead to entice her clients 'out into the open' struck me as being a staggeringly original act in this otherwise strait-jacketed world. I began to look more closely at these men who had fallen so hard for Marina and her agency that they were willing to debunk prostitution's conventions of male subterfuge. From the way they all looked at her, with the exception of Frankie, her new live-in lover who had just swept in through the front door with a beery 'Hello all!' greeting, it was clear that the men were there purely in deference to the wishes of Marina.

Frankie slumped down on the then still plush, unstained carpet and instantly clocked me a knowing look followed by, believe it or not, a wink. The effect was catching and I found myself winking back, without knowing why, at both Marina and Frankie. The arrival of her 'real man' seemed to settle Marina and, pulling in her pout, she quietly tapped the side of her long-stemmed wine glass.

'Gentlemen, my dear friends,' she began earnestly, 'I want to thank all of you for coming today. I know what it means for each of you to come out in public as the favourite clients of "Angels Of Love".' Rather than placating the men, Marina's words had the opposite effect by reducing her four clients, gathered round her in a conspiratorial circle, to blushing schoolboy-like shoe-shuffling and throat-clearing. The full impact of what each of them was doing sank in and, inevitably, the sudden rush of accompanying fear forced them to all look doubtfully across the room as Marina began to introduce me as 'a writer of integrity, someone who is here to understand our agency world and to explain it to others'. Although her intention was to both flatter me and, in turn, soothe her worrisome clientele, her words only succeeded in troubling us all even further.

It is a mysterious law of life that no sooner are you described as being full of 'integrity' than, as the eyes of people turn towards you to witness such principled behaviour for themselves, you break out into a shifty-eyed, collar-loosening rash of perspiring convulsions. As the doomed eyes of Marina's men lanced into me, I succumbed to that irrevocable rule. Beneath their gaze I seemed to metamorphose, Gregor Samsa-like, into what I was sure resembled an ulcerous *News Of The World* maggot, overflowing with Machiavellian plans to tear their guts out.

The men seemed to think so too, for they quickly averted their gaze to the more pleasant sight of Marina holding forth, her short, blonde hair bobbing expectantly with every sensually explicit sentence. She extolled the joys of 'liberated love-making' and the 'virtue of any sexual desire, no matter how depraved others might think it'. With us today, she confided, there was not only 'our writer of integrity', but some deeply sensitive men who were beginning to 'flower freely and beautifully as sexual beings'. They were no longer imprisoned by their desire; rather, they were starting to free those very same yearnings. They were ready to be dominated and devoured by women, to be whipped and flogged; they were no longer afraid to wear women's clothes or to release the most primal urges within themselves; they were so free that they could find beauty and joy in almost anything. Why, said Marina with almost cooing delight, there was even one man here unselfish and imaginative enough to desire the pleasuring of Goldie. Apparently this yearning still had to be fulfilled as Goldie himself had yet to be convinced of the allure of the man's proposal.

Goldie, a remarkably sane Golden Labrador, was at that very moment out in the back garden barking cheerfully at the next door neighbour's cat. It was difficult then not to marvel at the dog's sensible approach to life. Marina, meanwhile, pushed on down her emancipatory path of sexual passion although the attention of her audience had wandered to the more consuming thought of who amongst us was the aspiring Goldie-lover. Being new to this particular kind of erotic craving I struggled to identify the culprit for they all seemed to be fine gentlemen from, as Marina confirmed, the worlds of high finance, management consultancy, publishing and advertising.

As if keen to re-establish their otherwise impeccable credentials, the men began slowly to enter the conversation. Talk shifted curiously from bestiality to the pressures of tight business schedules, Picasso's 'Blue Period', the delights of a fine cheese-fondue dinner and late Victorian literature. The sub-text to this startling change of subject-matter was clear. Everyone was determined to prove himself to be both a responsible and cultured citizen rather than a sexual deviant. In the world outside this Surbiton front-room, these men were undoubtedly used to fawning respect; it was poignant to see them trying desperately to reaffirm their sense of decency and worth. But Goldie, reliable old barking Goldie, kept the pathos of the situation in check.

Frankie, of course, paid no attention to any of this but kept on giving me his laddish wink. Eventually he sidled over to me when the other men were diverted by a sudden interjection from Marina and hissed, 'You and me seem to be the only ones who don't have to pay for it round here, hey matey?' Luckily, Marina had just announced the arrival of some of the 'Angels' and Frankie and I were both distracted by the wash of silk and perfume flowing into the front room. Deborah, Gemma and Gillian, Marina's three closest 'Angels', swirled round the room, smiling, murmuring throaty 'Hellos' and kissing all of us lightly on our cheeks.

In the adjoining dining room, Marina had spread out an elaborate buffet, complemented by chilled bottles of white wine. As the drink flowed we loosened up and, in Marina's word, 'mingled'. The others even appeared to have forgotten the burning question relating to the identity of Goldie's unrequited lover.

The men had been given anonymous names for the night

by Marina. She called her two shorter clients 'Bill' and 'Bob' while their thinner, more elegant counterparts were tagged 'Claude' and 'Clive'. They were as much strangers to each other as they were to me. But somehow they began to open up and talk as if they had all known each other for a very long time.

The bizarre nature of their conversation deepened as they finally began to discuss male attitudes to prostitution over the last of the salmon and mushroom vol-au-vents and the rapidly sinking bottles of wine. Goldie still gambolled tantalisingly outside, amidst the shadows stretching across Marina's manicured lawn.

Both 'Claude' and 'Clive', firm chums now, refuted the notion that there was some kind of hypocrisy behind the fact that all four of them were married and yet still amongst Marina's most regular clients. 'You're very young, my boy,' 'Claude' pointed out helpfully, 'and so what seems contradictory to you now has much to do with youthful idealism. When you get older you'll find out that, fortunately, women are not made like us, they have different desires. Their sexual needs fade with the years. A woman of my age, the right side of fifty, does not retain the same urge I have for a full and varied sex life.'

Claude was depressing me and I looked over sympathetically at Goldie for I thought I knew what the old bounder meant when he said 'varied'. But then 'Bill' went and spoilt it all, just when I had begun to admire his stolid restraint, by backing 'Claude' to the hilt. 'It's not that we love our wives any less, it's just that we need a little bit of sexual stimulus on the side. This can keep the marriage on an even keel rather than destroy it.'

When I inquired whether the same process of equilibrium applied if the woman in the marriage fancied some 'stimulus on the side', a stunned silence was soon engulfed by a barrage of guffaws. They assured me that I had a lot to learn for this idea, at least in their marriages, was 'quite ludicrous'. I was shepherded over, in my innocent lamb guise, to the more sharp-witted company of Gemma and Gillian.

They were both in their late twenties, former 'office administrators' who had become disenchanted with the ceaseless innuendo and creeping sexual harassment of their day-to-day working lives in London. Three years ago they had answered an 'Escort Agency' advert together and, after a bewildering first few weeks of prostitution work, had settled into the work. Although careful to remain diplomatic while within earshot of the men and of Marina, Gemma and Gillian became less enthusiastic about agency work and especially their clients whenever a sudden burst of laughter from the others muffled the candour of their words.

But even in their disenchantment there was a bottom-line. 'It's Money, spelt with capital fucking M,' whispered Gemma. 'You quickly get used to the money because, after working in a nine-to-five office job, it's fantastic. I earn as much in a day as I used to in a week. And once it's in my hand I find I spend it — on clothes, on books, on holidays. I'm not wild about any of the men, and I get bored with them quickly, but to go back to my old life now would be almost impossible.'

Gillian provided a more subtle distinction: 'In our old lives we seemed to be so much more subservient to men. That might sound strange at first because the initial idea everyone has about prostitution is that the woman is exploited, she is the one being dominated. But I feel so much more in control here, in this environment, where I'm more in charge, where the men even want me to boss them around, than in a more conventional setting. To go back to that old office-politicking and sexual game-playing would be hard. But, sure, there are many, many times round here when it gets pretty distressing as well. Some days, some guy's sexual kink no longer seems mildly amusing and you just feel sick of it all . . .'

Bang on cue, 'Claude' wafted over, his fat face wreathed in ingratiating smiles. With a slight squeeze of Gemma's hand he asked if I had learnt anything new about women since we had last spoken. I was by now drunk enough to want to sneer back some pithy 'You sick old fuck, Goldie will *never* give in to you' one-liner. But I was also still sufficiently alert to see Marina waving girlishly across the room at me, in an affecting 'Are you having a good time, baby?' kind of way. I waved back and smiled pleasantly, if hopefully mysteriously, at 'Claude'.

Marina was over in a flash for, as she said, she and I had to get down to some serious interviewing while the two 'Angels' had 'dates' in the next hour. The four men were issued with my telephone number and an instruction from Marina that they were all to call me so that I could interview each of them personally. Once more she assured them of their anonymity and my integrity. This time, with the wine zinging through me, I felt myself subvert the norm. As they each pumped my hand I was sure that I had never looked more ethical or trustworthy. Even 'Claude' assured me that we would arrange a meeting.

Frankie, who seemed to become more menacingly sober with each beer he drank, led the men out into the night — he was taking them drinking and it was no secret that he wouldn't be paying. With dewy-eyed devotion, Marina watched him leave. 'Isn't he a love?' she murmured. Gemma and Gillian looked stonily back at her while I once again attempted my ambiguous shrug and smile routine.

With a promise that they would also keep in touch, the two 'Angels' disappeared into the back of a cab whisking them to the other side of London, to Hampstead and to St John's Wood — to work. Deborah, an ex-nurse in her early forties, was already answering the 'Angel Of Love' hotline which seemed to ring with increasing regularity as the hours slipped by and the night deepened.

Every twenty minutes or so, Deborah would call Marina to the phone so that she could take a call from an established client personally. Always, without fail, her greeting rang out with the words said in the very same sequence and with the

247

same pitch of bubbling sincerity. 'Well, surprise, surprise! Hello, my baby. How're we doing? Mmmmhmmm, but I can tell, baby, you'd like some *randy* company tonight . . .' Of course she was always right and after explaining that she herself would not be available for a few hours, winking coyly at me, she then proceeded to list a whole stream of alternative 'beautiful and randy young ladies' — breasty blondes, leggy brunettes, sensual Swedes, English roses, Turkish delights, matronly nurses, young secretaries, school teachers, university students, bisexual double-acts, single masturbating girls who were just dying to be watched . . .

Whatever the type of 'Angel' wanted, Marina said coyly, their price of heaven started with an agency introductory fee of £50. The remainder of the cost would have to be negotiated with the girl he chose. Once the caller had decided which 'Angel' should visit him at his home or hotel, Deborah would telephone the escort and, usually, her conversation would begin with a 'Hi, it's me. Listen, we've got a bit of a strange one for you but he sounds keen and the money should be good' preamble. The man's telephone number would be read out and then it was down to the woman to contact him and set up a 'date', usually within the hour.

As the telephone chirruped incessantly, with Deborah answering it unstintingly in her sexiest 'Hi, this is "Angels" — can I help you?' voice, I said to Marina that it seemed that she had hit on a booming kind of business. 'Oh, it is much more than that, my baby!' she crooned as she led me towards the privacy of the kitchen and another bottle of wine which would surely help us get our interview going at last. 'Did you hear what Deborah said? — "Can I *help* you?" I insist she says that to every caller. I'm not in this just to make money, baby, I'm here to help men, to offer them therapy. This is a place of *sexual healing*, my angel . . .'

Like Sara Dale, whom she strove to emulate, Marina's desire to heal was essentially bound up in her need to confront damage which had already been done. The common perception of prostitutes is that such damage has, in some way, been done to them and it is this which leads them to their seemingly ruinous 'sex for sale' way of life. While stressing that such generalisations wrongly assume that prostitution ruins people even further, Marina believed that embryonic hurt was often the most decisive factor in shaping people's lives.

'To do this work well you have to know about abuse and about the pain it brings. Yes, my baby, you have to have had a little damage done to you. There are some women who have always been protected, always been loved, and they do not become prostitutes. They would have difficulty in understanding the angry and fearful lust of men. But when such a man has stood over you when you are young you know these things, you are different to those luckier women.

'I was damaged but, baby, I believe that scars do heal. And this work here, at "Angels", is about healing — for we, all us "Angels", are here to help and to heal men of the damage that they have done to us and that society has also done to them.'

Marina, naturally, was more comfortable churning out nebulous paeans to sexual healing than in discussing her own hurt. However, after much obscure warbling, she returned sharply to the subject when describing her move from Poland to Sweden in the mid-1960s. 'It was around 1966 and I was about twelve years of age. My father died when I was much younger and things had been very bad for my mother and me in Warsaw. We were often struggling to just survive. My mother's brother had been transferred to Stockholm a few years previously — he was some sort of diplomat and he managed to arrange that we could join him in Sweden for a short holiday that summer. He paid for us to come over and even though I did not know it at the time, the intention was always that we would stay with him and his wife and not return to Poland. Of course, I was very excited and I quickly started to learn Swedish and to attend a local school.

'I was very grateful to my uncle and when he began to show me special attention, you know, doing little things like stroking my legs and giving me little kisses when we were alone together, I felt I couldn't say anything to my mother. He had been so kind to us so it was very hard for me to imagine that he would do anything wrong.

'One Sunday afternoon, still in the summer, he asked me to go with him for a drive into the countryside. After a while he pulls over into the woods and he takes out his penis which by now is very hard and, for me, you know, a little girl, very frightening to look at. He made me touch him and when he came it was all over my dress. I was very disturbed by this but, more than anything else, I was confused. So it was almost a relief when he told me exactly what I must do. We went down to the stream to wash my dress and then, while it was drying on a rock in the sun, he made me take off my underwear. Then he raped me.

'Up until then it had been an embarrassing experience. I had been afraid, but I would be lying if I did not say that I also felt the first stirrings of sexuality in me. I had seen the power I had when I touched his penis and made it jump! But of course he was the one in power. He proved this when he raped me. He hurt me terribly. I went into shock. I could hardly speak for days afterwards, even when my mother asked me what was wrong. My uncle had told me that my mother would have to go back alone to Poland if I told her what "we did". What could I do? I kept quiet and it never happened again. I think that his wife maybe guessed what happened for he never touched me again. It was very strange for then he treated me like an "ordinary" uncle. I hated him but I was also relieved that it had ended.'

Marina's resilience was such that she then enjoyed what she describes as a 'healthily promiscuous' teenage sex-life with boys her own age. However, she was raped again, in her early-twenties. After she had fallen awkwardly in a

Stockholm street she was dazedly helped to the near-by flat of a passer-by who promised to treat her cuts. Instead, he kept her prisoner there for the next twenty-odd hours, during which time he raped her repeatedly.

While not dismissing the damage that rape inflicts, Marina refused to draw any links between those grim episodes of sexual violence in her life and the catastrophic upheaval which finally drove her towards prostitution. Increasingly insecure after the second rape, Marina moved to Amsterdam where she met an Englishman whom she married little more than a month later. When she returned with him to England the marriage quickly went sour and, after a few months, he forced her out of his flat.

'I had no money, I had no friends, I had nothing. I was desperate. Either I must kill myself or else I must do something fast to get out of this mess I am in. I had seen this advert in the local paper a few weeks before. It was an escort agency in North London and they were advertising for new girls. I phoned and that same afternoon I had my interview with the agency owner. He was an Indian and soon after I had gone into his office he told me to take my clothes off and then he fucked me. He said that this was a test all the girls had to take. I didn't like him at all but I knew that I had to do it if I wanted a job. Soon after we finished he tells me that there's a special client of his at The Dorchester – an Arab sheik who I must go see.

'I feel like I've just been raped and now I have to go do it all over again. I hardly have time for a shower. I walk into The Dorchester and I feel terrible. I can hardly face it. And my heart sinks when I walk into the Arab's suite. He's a really fat and ugly man and I prepare myself for the worst. But that was when I learnt that preconceptions in this business are useless. He must have quickly guessed the situation for he was charming. I spent maybe four hours with him and I told him everything. He ordered wonderful food and then he gave me £300 and told me to take care of myself. When I said, ''But we haven't even had sex –

251

you don't need to pay me," he laughed and said that I would learn that this business was not just about fucking. I had given him pleasure just by talking to him and he felt it was not "appropriate" that I should have to have sex after all that had happened to me that day. I was really lucky to have him as my first client. It also made me understand that prostitution can be a good thing, a kind of therapy. That man helped me that first time and since then I have helped many men.'

With this almost naïvely 'helpful' attitude to her clients, Marina soon established herself as the agency's most popular escort. Her open-minded willingness to listen to the men's wildest sexual fantasies, and usually go as far as she could to fulfilling them, was accompanied by her steadfast 'Are you having a good time, baby?' banter. Marina also got on well with most of the women escorts whose spasms of envy at her money-spinning success were quickly blunted by their liking for her wit and optimism.

When the agency owner was jailed a year later for his simultaneous involvement in a drug-smuggling ring, it did not take Marina long to decide that she would set up her own business. 'I had all these clients and, also, all the girls I had worked with were then no longer with an agency so it seemed a natural thing to do to open up "Angels". First I went out and bought this house, here in lovely Surbiton. This means a massive mortgage repayment for me to make every month but I am more interested in creating the right kind of atmosphere for an agency like "Angels".

'I chose to move to Surbiton because I wanted to be close to London without being in the city itself. Also I thought the police wouldn't be too tough on agencies out here. So we were under way within a few months of the other agency closing down. All my old clients stayed with us and we now have about thirty girls on the books. I interview every one of them and I make sure that they are nice girls who understand my policy of sexual healing.

'Basically, my philosophy is that we should not try to bury

our fantasies. It's far better to bring them out into the open. That, of course, is not the British way. Here people repress their sexual desires so they come out all twisted. It is far better to listen to what the men want and then to try to help them release themselves from these fantasies. Maybe the other women are not quite as committed as I am to these ideals but then I see myself, like Sara Dale, as being a kind of sexual therapist rather than a prostitute. This is not meant to be just about profit for me — it is about helping to heal the men and, also, to heal the pain that has been done to my "Angels" in the past . . .'

As her telephone manner implied, Marina took great pride in her diversity of 'Angels'. Apart from more blatant sexual distinctions, the escorts were also differentiated by age, class and colour. The youngest of Marina's 'Angels' was a seventeen-year-old Arab girl, Sharma, whom Jackie would have loved to have met as she came from Fez, in Morocco. Her mother, Rosetta, also worked for Marina as a prostitute. But as the helplessly youthful Sharma became more popular, Rosetta began to cut back on her own work and act instead as a perverse kind of maternal manager, pimping her daughter from one trick to the next. Loath to pay Marina the standard £50 agency fee every time Sharma 'did business', Rosetta began to give out her family telephone number to more and more men and, eventually, she was running her own one daughter agency.

In contrast to Sharma, in virtually every way imaginable, 'Mrs Spinks' was Marina's least solicited escort. She was seventy-nine years old when she phoned Marina and asked her if she could work as an 'Angel'. Her husband had died nine months previously, after a marriage of nearly fifty years. They had had a serene half-century together and when he died Mary Spinks was devastated. During their retirement years, they had collected coloured bottles of glass. This seemingly pointless hobby assumed grotesque meaning for Mary Spinks in the most grievous months following her husband's death. Shutting herself away from the world she spent six months alone, smashing their collection of coloured, bottled glass and then pasting the shattered fragments all over the walls and ceilings of their cottagey home in Dulwich.

To walk into that house at night, with candles burning so that their light fell magically across the coloured glass lining every room, was an experience that money could never buy. But it was Marina rather than any man who paid money to her; money to keep her alive for, as an 'Angel', Mary Spinks said, she still had something worth living for. The gentle kind of madness in her was not sufficient for her to be institutionalised but, especially with her old age, it hardly constituted the ideal scenario for escort agency work.

'What could I do?' sighed Marina. 'She phones me up out of the blue and when I see her heart-breakingly beautiful home I will do anything to help this woman. Now when men say that they want an older woman they still get frightened if I say I have a seventy-nine-year-old waiting for you. So what I do is I send her money every week and say that the men had to cancel their appointments at the last moment for business reasons so she still gets her fee. She laughs like a young girl then and says she understands. She has obviously never had one client in her whole life but, to me, she is still one of my most special "Angels".'

For Gillian, this was 'a typical Marina-kind of thing to do. It's wonderfully kind and that's Marina. She's a very sweet woman and so hurt people always flock to her. But in this business you have to look after yourself first because, otherwise, it will just ruin you, it will destroy you. And then what good are you to anyone? This is the trouble with Marina — she so needs to help others that she forgets that this is the most unhelpful thing she could do to herself.

'I know I sound terribly hard but beneath all her "bubbly personality" bullshit, Marina is really fucked up. You can see it in the way this business of hers operates. It's shambolic, mainly because Marina spends too much time listening to that creep "Claude" begging to be allowed to fuck Goldie. Meanwhile, she's being ripped off left, right and centre — by the men and by the girls. If a man says to her he only has £80 with him instead of the required £120 she'll say, "OK, pay me next time." Fuck, man, that goes against every basic rule in this business. You never drop your price for these fuckers.

'Well, you could say that's her business but we're effectively employed by her and what she does affects us. Even worse, she'll do something like anal sex and will hardly charge anything more. It's crazy — especially when you think of AIDS. I've lost a lot of regulars because either I won't do anal sex or else I drop them because I know she had already done it with them. I'm not gonna die because of her sexual healing bullshit!

'I'm only in this business for another year or two — tops. So far I've saved £20,000 which I keep in a high-interest account. I reckon I need forty grand and then I'll be free. I won't need to do work I hate any more, either in an office or in the bedroom. So I keep very much on the straight and narrow. I do my thing but I know how fucked the world is and I know I can't heal it. I'm not Marina, thank God!

'Maybe if things had turned out differently for her when she was younger she would have been someone really special. But as a prostitute she's hopelessly misguided. Sure, this made her wildly popular when she first started out but the men aren't fools — the sensible ones soon move away from her because they know that she takes risks. So she just gets the anal specialists and the dog-fucking creeps and she thinks she's Mother fucking Theresa on some kind of healing mission from God.

'But all the time she's getting deeper into debt. I'm one of the few girls who still pays her the £50 agency fee. I've seen the rest of them — even Gemma, you know — they just keep the money for themselves. And if she does ask, they just say, "Next time, Marina, next time, I promise." And she says, "OK, my baby, don't you forget now, my baby . . ." Of course, she's the one who forgets and she'll never listen to me when I try to reason with her. I can't imagine how she manages to pay her mortgage every month especially with that fucker Frankie scrounging every pound she makes for himself. And the police do nothing when he beats her up — to them she's not an angelic sex-therapist, she's just a prostitute who's lucky they're not shutting her business down. It's little wonder that she's drinking so heavily . . . she can only go one way now and that's down, all the way down to very bottom.'

That scathing indictment of Marina's deluded business sense, which encouraged her to think in almost mystical 'Angel' terms rather than with more hard-headed 'Agency' practicality, was borne out in later months by the clients themselves. Even the doggedly deceitful 'Claude' admitted that he stopped paying Marina for her services despite his own business investments amounting to more than a million pounds.

'It no longer felt fitting to think of her as a prostitute, my dear boy,' burbled 'Claude'. 'She was much more than that; she had become a very dear and trusted friend. I would listen to her troubles, she would listen to mine. It was give and take, real friendship. Money didn't come into it any more.'

Aside from this gullibility, Marina's fatal flaw as a prostitute was her inability to separate her personal life from the ingrained impersonality of prostitution. Ironically she was ruined by her failure to deaden herself to others. She listened to them, she believed them, she thought she could help them. Inevitably, she found herself falling in love with some of her clients, the best of whom, as she now concurs, was Roger, an earnest builder from Bow in East London.

'I first started to go to escort agencies the year after I got divorced,' Roger explained. 'Marina was one of the first prostitutes I slept with. Really, there was no-one else like her. She was terrific in bed, she really made you feel special and, even stranger for a prostitute, you also got the feeling that she was getting pleasure from you. That's what made me think of her as a woman, rather than just as a "prostitute". She liked me, I think, because I wasn't married or anything. So we started to see each other regularly and she refused to take money from me any more. I was pleased about that — not because I was saving my dosh but because it made me feel that we really were lovers.

'As I found myself falling more and more in love with her I begged her to stop the agency work. I couldn't bear the thought of her being with other men, especially the type of perverts who used to turn up on her doorstep. But she wouldn't stop, or she just couldn't. She went on that whole "sexual therapy" malarkey. What could I do? I said, "It's either me or them." She said they needed her help more than I did. Now I would have understood it if she was making piles of money off these other blokes but they were just ripping her off. Financially speaking, she would probably have been much better off living with me. But it wasn't to be.

'I was shattered for months afterwards but then I pulled myself together. I see Gillian now — she left "Angels" just before the crash. She works at this other agency round Surbiton way. Different set-up altogether. Business all the way. That's how it is with me and Gillian. There's no real lovey-dovey stuff between us. She's not out to heal me or anything. Anyway, I reckon she knows that I'm basically a pretty together sort of guy. I just can't be bothered trying to pull someone down the pub. This is more upfront. But I also do respect her and Gill and I have a sad kind of laugh now and then about Marina and the "Angels Of Love". Despite ourselves we still really miss her, you know . . .'

Lost within anguished cycles of violence and debt, Marina Studzinski began to crumble a few months after our first meeting. As her 'Angels Of Love' dream slowly disintegrated beneath the relentless demands of her building society and the similarly percussive pressure administered to her face and body by the drunkenly psychotic Frankie, Marina slipped away into the most personal kind of ruin.

She could have saved her house and herself from physical harm by changing, by taking the money she rightfully earned as a prostitute and by forcing Frankie out of her life. Yet Marina was lost in far deeper ruin, within the morass of illusion that had set into her head like the subsidence which began to sink Mary Spinks' beautiful home of coloured glass.

It's uncertain exactly when Marina's own collapse originated but the mazy patterns of brutality and sex running through her life pull one inexorably back to that Sunday afternoon in Sweden with her dress drying on a rock in the summer sunshine, to that moment when she was first raped. It can be said that millions of other women have been subjected to the potentially ruining terror of rape and yet have not followed the path taken by Marina Studzinski. 'But who can really tell,' Marina herself asked that final afternoon in her lost Surbiton front room, 'what drives one woman one way and another a different way? All I know is that I had this dream, to be a sexual healer. I thought I could change people and even now I still believe that I did that. It wasn't all about my "Angels" deserting me without paying me or the debt-collectors banging on the door or Frankie hitting me again and again or me getting drunk night after night. No, no, my baby, it was about something better than all that.

'I remember one day this man came to the door. He was a postman, maybe thirty-five years old. So painfully shy he made even me want to curl up with embarrassment. I spent one whole day with this man. He is broken. He has never even been able to look at a woman, much less hold her. Slowly, he begins to become a little more confident. It's beautiful to me. He holds my hand and then an hour later we kiss and then two hours later we make love. He was crying all the time — with relief, with joy, he said. He never knew it could feel this good. We did it again and then once more. I told him not to pay me — you should not pay on your first time. Sure, it was bad business sense but, my baby, I was like a fucking angel that day — who can put a price on that sort of healing? Only ruin can be measured by money, by how much you have lost . . .'

Yet even ruin cannot really be quantified. How do you measure the inward debt occurring when Marina Studzinski's face falls into those powerless ripples of twitches and frowns? How certain can you be that the ruin has been washed away forever now that Frankie is in jail and she lives as an 'ordinary one-man woman' with one of her former clients, with 'no chance' of ever returning to her dream of sexual healing? She is cared for, she has as much money as she needs but, as she says, 'I have lost something, I know that I will now never be a sexual healer. That dream is gone, it is ruined. What can I do, my baby, what can I do? That sadness will still not leave me . . .'

Chapter Ten

Money Pumping

During those same winter nights, while 'Angels' slowly turned to ashes, a different kind of vision burned brightly across the city. Far from the suburban backstreets of Surbiton, beyond the ethereal dreams of sexual healing, Howard Lambert's money-spinning fantasy burst into radiant reality every night of the week.

I remember, in the last weeks of Marina Studzinski's agency-decline, making that ponderous journey across the frozen wastes of London from Surbiton to Highgate. No matter how many times I subjected myself to that interminable trek, to the bleak waiting for cancelled trains and the sourly sighing delays in darkened tunnels, each new journey became worse than the last. And when I'd finally make it to the end of the line, only one thing stopped me from making a last wrist-opening walk into the cemetery-centred woods of Highgate; the realization that I had travelled in the 'right' direction, from ruin to fulfilment, from chaos to clarity, from 'Angels' to 'Pumps'. I resolved never to make that particular journey in the opposite direction, from Howard Lambert to Marina Studzinski, for the contrast would have been unbearable.

Yet, even as I was being swept along the Turkish-carpeted hallways of Howard's unmortgaged home, it was hard not to think of Marina; not to fear that before the night was through Frankie might leave her face swollen and streaked with colour again. The tragedy in that thought would invariably coalesce with the music I'd hear billowing through the house, growing ever louder as we neared the room where Howard worked the phones. I soon learnt to recognize those sounds, that music of beautiful ruin, for Howard would be 'on another Mahler and Schubert binge'. When the theme from *Death in Venice* — or Mahler's *Fifth*, as Howard sniffily informed me — echoed down those long passages I found myself seeing the absurdly young face of the boy leading me through the house dissolving into that of Marina. At other times, Schubert's forlorn *Die Winterreise* would wear us down until we reached the heavy oak door which the boy swung open. With a smile he would disappear into the unknown reaches of the house — where I never saw him again until the next time I arrived at Howard's front door.

Inside Howard's room, the surrounding blackness was broken only by the steadily climbing red light of the amplifier and, more sporadically, by the flashing beacon on top of the telephone. Howard's eyes must have stayed open in the dark for whenever the telephone sparkled he would instantly whirl his revolving chair round, swing his feet back onto the desk, lower the volume of the music with his slim remote-control stick, lift the phone from its blinking cradle and say those words he must have said a million times.

'Yeah, this is "Pumps" and my name's Howard. What can I do for you?'

He said these words naturally, as if this was what he would say even if the voice on the other end of the phone belonged to his mother. Even the 'yeah', a word which can give in all too easily to contempt or lethargy when used as the very first in a telephone conversation, fell from his lips with brightness, a 'yeaarhhh!' sort of oomph, which shone naturally from him. In a room so dark, this flaring liveliness felt all the stranger when the call ended. Still in the blackness, Howard would half-turn to me as if continuing a briefly interrupted conversation of our own. He'd say something over his shoulder like, 'Fuck, kid, didn't this guy come up with the music to end all music? You can even hear it in his titles — *Frozen Tears, Loneliness, Last Hope, Deception, Numbness* — it's all here, boy!' And before I could ever think of an adequate reply he would lift his legs from the table, skirt round a semi-circle in his chair and send the red light on his sound system spiralling up into the highest reaches of the small display window. As a desolate tenor rolled out into the night, Howard would motion me to sit on a settee in full striking distance of the huge speakers pounding out Franz Schubert's *Winter's Journey*. We'd sit there silently, Howard and I, face to face in the dark, with me thinking that Franzie himself must have made the grim equivalent of a few British Rail Surbiton-to-Highgate winter journeys to have written music this sad.

Eventually, the flickering phone would set the whole whirling, foot-lifting, volume-tweaking process in motion again. Then, and only then, as if it were a prerequisite that we shared those opening moments of musical intimacy, Howard would stretch out his hand to shake mine. With an almost touching seriousness he would ask, 'So, how are you, kid?' And no matter how often I reduced my answer to a flippant 'Fine', he would nod gravely and say how pleased he was to hear this supposedly significant news. When his turn came to reply to the same question he would almost always gently raise the level of the music a couple of notches and, with the slabs of jowly flesh on his face splitting open into a wide grin, say, 'Things are pumping here, boy, they're *really* pumping!'

Whenever I visited Howard's house I felt that pump; it was there in the music, especially when he swapped Mahler and Schubert for The Gap Band and Funkadelic, when *Death In Venice* and *Winterreise* faded into the massive blocks of funk pumped out on *Burn Rubber On Me* and *Work That Sucker To Death*. It was there even when the volume was turned down, for then you would hear the phones ringing, almost pumping with desire, as one caller after another phoned the best gay escort agency in town. As much as this was a house overflowing with music and ringing phones, it was also a place full of men — the men, some of them trying to look more like boys, who worked for Howard; and their wayward friends.

Unless it was very late at night, they were always popping by, to drop off or to pick up some money. While they were there they'd chill out for a few hours. A couple of them would even take turns manning the phones so that Howard could take a break. Every now and then a job would turn up for someone who had to be reluctantly prised away from finding out the extent to which the house was well-stocked with food and drink that specific week. Yet, even though they were free to help themselves to more than the odd snack, the circle of escorts and hip hangers-on never appeared to take Howard's generosity beyond the limits he himself had set. It was as if they were dwarfed by his presence in that house of music and phones. Although he was not a particularly tall man, there was an assured solidity about everything he did. This, coupled with his singular kind of commanding warmth, encouraged the pumping boys to show due deference to his hospitality. There was never any other feeling than that this was Howard's place, that you were lucky to be in his 'Pumps' space.

For, if they fucked up, they knew they were out; they knew that there was a queue of boys ready to take their slot. One night, when we were in his room at the back of the house where Howard liked to listen to classical music and take the last few hours of calls, I asked him about his apparent altruism.

With a smile that suddenly glinted with the steel beneath his big open face, he said simply that, 'They're welcome here, they know that. I'm happy for them to come round. They're my boys, they're the guys that make this agency. And I like to see them, to hear how they're doing, it keeps us in touch. It's what makes it a rare kind of agency, it's what makes it the best. They can bring their friends with them, they can have a drink, a meal even, watch a video, whatever. But they know, if they let me down then they're